LEV
COG
DEVEL

LEVELS OF COGNITIVE DEVELOPMENT

TRACY S. KENDLER

University of California, Santa Barbara

Routledge
Taylor & Francis Group

LONDON AND NEW YORK

First published 1995 by Lawrence Erlbaum Associates, Inc.

Published 2018 by Routledge
2 Park Square, Milton Park, Abingdon, Oxon OX14 4RN
52 Vanderbilt Avenue, New York, NY 10017

First issued in paperback 2018

Routledge is an imprint of the Taylor & Francis Group, an informa business

Library of Congress Cataloging-in-Publication Data

Kendler, Tracy, S.
    Levels of cognitive development / Tracy S. Kendler.
      p.   cm.
    Includes bibliographical references and indexes.
    ISBN 0-8058-0680-6 (alk. paper)
    1. Cognition. 2. Human information processing. 3. Thought and thinking. 4. Psychology, Comparative. I. Title.
    BF311.K38 1995
    153—dc20   95-17297
                                            CIP

ISBN 13: 978-1-138-99537-6 (pbk)
ISBN 13: 978-0-8058-0680-9 (hbk)

Contents

Acknowledgments

The ideas discussed in this book emerged gradually from years of research that could not have been conducted without the creative cooperation of others. There were graduate assistants, especially Beulah Learnard, Martha Carrick, and James Ward, who not only helped to conduct the experiments, but also contributed to designing the procedures and analyzing the data. I wish to recognize the inspiration received from all of my PhD students, in particular. Barbara Basden, Lila Tabor, Candida Peterson, and Kam Rust, whose original research and astute thinking contributed in considerable measure to the ideas expressed in this book.

There were others who were more than helpful; they were essential. Doris Phinney served as a Staff Research Associate supported by the National Science Foundation for over 10 years. During this time she collected and organized the bulk of the children's data presented here. She was wonderfully resourceful, loyal, intelligent, good humored, and dependable.

Judith B. Bruckner, mathematician, computer scientist, and good friend. Dr. Bruckner collaborated on the mathematical model of discrimination-learning that plays a central role in this book. More recently she wrote the computer program for the simulations that form the body of chapters 7 and 8, which brought the mathematical model to life. I am grateful for the exhilarating stimulation this collaboration produced.

To the third essential person, my husband Howard Kendler, I am indebted for putting up with me all these years without losing his sense of humor. He encouraged me to begin this line of research and we collaborated on all the early experiments as well as on the early theorizing. Although the scientific collaboration eventually ended, he remains my best friend and dearest companion, as well as my severest critic.

I also appreciate the very early support, as well as the sustained forbearance, provided by Lawrence Erlbaum, my publisher, and Sondra Guideman, my production editor, who guided the book through publication.

Tracy S. Kendler

CHAPTER ONE

A Preview

There is a Zen principle that says there are big truths and small truths, and the way you tell the difference is this: The denial of a small truth is clearly false, but the denial of a big truth is also true.

—Anonymous

Since its inception as a science, psychology has been bedeviled by four recurring, fundamental, unresolved controversies. Are living organisms passive recipients or active interpreters of the information they receive from the environment? Does behavior consist of automatic responses to specifiable conditions or intentional actions based on rational decisions? Is cognitive development essentially qualitative or quantitative? Is cognitive development a function of innate or environmental determinants?

Recurrent controversies like these will continue to plague our science until we recognize that each side is a "big truth whose denial is also true." The developmental theory proposed here has, as its broadest purpose, the provision of a paradigm for the resolution of each controversy by incorporating both sides in a levels-of-function format that allows ostensibly incompatible versions of the "big truths" to coexist harmoniously. The narrower purpose is to explain certain objective, empirical facts—"small truths"—about developmental changes in basic aspects of cognition, namely the capacity to abstract information and the capacity to provide rational solutions to problems. The general premises of this theory and the nature of the supporting empirical evidence are broadly outlined at the outset in order to sketch in the whole picture before fleshing out some of the requisite manifold particulars.

Empirical Base

Intellect is defined in common parlance as the knowing and reasoning faculties of the mind. The term derives from the Latin *intelligere*, meaning to choose among and therefore to understand, to perceive, or to know. The empirical bedrock on which this theory rests comes largely from years of research on how infrahuman animals and humans of different ages behave when confronted with simple problems that require choosing between two visual displays. One display is correct and the other incorrect; the problem calls on the solver to discover which is which.

The information in these displays, as in real-life, contains both relevant and irrelevant elements. The problems can be solved whether the information is processed actively or passively. Active information processing abstracts and selectively encodes the relevant information and ignores that which is, or appears to be, irrelevant to the solution of the problem. Passive information processing nonselectively encodes all of the perceptible information, relevant and irrelevant alike, in parallel. In a complementary manner, the problems permit solutions by means of automatic associative learning or by means of rational hypothesis testing.

When these problems were presented to infrahuman animals they mostly tended to process the information in the displays nonselectively and to solve the problems in the automatic associative mode. When human adults were presented with the problems they typically abstracted the relevant information and solved the problems in the rational hypothesis-testing mode. How human children encoded the information and solved the problems depended on their age. The youngest children, like the infrahuman animals, mostly tended to encode the information nonselectively and to solve the problems in the associative mode. But between early childhood and young adulthood there was a gradual, systematic, quantitative increase in both the tendency to abstract the relevant from the irrelevant information and in the tendency to solve the problem by testing plausible hypotheses.

Premises

The theory that gradually emerged from this research can be summarized in seven basic premises about the structure, function, and development of the psychological system that governs how these ostensibly simple problems are solved.

Premise 1. This psychological system is differentiated into separable but interacting components. The basic differentiation is into an information-processing system and an executive system analogous to the differentiation of the nervous system into afferent and efferent systems. The function of the information-processing system is to receive, store, and transmit sensory input from the external world and also from internal bodily receptors to the executive system. The executive system uses the transmitted information to generate a suitable response. Simply put, the information-processing system regulates what one perceives and the executive system regulates what one does.

Premise 2. The information-processing system is further differentiated into structural levels, with the higher level, in part, duplicating the function of the lower level, but in a more plastic, voluntary, and efficient manner. For the present the theory is limited to two levels. The lower level provides the organism with the capacity to encode, in parallel, all of the impinging information to which it is sensitive. There is no abstraction of the information pertinent to the task in hand. Processing at this level is passive in that it is governed by the sensory system of the organism; motivation has little or no effect.

The higher level provides the capacity to select only the relevant portion of the information for further processing. This level is active in that what is relevant is determined jointly by the context in which the problem is presented and the motives of the organism.

Premise 3. Although the two information-processing levels have different functions, their operations are complementary rather than mutually exclusive. Instead of replacing lower-level encoding, which continues to be necessary for the reception of all the perceptible information, higher-level encoding increases the capacity of the system by abstracting the relevant information from the total input.

Higher-level encoding is manifested in ordinary experience by the ability to concentrate selectively on a particular conversation in the midst of, say, a noisy cocktail party. Although the many other conversations, noises, and general distractions in the surround are ostensibly ignored, you are nevertheless very likely to hear your name if spoken across the room. Thus while, prior to that time, you seemed to "hear" only the conversation in your own group, the rest of the information impinging on your sensorium is also being encoded at the lower level.

Postulating two compatible levels of information processing allows the passive–active antithesis to be resolved by integrating the ostensible incompatibility between selective and nonselective encoding within a higher synthesis in which each mode has its place and its function.

Premise 4. The executive system is also differentiated into two levels. The lower executive level provides for the capacity to modify behavior by virtue of gradual, automatic changes in stimulus–response associations subject to the laws of associative learning. This level operates in an automatic mode, meaning it governs the evocation of responses that can be executed with little or no prior thought. The associative mode is manifested in the many automatic responses one eventually learns to make when driving a car or typing on a keyboard.

The higher executive level operates in a rational mode providing sensible solutions to problems for which no suitable automatic response is available. The rational mode is manifested when one successively tests various reasonable hypotheses until a workable solution is discovered.

Premise 5. The higher level of the executive system, instead of replacing the lower level, enhances the capacity of the organism by producing more efficient and wider ranging problem solving. However, the lower mode continues to serve two functions. One function is to provide for associative learning when circumstances require it, as in the acquisition of a new vocabulary. The other function is to permit rational solutions to gradually to become automatic as a result of practice.

A familiar example of cooperation between the two levels of the executive system is presented by the student typist, who begins by deliberately and rationally choosing to learn the rules about fingering and uses these rules wittingly to produce correct responses by invoking the higher executive level. Eventually, as a result of continued practice, the correct fingering becomes automatic by virtue of the action of the lower executive level, leaving the typist free to concentrate on the content of what is being typed or to daydream.

Postulating two executive levels resolves the automatic-intentional antithesis also by integrating the two theses into a higher thesis, giving them both a place and a function.

Premise 6. The next premise assumes that understanding human cognitive processes will be informed by an evolutionary perspective that ultimately relates changes in cognitive capacity to changes in brain structure and function. Specifically, the differentiation of the information processing and executive systems into different functional levels is presumed to have occurred sometime during the evolution of mankind with the higher level evolving later than the lower one as the central nervous system became increasing encephalized.

The conception of different functional levels regulated by different neurological infrastructures that evolved over the course of mammalian evolution has a long history. Jackson (1834–1911), the founder of modern neurology, proposed that the central nervous system evolved into several structural levels, with each level controlling the entire bodily function in a different manner. The lowest level consists of the spinal cord and brain stem and controls reflex function. The second level contains the motor and sensory areas of the cerebrum and is concerned with movements and sensation. The third and highest level, localized in the highest cerebral centers, concerns consciousness and volition. There are more contemporary advocates of the idea that the brain is organized into functionally and structurally differentiated levels that evolved sequentially. Maclean (1968) proposed that man's brain has inherited three basic types of structures which, for simplification, he referred to as reptilian, old mammalian, and new mammalian. He imagined the brain to have evolved like a building to which wings and superstructures have been added. All three types differ in structure and chemistry. Yet in humans they mesh and function together as a "triune" brain in which each level has its own peculiar form of subjectivity and its own intelligence. Altman (1978), postulated that "three levels of mentation" can be ascribed to three different neuropsychic systems that emerged in the evolution of vertebrates from the early beginnings to man. Petri and Mishkin (1994) present neuropsychological evidence that the brain contains "more than one system for learning and retention." They interpret this evidence as supporting "both the behaviorist and cognitivist approaches by suggesting that each is consistent with a different mechanism and a different neural system."

The levels theory proposed here shares some aspects of each of these theories. Unlike stage theories in which the more advanced stages replace their predecessors, in a levels theory each successive, superimposed level extends the repertoire of the species without depriving the lower level of its function. Among human adults all levels are assumed to function in an integrated fashion.

Premise 7. The last premise is that, in the course of human ontogeny, the higher levels of the information processing and the executive systems each develop later and more slowly than their lower-level counterparts. This assumption also traces back to Jackson who conceived of development in the human nervous system as the passage from the comparatively well organized lower nerve centers at birth, to the highest nerve centers, that are continually organizing throughout life. The transition is from the simplest to the most complex, from the most automatic to the most voluntary (cited in Lassek, 1970). More articulated, contemporary versions of the same notion can be found in the work of Hebb (1972) and Luria (1973), the cofathers of modern neuroscience. The present levels theory can be considered as filling in some particulars of behavioral development within the schemes originally proposed by these distinguished forebears.

While infants are born with most, if not all, major neurological structures in the central nervous system in place, the rate at which they mature varies. The more recently evolved structures begin to mature relatively late and proceed with the maturation relatively slowly (Luria, 1973; Mishkin, Malamut, & Bachevalier, 1984; Yakovlev & Lecours, 1967). Presumably, in humans the neurological infrastructures of the higher information processing and executive levels mature at a slower rate than the neurological infrastructures of the lower levels. The efficiency with which these structures function is assumed to be related to their maturational status.

This premise would resolve the controversy about whether cognitive development is quantitative or qualitative by showing how both sides could be true. Cognitive development is qualitative in that the higher levels of function entail qualitatively different modes of operation. In the information-processing system, the lower mode is nonselective and the higher mode is selective; this is a qualitative difference. In the executive system, problem solving is associative in the lower mode and rational in the higher mode, also a qualitative difference. But because the higher levels in each system mature quantitatively, in a gradual manner, the consequent cognitive development is both qualitative and quantitative simultaneously.

Consider finally the controversy surrounding the role of heredity and environment in ontogenetic development. This is not the usual hereditary–environment controversy about which contributes more to individual differences in cognitive capacity. The reference is rather to the species-general increase in the tendency to perform on the higher levels. Invoking maturation of the neural substrates to explain this increase implicates heredity in the form of genetically determined, preprogrammed development. But this by no means excludes the role of environment. As in the case of physical growth, the environment—broadly defined to include experience—can act to determine the course of maturation by affecting the rate at which the maturation proceeds, the ultimate level it attains, or, more rarely, the form it takes (Gottlieb, 1983). In this way the theory allows for the concurrent action of heredity and environment on the course of cognitive development.

Together these premises, if adequately detailed, interrelated, and empirically supported, could explain the truism that adult humans are better at abstracting relevant information and solving problems than lower animals and young children. Validating these premises can also resolve some of the persistent, recurring controversies in the history of scientific psychology. The rest of the chapters discuss how and why this formulation was generated and also provide the presently available necessary details and empirical evidence.

CHAPTER TWO

Selective and Nonselective Encoding

How odd it is that anyone should not see that all observation must be for or against some view if it is to be of any service.
—Darwin in a letter to Fawcett (1861)

Research leading to the levels theory began in the neobehaviorist tradition, a tradition committed to the application of natural science methods to psychology. The purpose was the production of testable theories about the effects of experimentally manipulable variables on learning. Had neobehaviorism become a successful paradigm, this early research would be typical of the "normal science" phase of scientific development (Kuhn, 1970). But neobehaviorism has been superseded by the presently dominant cognitivist school. Nevertheless I shall claim the neobehaviorists did solve some problems and at least part of that achievement will prove to be permanent.

Neobehaviorism

Although neobehaviorists sometimes studied human behavior, they mostly used laboratory animals because without animal research establishing a natural science of behavior would be difficult, perhaps impossible. Restricting research to human subjects closed off too many avenues of controlled experimentation for practical or ethical reasons. Like the radical behaviorists led by Skinner, neobehaviorists were convinced that scientific psychology should explain publicly observable behavior rather than covert mentation. The stimulus–response association served as the unit of behavioral analysis.

This unit had three constituents: an initiating stimulus (*S*), a consequent response (*R*), and a connection (–). Learning entailed modification of the connection by experience. Unlike the radical behaviorists, neobehaviorists undertook to produce a rigorous, testable, black-box theory of how experience acts to modify these connections.

In black-box theories the system that mediates between the stimulus-input and the response-output is treated as impenetrable, leaving how it operates to be inferred from publicly observable input–output relations. Neobehaviorists used hypothetical constructs to develop elaborate, deductive theories about how the system works. These theories were to be validated by their capacity to predict observable behavior. Explanations that included either biological or mental processes intervening between stimuli and responses were not excluded in principle, as long as these processes were clearly defined and measurable. The emphasis on black-box theories was based on the belief that a valid, objective, strictly psychological theory was possible. There was no profit to be gained from either vaguely defined mentalistic or prematurely conceived biological constructs at this stage in its development.

The most prominent of the neobehaviorists, Hull (1943, 1952) produced a mathematical theory of learning intended to explain a variety of simple learning behaviors based on a series of explicit postulates from which testable deductions were derived. His theory began with noting that organic evolution provides the normal organism with receptor organs capable of responding to the important stimuli in its environment (*S*), motoric organs that can make the necessary responses (*R*), and a nervous system that connects these stimuli and responses (–). Adaptive connections between stimuli and responses are of two types. There are unlearned *S–R* reflexes adapted to rapid response to emergency situations. The other type are learned *S–R* connections which provide a slower means of adjusting to less acute situations but are more suitable for adapting to the changing circumstances an animal might face.

To explain how learning occurs Hull proposed a number of principles. Only a few of the pertinent, basic principles are described here, in their most general form, to provide a sense of this kind of theorizing. There was the *habit family hierarchy* principle that assumed innate response tendencies to a stimulus could be arranged in a preferential order. For example, an organism could have both an innate tendency to approach and to avoid a novel stimulus, but the tendency to approach might be stronger than the tendency to avoid. There was also the principle of *extinction*, the tendency for an unrewarded *S–R* connection to become weakened, and the principle of *reinforcement*, the tendency for a rewarded response to be strengthened. Extinction coupled with the habit family hierarchy predicts an ordered succession of different responses until a rewarded response is evoked. Repetition of the rewarded response, coupled with the reinforcement principle leads to an adaptive reorganization of the response hierarchy, commonly known as trial-and-error learning.

The innately determined hierarchy could vary for different species due to genetic differences. The effective hierarchy could vary for different individuals in the same species due to different experiences. But the principles underlying the change in the hierarchy were assumed to apply in general to all organisms equipped with the capacity to learn. Therefore, how these and other related mechanisms worked could be investigated experimentally in controlled laboratory conditions, using convenient laboratory animals. Despite his belief that all organisms operate according to a common set of primary behavioral laws, Hull acknowledged that humans have the added capacity of speech, symbolic behavior, with its accompanying advantages to the higher mental processes. He also admitted that whether this added capacity introduces any additional primary behavior laws remains to be determined.

Mediating Responses and Higher Mental Processes

One of the theoretical constructs proposed by Hull, was the *fractional anticipatory goal response* (r_g), which together with its stimulus correlate (s_g) was assumed to mediate between the observable stimulus and the measurable response. To illustrate how this hypothetical response was supposed to work, suppose a laboratory rat is presented with a tone followed by a shock. The shock can be avoided by moving to an adjoining chamber at the onset of the tone. According to the principle of reinforcement, the animal can learn to move to the other chamber to eliminate the shock because reducing pain is reinforcing. But the reinforcement principle by itself will not explain how the animal learns to escape the shock before it occurs.

Another prominent neobehaviorist (Miller, 1951) explained anticipatory escape responses by postulating that the pain-producing shock elicits a covert fear response (r_g). The r_g has a noxious, internal stimulus correlate referred to as anxiety (s_g). The s_g becomes anticipatory when the r_g becomes classically conditioned to the tone that precedes the shock. The noxious s_g is reduced by escaping to the other chamber at the onset of the signal. Reducing noxious stimulation is reinforcing, hence the animal learns to escape at the onset of the tone-signal thereby avoiding the shock altogether. This chain of events can be represented as follows: $S_{tone}-r_{fear}-s_{anxiety}-R_{escape}$.

This anticipatory mechanism was important because it provided an automatic device for explaining ostensibly intentional, purposive, anticipatory infrahuman behavior without resorting to anthropomorphic mentalisms. Presently this mechanism was used to explain higher mental processes among humans as well. The r_g was more generally characterized as a mediating or cue-producing response (r) whose function was to generate feedback (s). The feedback, in turn, stimulated overt behavior (R), as in the use of a mnemonic device to prompt recall. Because mediating responses functioned only to produce feedback, they could become as covert and as minimal as biological economy would dictate. Hull went so far as to suggest that covert mediating responses could diminish until nothing but a neural vestige remained. Note that a mediating response changes the locus of control from the "passive" regulation of behavior by the external environment to a more "active" regulation produced by self-generated stimuli.

At first the mediating response (r) applied to higher mental processes was mostly conceived to be linguistic in nature but later these mediating responses were extended to encompass imagery, perception, and response-induced drives (Miller, 1959). The research that eventually led to the levels theory began with the intention of testing the applicability of the broadened conception of mediation to human problem solving. Two processes basic to human problem solving, namely abstraction and reasoning, were differentiated. The strategy was to find out how far neobehaviorist learning theory, amplified by the covert mediating response mechanism, could go toward explaining each of these processes. Discrimination learning, a standard laboratory procedure usually used with infrahuman animals, was used to investigate abstraction.

Discrimination Learning and Abstraction

Discrimination learning served initially to measure the sensory capacities of infrahuman animals by testing whether they could learn to choose between two discriminanda that differed on some dimension. For example, to determine whether a certain animal species is color sensitive, a representative sample could be trained to choose between two simultaneously displayed discriminanda, one red and the other green. Half of the sample would be rewarded with food or water for choosing *red*, the other half for choosing *green*. To ensure that the animals learn on the basis of color, not position, each discriminandum would appear equally often on the right and on the left during training. If the animals could learn to make the correct choice, one can infer they are capable of discriminating between those colors, providing that all other possible cues are controlled. Variations on this procedure were later used extensively to investigate the learning process *per se* but continued to be referred to as discrimination learning.

The discrimination learning procedure we used as a *modus operandi* for the study of abstraction consisted of two or more phases. In the first phase the discriminanda differed simultaneously on two visual dimensions, say size and brightness, but only one of the dimensions was relevant to the reinforcement contingencies. The learner was trained to a pre-established criterion. The next phase, which followed after this criterion was attained, consisted of a transfer-of-training test. This test was designed to determine whether the cues on the relevant dimension had more influence on choice-behavior than the cues on the irrelevant dimension.

This experimental vehicle was considered suitable for several reasons. First, because it was a standard procedure there were a number of established facts about how learners respond to this procedure. Second, the discriminanda, which can be made more or less complex, allow for controlled, experimental manipulation of the information to be encoded. Third, applying transfer-of-training measures allows one to measure how the information in the discriminanda is encoded. Fourth, because spoken instructions are not necessary, the procedure can be used with infrahuman and human learners as well as with human learners over a wide range of ages. Last, and probably the most important reason for using discrimination-learning lies in the theoretical significance of the continuity–noncontinuity controversy.

THE CONTINUITY–NONCONTINUITY CONTROVERSY

Noncontinuity Theory

This controversy had its origin in some incidental observations made by Karl Lashley (1929). While using discrimination learning to investigate sensory capacities in rats, he noticed some systematic presolution behaviors that seemed to refute trial-and-error learning theory. When he plotted the errors made by individual rats about half showed a rather sharp drop from chance to almost perfect performance. The remaining animals manifested other systematic behaviors, which he interpreted as denying the random and haphazard responses he considered to be the defining characteristic of trial-and-error behavior. Instead, Lashley (1929) compared the rat's behavior with how a mathematician might respond when he opens the hood of a car that will not start:

> The mathematician consumes time with this and that experimental adjustment; but once he discovers dirt in the distributor, the habit of turning first to that point is quickly established. So it is for the rat in the discrimination apparatus; responses to position, to alternation, or to cues from the experimenter's movements usually precede the reactions to (the correct cue) and represent attempted solutions that are within the rat's customary range of activity . . . such behavior suggests that the actual association is formed very quickly and that both the practice preceding and the errors following are irrelevant to the actual formation of the association. (p. 135)

Besides denying the role of practice in learning Lashley (1938) also proposed that the rat attends selectively to one cue at a time:

A definite attribute of the stimulus is "abstracted" and forms the basis of the reaction: other attributes are either not sensed at all or are disregarded. So long as the effective attribute is present, the reaction is elicited as an all-or-none function of the attributes. Other characteristics may be radically changed without affecting the reaction. (p. 81)

Inspired by Lashley's incidental observations, Krechevsky (1932a, 1932b) undertook a series of studies to test their reliability and succeeded in replicating the nonrandom character of individual rat behaviors. Like Lashley, he concluded that the animal attempts to solve the problem in a systematic manner from the beginning. These systematic attempts he labeled "hypotheses." Hypotheses were defined as systematic, purposive behavior that involves a degree of abstraction and does not depend entirely upon the immediate environment for its initiation and performance.

Continuity Theory

Kenneth Spence, a young neobehaviorist of that era, took up the challenge posed by Lashley and Krechevsky. In a seminal article entitled "The Nature of Discrimination Learning in Animals" (Spence, 1936) he pointed out that systematic presolution behaviors were entirely consistent with modern, incremental, associative learning theories. These theories would expect individual animals to respond systematically in accordance with either their innate predispositions or previous learning. Moreover, he demonstrated how a mathematical model of incremental, associative learning could account for the rat behaviors described by Lashley and Krechevsky, without attributing to these animals either the capacity to abstract or to test hypotheses.

The theory began with noting that discriminanda in a simultaneous, visual, discrimination learning problem are composed of both relevant and irrelevant cues. For example, if a rat is trained to choose between a black (+) and a white (−) discriminandum then *black* and *white* are the relevant cues. Relevance is defined with respect to the reinforcement contingencies. In this example choosing *black* always leads to food and choosing *white* never does. Position, *left* or *right*, is irrelevant because, in a properly designed experiment, its relation to the reward is randomized. Consequently, left and right choices will each be rewarded whenever they happen, by chance, to coincide with the correct cue and frustrated whenever they happen to coincide with the incorrect cue. Therefore:

Discrimination learning does not consist . . . in the strengthening of one response relative to another or others . . . but involves rather the relative strengthening of the excitatory tendency of a certain component of the stimulus complex as compared with that of certain other elements until it attains sufficient strength to determine the response. (Spence, 1936, p. 430)

Accordingly, discrimination learning in this example consists in the strengthening of the excitatory tendency to choose *black* relative to the excitatory tendencies to choose *white, right,* or *left.*

To explain how such strengthening occurs, Spence invoked two major principles of *S–R* learning theory. The *principle of reinforcement* states that, if a response is followed by a reward, the excitatory tendencies of *all* the immediate stimulus components impinging on the organism's sensorium are strengthened by a certain magnitude. The *principle of inhibition* states that, when a response is not rewarded, the excitatory tendencies of *all* impinging stimulus components are weakened by a certain magnitude.

The theory also assumed the total excitatory strength (E) of a stimulus compound is the sum of the component E strengths. For example, the E for black-on-the-left equals E_{black} plus E_{left}. When the rat has to choose between two compounds, say black-on-the-left *versus* white-on-the-right, the compound with the greatest total E will evoke the choice response. A correct choice will occur if $E_{black} + E_{left}$ exceeds $E_{white} + E_{right}$.

This analysis might seem to involve abstraction in that one element in the stimulus complex eventually attains control over the behavior. Yet the theory calls for no higher-order capacity than the capacity to distinguish between the cues and to modify choice behavior in accordance with the principles of reinforcement and inhibition. No sagacity, no ability to abstract, or to test hypotheses is attributed to the animals.

With the help of a model that provided some approximations to the mathematical functions relating excitatory increments and decrements to the number of rewarded and nonrewarded trials, Spence was able to show that his theory could simulate the behaviors Lashley interpreted as abstraction and Krechevsky interpreted as hypothesis testing. For instance, among rats the most common presolution "hypothesis" is a position habit. An animal with a left-going position habit will persist in choosing the discriminandum on the left for trial after trial, regardless of whether it is *black* or *white.* According to Spence, because position is irrelevant left choices are randomly rewarded on half the trials and frustrated on the other half. Adventitious reinforcement for choosing left on a few trials could create a position habit, especially if position is salient—which it is among rats—and the increments early in learning are greater than increments later on. The position habits observed after a few trials could have been produced by adventitious reinforcement. However such intermittent reinforcement and nonreinforcement should cause the difference between E_{left} and E_{right} to gradually decrease. The result should be an incremental decrease in the strong left-going position habit.

Meanwhile a *black* choice is always rewarded and a *white* choice is always frustrated so that every trial either increases E_{black} or decreases E_{white}. Thus, while the position habit is gradually eroding, the tendency to choose *black* over *white* is gradually growing. But this tendency may not be manifested because *left* choices will persist until the difference between E_{left} and E_{right} becomes smaller than the difference between E_{black} and E_{white}. The animal will satisfy the criterion of learning when the difference in favor of *black* over *white* is large enough to consistently offset the difference between the two position habits.

In this way Spence demonstrated in detail how an incremental, association theory could explain systematic presolution behaviors in infrahuman animals. Unlike the more cognitive theories of Lashley and Krechevsky, this theory also explains the fact that when an animal breaks a position habit it is much more likely to choose the correct than the incorrect visual cue (Sutherland & Mackintosh, 1971).

He also wrote that to characterize these behaviors as "hypotheses" did not further our understanding. To claim that these so-called hypotheses are selective, purposive, and self-initiated, merely because behavior is systematic goes well beyond the data. Nevertheless, he went on to say, one can propose that the animal sets out to solve the problem insightfully by systematically trying out one after another from its repertoire of hypotheses until the correct one is hit upon. Although this view ignores such critical questions as what determines the order of attempted hypotheses, and what leads to the eventual abandonment of the incorrect hypotheses, it nevertheless leads to certain testable implications.

One such implication concerns the reversal of reinforcement contingencies before the animal begins to respond above chance to the correct discriminandum. For instance, what should be the effect if, after a number of training trials, the reward is switched from *black* to *white* while the animal is still presumably responding systematically to a left-is-correct hypothesis? If the animal selects and tests one possible hypothesis after another and does not test the correct one until just preceding solution, then the reversal of reward on the relevant dimensions prior to solution should have no effect. For, as Lashley stated, the practice preceding the correct hypothesis is irrelevant to the actual formation of the association.

The prediction about the effect of reversing reinforcement derived from Spence's model begins with invoking the *learning-performance distinction.* This distinction, introduced into learning theory by Tolman, emphasizes that performance is not necessarily a direct index of learning. Although learning is an important determinant of choice behavior, there are other determinants to be taken into account, including motivation and competition with other responses. *Learning* in Spence's theory refers to changes in the strength of the hypothetical excitatory tendencies that occur during the course of training while *performance* refers to the observable choices of the animal. Thus, while every choice the animal makes should increase the difference between the E's for the correct and incorrect cues, it may require a number of training trials before this difference is great enough to produce a consistently correct choice.

For example, if one plotted a learning curve for an animal with a strong, left-going position habit, the probability of choosing the correct discriminandum would hover noisily around chance for a while because *black* would be on the *left* for a random half of the trials. Learning would nevertheless be taking place. But it would not be reflected in performance until the difference between E_{black} and E_{white} exceeds the difference between E_{left} and E_{right}. Only then would the animal choose the black discriminandum regardless of whether it was on the right or the left. Hence, according to Spence's theory, early reversal of rewards should increase the trials required to learn.

Reversal Shift Procedure

To test these two opposing theories Spence proposed a critical experiment. Suppose an experimental and a control group of rats are exposed to a discrimination learning problem. Let the control group be trained throughout with the same reinforcement contingencies. Let the experimental group have the reinforcement contingencies reversed after some training trials have been presented but *before* the animals begin to respond correctly above chance. Association theory predicts that the reversed group will learn more slowly than the nonreversed control group.

This experiment crystallized the difference between Spence's neobehaviorist theory of animal discrimination learning and the more cognitive, Lashley–Krechevsky theory. The difference generated what Krechevsky (1938) dubbed the continuity–noncontinuity controversy. The neobehaviorist theory represented the continuity side of the controversy because it assumed that the excitatory tendencies change continuously throughout training. Moreover, as Krechevsky (1938) emphasized, in continuity theories "Nothing is said about the 'attention' of the animal, nothing about the 'awareness' of the animal with respect to the important stimuli" (p. 111). He characterized the theory proposed by Lashley and himself as noncontinuous because the animal learns only about the stimuli to which it is attending. If these are not the relevant cues, the animal eventually gives up responding to them. Learning is discontinuous because nothing has been learned about the correct cue while the animal is attending to the incorrect one. As to testable predictions, Krechevsky (1938) agreed that

> if the significance of the stimuli are reversed before the animal begins to 'pay attention to' them (i.e., during the presolution period), it should not necessarily make for any slower learning of the reversed problem. (p. 112)

The way Krechevsky formulated the controversy emphasized the difference between how the two theories interpret the encoding process. Continuity theory assumed that information processing in animals is nonselective and noncontinuity theory assumed it is selective. Continuity theory conceived of discrimination learning as a gradual change in the association between nonselectively encoded information and choice behavior. Noncontinuity theory conceived of discrimination learning as a change in what the animal is attending to. As in contemporary cognitive theories, the distinction between learning and perception was blurred.

Because the controversy concerned such ostensibly clear differences both sides agreed they could be resolved in a critical experiment. Many reversal–nonreversal discrimination learning experiments were performed. Unfortunately, no unequivocal evidence acceptable to both sides emerged, due largely to lack of agreement about the proper controls. Nevertheless, for a brief interlude it seemed as though the controversy was resolved in favor of continuity theory, partly because Spence's formulation was more precise and elegant and partly because the evidence mostly showed learning to be slower among reversed than nonreversed animals (Deese & Hulse, 1967; Riley, 1968). Presently the zeitgeist shifted again toward more mentalistic, cognitive versions of learning and memory and the noncontinuity version is currently prevalent.

Reversal Shifts and Symbolic Mediation Pretheory

Spence acknowledged that a complete account of discrimination learning would require a more complex theory than he had provided. Nevertheless, continuity theory successfully demonstrated that the discrimination learning of animals did not demand high-level intellectual powers of the sort postulated by noncontinuity theory. At the same time Spence was especially careful to limit the application of continuity theory to infrahuman animals and to "preverbal children." Like Hull, Spence expected language to have a profound effect on human discrimination learning.

Our early research set out to test the hypothesis that, while continuity theory applied to discrimination learning in infrahuman animals, human adults acquired mediating representational responses that result in selective control of their choice behavior by the relevant dimension. We used the reversal shift procedure but, instead of reversing the reinforcement contingencies while the learner was still responding at chance, the reversal was delayed until *after* the preshift discrimination was learned to criterion. And instead of using discriminanda with only one visual dimension, the discriminanda differed on two visual dimensions, only one of which was relevant.

When the learners reached criterion on the preshift discrimination they were presented with the shift phase using the same discriminanda but the reinforcement contingencies were changed. For half the subjects, the reversal-shift group, the rewards were reversed within the relevant visual dimension. For the other half, the nonreversal-shift group, one of the values on the previously irrelevant dimension became correct. The question was which would be learned more easily, a *reversal shift* within the previously relevant dimension or a *nonreversal shift* to a value on the previously irrelevant dimension?

Spence's continuity model predicts a reversal-shift should require more trials to learn than a nonreversal-shift (H. Kendler, Hirschberg, & Wolford, 1971). The prediction follows because learning to reverse a previously well-learned choice on the relevant dimension should be more difficult than learning to choose between two neutralized values on the previously irrelevant stimuli. Kelleher (1956) compared the ease of learning reversal and nonreversal shifts in rats and confirmed the prediction. The animals learned reversal shifts significantly more slowly than nonreversal shifts. Other investigators have since replicated this result with rats (Tighe, Brown, & Youngs, 1965), as well as with other infrahuman animals, including chickens (Brookshire, Warren, & Ball, 1961), pigeons (Schade & Bitterman, 1966), cats (Coutant & Warren, 1966), and both infant and mature monkeys (Tighe, 1964, 1965). In each experiment the animals required more trials to learn reversal than nonreversal shifts.

On the other hand, when human adults are presented with a suitable variant of the reversal–nonreversal-shift procedure they learn the reversal shift relatively easily. For instance, Buss (1953) performed an experiment on college students in which the discriminanda consisted of wooden blocks differing in height, form, color, and size. Half the students learned a height discrimination followed by a reverse height discrimination (reversal shift). The other half learned a form discrimination followed by a height discrimination (nonreversal shift). The reversal group learned the shift discrimination in less trials than the nonreversal group. Other experiments controlling for one artifact or another have since been conducted with human adults using some variant of the reversal–nonreversal procedure (e.g., Gormezano & Grant, 1964; Harrow, 1964; and H. Kendler & D'Amato, 1955). All obtained the same result; among human adults, a reversal shift was easier than a nonreversal shift.

Our early discrimination-learning research explored a simple pretheory of learning and problem solving, which we then thought could be elaborated to account for the qualitative difference between how adult humans and infrahuman animals responded to the reversal–nonreversal procedure (H. Kendler & Kendler, 1962). This pretheory utilized the hypothetical mediating response mechanism to distinguish between two learning modes: a single unit (S-R) mode and a mediated (S-r-s-R) mode. We assumed the single-unit mode operates according to continuity theory and therefore processes all discriminable sensory input nonselectively and in parallel and the association between the stimulus and response is relatively direct. Encoding in the single-unit mode is therefore nonselective.

In the mediating mode the association between the extrinsic stimulus and the overt response is interposed by a learned hypothetical representational response (r). This r, unlike the r_g usually applied to animal learning, forms a symbolic representation of the stimuli in the discriminanda. The mediating representational response, which could be overt or covert, was assumed to generate some kind of hypothetical stimulation (s), which, in turn, could become associated with an overt response. The effect of this mediation was the selective encoding of the cues on the relevant dimension. In the language of current-day connectionists the r would be a kind of hidden unit.

The original presumption was that such hypothetical, covert associations obeyed the same laws of learning as overt $S-R$ associations. Accordingly, the correct response becomes associated with the stimulation produced by the relevant representational response rather than with the extrinsic stimulus, *per se*. One obvious implication of this presumption was that the mediating representational response behavior was learned.

Such a formulation naturally leads the investigator toward the study of when and how humans acquire mediating, representational responses. Kuenne (1946), one of Spence's doctoral students, had already began this quest by adapting another type of discrimination learning procedure to children. Her results suggested that very young children responded in the so-called single-unit mode while older children responded in accordance with the mediated mode. This interpretation was tested by investigating how children respond to the reversal–nonreversal shift procedure.

INITIAL REVERSAL SHIFT RESEARCH WITH CHILDREN

When discrimination learning procedures are used with laboratory animals, each animal usually gets a stipulated number of trials per day until a criterion of about 80% correct choices on a given day is attained. Attaining criterion can take many trials per day and many successive days of training, particularly when there are irrelevant, visual dimensions. Working with children required adapting the procedure to this new species in a way that allowed for valid interspecies comparisons. The procedure we used in the first experiment with children (T. Kendler & Kendler, 1959) is described here in detail to provide the reader with a sense of the problem from both the child's and experimenter's perspective. As our experience grew and laboratory technology increased we varied the procedures and automated the controls, but in this first experiment we used the simplest apparatus: four metal tumblers that differed simultaneously in size and brightness, as illustrated in Fig. 2.1. The tumblers were set out in pairs, one pair per trial, on a turntable with a shield in the center.

The learners were kindergartners drawn from public school. Each child was brought individually to a room in the schoolhouse and seated in front of the turntable. When the child was comfortable, the experimenter said,

> This is the game we are going to play, (child's name). Before we start, listen carefully and I will tell you how the game is played. See there are two things

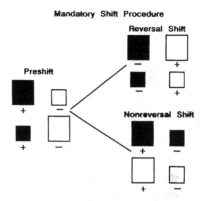

FIG. 2.1. Illustrative discriminanda and the associated reinforcement contingencies in the two phases of the mandatory shift procedure.

here (pointing to a large black and a small white tumbler on the turntable). When we start the game you will choose one of them and pick it up. If you are right you will find a marble under it; if you are wrong you won't find anything under it. Each time you may choose only one. Then I will turn it around like this and you will have another turn.

Turning the table allowed the experimenter to change the position of the discriminanda and bait one of them with the marble behind the shield out of the child's sight. When the next pair of discriminanda were displayed the experimenter went on to say, "On each turn you may choose only one. The game is to see how soon you can get a marble every time you choose." After a correct choice the child was shown how to place the marble in a receptacle that displayed all of the marbles won in the course of the game. This receptacle was placed next to the apparatus where the accumulating marbles could be admired. Judging from their eagerness to play, the children enjoyed the game, although it was understood from the outset they would not keep the marbles they won.

The Mandatory Shift Procedure

A discrimination shift experiment can be designed in several different ways. The mandatory shift design used in the first experiment with children is illustrated in Fig. 2.1. The discriminanda are always presented in pairs but only one pair is presented per trial. One member of the pair is correct and the other is incorrect. Which pair is presented is randomly determined with the proviso that the same pair is never presented, and the correct choice is never in the same position, on more than three successive trials. Let it be understood that in this design, and in all others to follow, the position (left or right) of the correct discriminandum always varies from trial to trial so that the correct cue is on the left and right a roughly equal number of times.

Training in the mandatory design is divided into a preshift and a postshift phase. During the preshift the discriminanda are paired so that one visual dimension is relevant to the reinforcement contingencies, while the other visual dimension is irrelevant. In this example *brightness* is relevant during the preshift phase because *black* is correct, and *white* is incorrect. *Size* is irrelevant because *large* and *small* are each correct and incorrect on a randomly determined half of the trials. One could say the brightness cues provide information about which discriminandum is correct and the size cues do not. In all experiments a counterbalanced design was used so that each feature, say, *black, white, large,* and *small,* was correct during the preshift for a randomly assigned quarter of the learners.

Training on the preshift continued until the child attained criterion, which in the first experiment was 9 out of 10 successive correct choices. Immediately after criterion was attained, training on the shift phase began without any forewarning or comment. A random half of the learners were presented with a reversal shift within the relevant dimension; the other half were presented with a nonreversal shift. The reversal group had to learn to reverse their choices within the relevant dimension, say from *black* to *white.* The nonreversal group had to learn to choose one of the previously irrelevant cues, say *large.*

Which experimental group should learn the shift more rapidly? If the children responded in the mediated mode, like the adults, the reversal group should learn relatively rapidly. If they behaved in the unmediated mode, like the rats, the nonreversal group should learn relatively rapidly. To my initial consternation, there was no statistically reliable difference between the two groups. It almost seemed as though neither mode characterized children's learning. Another possibility was that children at the kindergarten level were in a transition stage such that approximately half were responding in each mode. If the two sets were combined into a single group they would cancel each other out.

To test the transition hypothesis the data were sorted into fast and slow learners according to whether number of trials required to learn the preshift discrimination were above or below the median. The fast learners were expected to perform like the human adults, to learn the reversal shift relatively rapidly. The slow learners were expected to perform like the infrahuman animals, to learn the *non*reversal shift relatively rapidly. Both expectations were realized.

This *post hoc* analysis suggested the tendency for choice behavior to be mediated by representational responses develops sometime during childhood. The obvious next step was to see how younger children performed. If there is a developmental difference the younger children should learn nonreversal shifts more rapidly than reversal shifts. The next experiment was with preschool children about a year younger than the kindergarten children (T. Kendler, Kendler, & Wells, 1960). Taken as a group the expectation was confirmed. Yet, even at this young age, some children were learning the reversal quite rapidly. There seemed to be an interesting developmental phenomenon here but to pursue it further required a procedure that could more directly assess which mode was operative in the individual child.

The Optional Shift Procedure

The mandatory shift procedure randomly assigns each subject in a sample to learn either a reversal or a nonreversal shift. Comparing the mean trials of the reversal and nonreversal shift groups tells which kind of shift is executed more rapidly on the average. If, say the reversal shift is executed significantly more rapidly than the nonreversal shift, the implication is that the sample, as a whole, is somewhat disposed to encode selectively. But no information is provided about how this disposition is distributed within the sample. Take, for instance, the first experiment, where there was no significant difference between the mean number of trials to learn the mandatory reversal and nonreversal shifts. While this outcome is consistent with the hypothesis that half the children learned in one mode and the other half learned in another mode, a better procedure would measure these proportions directly by diagnosing which mode was operative in each individual learner. The optional-shift procedure provides such a method by allowing each individual the option of making a reversal or nonreversal shift.

This procedure, illustrated in Fig. 2.2, consists of three phases: a preshift phase, an optional shift phase, and a test phase. The three phases follow in succession without any break or warning. Because the optional shift is referred to often throughout, the three phases are described in some detail.

Preshift Phase. The preshift phase is exactly the same as in the mandatory shift. The paired discriminanda differ simultaneously on two visual dimensions; one dimension is relevant and the other is irrelevant to the

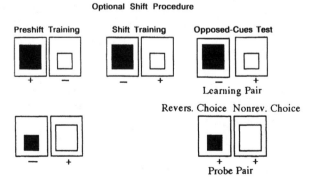

FIG. 2.2. Illustrative discriminanda and the associated reinforcement contingencies in the three phases of the optional shift procedure.

reinforcement contingencies. The two pairs are randomly alternated from trial to trial, as is the position of the correct cue. One value on one of the dimensions, say *black*, is correct for a given subject, and the learner is trained to criterion. In this example, the learner who "mediates" is presumably selectively encoding the values on the relevant dimension. This learner would learn to choose *black*, to avoid *white*, and to ignore the size differential. The learner who does not mediate is learning to choose the correct and avoid the incorrect compound while presumably responding nonselectively to all of the features in the discriminanda.

Shift Phase. When criterion is attained on the preshift phase, the shift phase is introduced without warning. In this procedure all of the learners are presented with the same shift training. Only *one* pair of discriminanda is presented but the reinforcement contingencies are reversed for everyone. Because there is only one pair, both visual dimensions become relevant and redundant. For example, both *small* and *white* become correct and both *large* and *black* become incorrect.

This phase allows the learner to attain criterion in one of two ways, depending on whether or not one selectively encoded the cues on the initially relevant dimension, The learner who selectively encodes the relevant, brightness cues, should transfer choices from *black* to *white*, and ignore the size cues. This kind of transfer is referred to as an optional *reversal shift*. On the other hand, the learner who encodes all of the stimuli nonselectively, should not spontaneously do the opposite of what was previously learned. (A more complete explanation is spelled out in detail in chapter 8.) This kind of transfer is referred to as a *nonreversal shift*.

Test Phase. Because the subject can learn to respond correctly on the shift phase by making either a reversal or a nonreversal shift, diagnosing which shift occurred requires the addition of a test phase after criterion on the shift is attained. On the test phase the pair of discriminanda omitted during the shift phase (the *probe pair*) is reintroduced without warning. The probe pair is alternated with the pair presented in the shift phase (the *learning pair*). Responses to the learning pair continue to be rewarded as in the shift phase in order to encourage the learner to continue responding as in the shift phase. On alternate trials when the probe pair is presented either choice is rewarded. These alternating trials are continued until the probe pair has been presented 10 times.

Which member of the probe pair the learner chooses provides the information that distinguishes the selective from the nonselective encoder. For example, a learner who selectively encodes the relevant brightness cues and ignores the irrelevant size cues should choose the large *white* discriminandum (reversal choice) rather than the small *black* one (nonreversal choice). Hence, a selective encoder is likely to make a reversal choice on the first probe trial and be rewarded for doing so because either choice is rewarded. The tendency to sustain the same choice on subsequent probe trials is buttressed by the alternating learning trials so that selective encoders should tend to make significantly more reversal than nonreversal choices. The probability of making 8 or more reversal choices in the 10 allotted probe trials by chance is only .05. On this basis a learner who makes 8 or more reversal choices on the 10 test trials can be diagnosed as having made a reversal shift within the initially relevant dimension. Given the proper controls, we can infer, with a slight margin of error, that this learner has selectively encoded the features on the relevant dimension. Any other pattern of choices is classified as a nonreversal shift. Nonreversal shifts are likely to occur if a learner responds nonselectively to all of the cues in the discriminanda, as assumed by continuity theory.

The group measure yielded in this procedure is the proportion of learners who make optional reversal shifts. When applied to children at different age levels, this proportion is treated as an estimate of the probability that the selective encoding mode will prevail at each age level. Before the optional shift procedure was adapted to children, we already knew that human adults are highly likely to make optional reversal shifts (Buss, 1956; Harrow & Friedman, 1958; H. Kendler & D'Amato, 1955). The first optional shift experiment with children (T. Kendler, Kendler, & Learnard, 1962) used a semiautomated apparatus that replaced the tumblers from the first experiments with two-dimensional discriminanda, each displayed in its own window. The learners were 3, 4, 6, 8, and 10-year-olds. The question was would the tendency to selectively encode be related to age?

To compare how infrahuman animals would respond under comparable conditions we also performed a similar experiment using the same, size-brightness discriminanda with rats (T. Kendler, Kendler, & Silfen, 1964). The left-most bar of Fig. 2.3 shows that only 5% of the rats made an optional reversal shift, which was no greater than chance alone would allow. That rats are disposed to make optional nonreversal shifts was later replicated by two independent laboratories (Tighe & Tighe, 1966; Sutherland & Mackintosh, 1966).

But, as shown in the right side of Fig. 2.3, among the children there was a statistically reliable, monotonic, age-related increase in the proportion of children who made optional reversal shifts. These experiments provided additional support for the existence of two qualitatively different encoding modes. They confirmed that rats are disposed to respond in the nonselective mode. The children's data indicated that whether humans are disposed to encode selectively or nonselectively depended on their age.

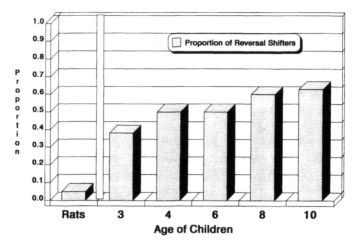

FIG. 2.3. Compares the proportion of learners who made optional reversal shifts among rats and among children at different age levels.

CONCLUSIONS

These data suggested that the continuity–noncontinuity controversy could be resolved by postulating two information-processing modes. The relatively passive, nonselective mode processes all the information to which the organism is sensitive. The relatively active, selective mode abstracts the relevant from the irrelevant input. When presented with visual, discrimination learning problems infrahuman animals are prone to respond in the nonselective mode. Human adults are prone to respond in the selective mode. The early evidence also suggested that the tendency for humans to respond in the selective mode increases gradually over age, but this suggestion required further confirmation.

CHAPTER THREE

Developmental Trends in Information Processing

If the vital centers of the lowest levels were not strongly organized at birth, life would not be possible; if the centers of the highest levels ("mental centers") were not little organized and therefore very modifiable we could only with difficulty and imperfectly adjust ourselves to the circumstances.

— F. Hughlings Jackson from J. Taylor (1932)

Because information processing by living organisms is not directly observable the nature of the process must be inferred from publicly observable behavior under specifiable conditions. Scientific understanding of hidden processes rests on a theory that relates observable inputs and outputs. A good theory organizes the available data, makes testable predictions, and suggests the means for testing them. The *S–R* mediational pretheory organized the early data by assuming that two kinds of discrimination learning could be distinguished, mediated and unmediated, and provided a procedure for distinguishing one from the other. The mediated mode selectively encodes the cues on the relevant dimension while the unmediated mode encodes all of the perceptible cues nonselectively. Mediation was assumed to depend on a learned, representational response interceding between the reception of the stimulus and the overt choice response. Reversal shift procedures provided an objective, controlled method for measuring selectively encoding in infrahuman animals as well as in humans of different ages. The first experiment using the optional reversal shift procedure with children found the tendency to make optional reversal shifts depended on their age. But the transition from nonselective to selective encoding seemed to take place over a longer time period than the commonly accepted critical 5- to 7-year period suggested by a number of experiments summarized by White (1965).

The next step investigated the reliability and generality of this unexpectedly long-term transition in a combined experimental–developmental format using the optional shift procedure. A new, more automated apparatus was built and housed in a mobile laboratory that could be moved from school to school. The discriminanda were now electronically projected onto two small windows, approximately 2.5 sq. inches, in front of which the learner was seated. The learner tripped each trial by touching a start platform placed between the two windows. The "game" became more amusing because the displays were not only more attractive but a correct choice automatically produced the reward, a varicolored marble, and the trials could be presented in quick succession as soon as the learner was ready. The order of stimulus presentation was preprogrammed and each choice was automatically recorded on tape. The automation also enabled the experimenter to stay behind and out of sight of the learner thereby reducing the possibility of unintentional cues.

The instructions given to the learners were essentially the same as before except for the necessary adaptation to the automated apparatus. The only change in the basic procedure was to increase the criterion for learning to 10 successive correct choices. Although automation reduced the time to train each learner and also made the game more amusing, the preshift phase remained difficult for some of the youngest children to learn. Consequently, a child who had not learned within a hundred trials was taken back to the classroom with the promise of resuming the game the next day or soon thereafter on as many successive days as required to attain criterion. This markedly reduced the bias introduced by eliminating children for failure to learn.

The research now had two purposes. One purpose was to determine the reliability and generality of the developmental trend by comparing perform- ance at the different age levels. The other purpose was to provide insights into the process that produces selective encoding by comparing different experimental conditions. This chapter concentrates on describing and inter- preting the developmental trends that emerged. The effect of the various experimental manipulations is taken up in chapter 9.

GENERALITY AND FORM
OF THE DEVELOPMENTAL TREND

The first experiment with the automated apparatus (T. Kendler & Kendler, 1970) tested the replicability and generality of the developmental trend found earlier, which had been challenged by a number of investigators (e.g., Shepp & Turrisi, 1966; Smiley & Weir, 1966; Wolff, 1967). To test for generality three dimensions were represented: *size*, where the area of the larger discriminandum was approximately 2.5 times that of the smaller one; *form*, where one discriminandum was circular and the other triangular; and *color*, where one discriminandum was bright red and the other bright green. These three dimensions were used to produce three sets of paired discriminanda. One set differed only in size and form, as illustrated in Fig. 3.1. A second set differed only in color and form; the third set differed only in size and color.

The procedure entailed a two-choice, simultaneous, visual discrimination between bidimensional compounds. Everyone was trained on the three phases of the optional shift procedure described in detail chapter 2. Recall that the preshift phase establishes one visual dimension as relevant and the other as *ir*relevant to the reinforcement contingencies. The shift phase makes both dimensions relevant and redundant but reverses the reinforcement contingencies. The test phase is essentially a continuation of the shift phase except that 10 opposed-cues probe trials are unobtrusively interspersed between the learning trials. On each probe trial the learner must make either a reversal or a nonreversal choice. A reversal choice implies dominance of the previously incorrect cue on the initially relevant dimension. A nonreversal choice implies dominance of the previously neutral cue on the initially *ir*relevant dimension. A learner who makes at least 8 out of 10 reversal choices is considered to have made a reversal shift within the relevant dimension. Given the proper controls, a reversal shift is assumed to reflect the selective control of the relevant dimension on the learner's behavior.

Four nonoverlapping age levels, drawn from kindergarten, second grade, sixth grade, and undergraduate university classes, were represented. The mean chronological ages of the children were 5.8, 7.8, and 11.8 years; the university students were arbitrarily assigned a chronological age of 18. Each learner at each age level was randomly assigned to training on only one of

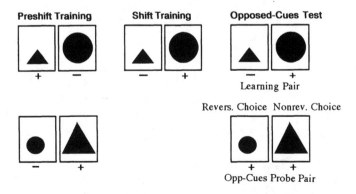

FIG. 3.1. Illustrative reinforcement contingencies in the three phases of the optional shift procedure, when the discriminanda differed in size and form and form was the relevant dimension.

the three sets of discriminanda. Within each set which dimension was relevant and which value was initially correct were completely counterbalanced. There were in all 348 learners and each learner was trained individually.

The results confirmed and extended upward the developmental trend manifested earlier; there was a statistically reliable overall increase over age in the proportion of learners who made optional reversal shifts under each of the three stimulus conditions. A second study (T. Kendler & Ward, 1972) followed using the identical procedure with nursery school children, which extended the age range downward to include two more nonoverlapping age levels whose mean chronological ages were 3.6 and 4.5 years. When these data were merged with the data from the previous experiment, the overall ordered age differences remained statistically significant. That is, there was an ordered increase in the proportion of reversal shifts between 3 years of age and young adulthood in each stimulus condition taken separately.

Quantifying the Developmental Trend

The trend began to seem orderly enough to be quantifiable. To test this possibility an exponential function, a power function, and a log function were each fitted to the data from all three experimental conditions combined (T. Kendler & Ward, 1972). The best fit was obtained with a simple log function of the form:

$$y = a + b \ln x$$

where y refers to the probability that an individual will make an optional reversal-shift, a represents the intercept and b the rate parameters, and $\ln x$ refers to the natural logarithm of chronological age in months.

Figure 3.2 presents the log functions subsequently fitted to the data for each stimulus condition separately. To produce these functions five age levels between 4 and 18 years were represented. The youngest age level was drawn from nursery schools. The eldest age level consisted of undergraduate university students, whose age was arbitrarily set at 18. The children between these two levels were drawn from public schools. To keep the format uniform all of the developmental trends presented here follow the same format. By transforming the age to logarithms the log function becomes linear, which permits the use of a chi-square test of goodness of fit (Maxwell, 1961). This test partitions the total chi-square into a linear component and a remainder component. If the linear component is significant, the age trend may be considered reliable; if the remainder component is *not* significant the fitted log function may be considered tenable. Each of the age trends proved to be statistically significant and each fitted function proved to be

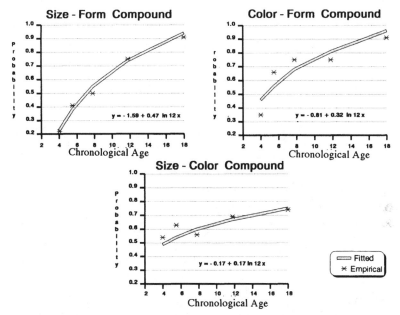

FIG. 3.2. Developmental trends fitted to the proportion of learners who made optional reversal shifts under three different stimulus conditions.

statistically tenable for each compound taken separately as well as for all compounds combined.

Fitted functions not only quantify the developmental trends, they simplify description and allow for interpolation and extrapolation. Interpolation enables one to predict performance anywhere on the age scale. Extrapolation down the age scale makes it feasible to estimate performance at the very youngest age levels where the practical problems of data collection become prohibitive. More than that, fitting the functions to these trends brought about another way of thinking about the data. Looking back now this difference could be attributed to differentiating between the form of the function and its parameters. The form of the function, which held over each stimulus condition, indicated that the disposition to encode nonselectively increased gradually at a decelerating rate over a long time period. This gradual increase is the expression of a long-term, age-related process. The parameters, on the other hand, measure the effect of the immediate stimulus conditions on the probability that selective encoding will occur. The implication is that a theoretical account of these data requires explanation of two separable factors, the form of the long-term developmental trend and the immediate effect of the stimuli to be encoded.

Extending the Generality of the Developmental Function

To test the generality of the fitted function further, the developmental trend was tested under two different training conditions (T. Kendler, 1983). One condition instructed the learners to label the relevant cues; the other over-

29

trained the learners on the preshift phase. The effect of both experimental manipulations were evaluated against the same control condition in which there were no instructions to label and the learners were not overtrained.

The discriminanda in this experiment differed in size and form, as illustrated in Fig. 3.1. The learners were grouped into five nonoverlapping age levels drawn respectively from nursery school, kindergarten, second grade, sixth grade, and university classes. Within each age level each learner was randomly assigned to one of the manipulated conditions.

Effect of Labeling. The label condition required the learners to supply verbal labels for the values on the relevant dimension. Assigning a distinctive role in the learning process to linguistic labels has a long history. Pavlov, for instance, considered words to be abstractions of reality, resulting in a kind of generalization that required a different principle of conditioning available only to language users. Spence (1937) also surmised that verbal processes could transcend the simple mechanisms of discrimination learning. There was evidence that instructions to label the relevant cues could potentiate reversal shifts (H. Kendler & Kendler, 1961; T. Kendler, 1964; Silverman, 1966). At the time this evidence was construed as supporting the hypothesis that selective encoding was produced by the mediation of a learned representational response. This experiment was designed to determine, among other things, how the introduction of verbal representations of the relevant cues interacted with age.

Each learner in the relevant label condition was instructed at the outset of the preshift phase to say aloud, after the discriminanda were displayed but before the manual choice, which of the two values on the relevant dimension he or she was going to choose. For instance, if the relevant dimension was form, the learner was told to say on each trial whether he or she would choose the *circle* or the *triangle*. During the preshift phase, a learner who omitted the label on a given trial was reminded once again to "say aloud. . . ." These reminders were limited to the preshift phase. As it turned out, all of the children, even the youngest, had appropriate verbal labels in their repertoire and proved capable of using them as directed.

The first graph in Fig. 3.3 presents the empirical proportion of reversal shifters at each age level in the relevant label condition along with the fitted log function. Invoking relevant labels did not did not change the form of the developmental trend, which remained statistically significant. The fitted log function was also statistically tenable. Although the emphasis here is on the developmental trend, it should be mentioned that when this function was compared to the function fitted to the control group, there was a significant difference in the parameters. The difference indicated that labeling potentiated selective encoding somewhat at the younger ages but this potentiation gradually diminished over age until it presently disappeared. Thus on the one hand the potentiation seems to support the notion that selective encoding depends on the mediation of a learned, representational response. On the other hand two findings raised questions about this notion. One was finding that the appropriate linguistic representations were already in the repertoire of all of the children. The other was that requiring everyone to use these representations by no means eliminated the developmental trend. Apparently linguistic labels can potentiate selective encoding but they are not the *sine qua non.* Some other age-related factor is also operative.

Effect of Overtraining. Another experimental condition in this experiment investigated the effect of overtraining on the preshift phase. The only difference was that, instead of requiring each learner to label the relevant cues in the preshift phase, the criterion run in this phase was followed by 30 overtraining trials. Several studies using rats had shown that, under certain conditions, overtraining in the preshift phase of a mandatory shift procedure facilitates reversal learning (e.g., Capaldi & Stevenson, 1957; Mackintosh, 1964; Reid, 1957; Shepp & Turissi, 1966). This phenomenon, known as the "overlearning reversal effect," was at the time considered to support a modified version of noncontinuity theory that assumed all discrimination learning entailed a gradual strengthening of selective attention to the relevant dimensions but might require overtraining to become manifest (Sutherland & Mackintosh, 1971). Prior research had also shown that overtraining potentiates the probability of reversing among children (Eimas, 1969a; Shepp & Adams, 1973; Tighe & Tighe, 1966).

The second graph in Fig. 3.3 presents the empirical proportion of reversal shifters at each age level in the overtraining condition along with the fitted log function. Again, the developmental trend in the overtrained condition was statistically significant and the fitted function was tenable. Again, relative to the control (no overtraining) condition the slope parameter was somewhat decreased but did not change the form of the developmental trend. Apparently overtraining also potentiates selective encoding but does not eliminate the developmental trend.

Intradimensional Shifts. The third graph in Fig. 3.3 presents the results of another experiment with another sample of learners drawn from the same five age levels. This one investigated the effect of a procedural variation known as the optional intradimensional shift on the developmental trend. In this variant the preshift phase is the same as in the reversal shift procedure; the difference lies in the transfer test. Instead of reversing the reinforcement on the same set of discriminanda, in the intradimensional shift the dimensions remain the same but the values on each visual dimension are changed. For instance, in the cited experiment the discriminanda differed in color and form (see Fig. 9.2 for an illustration). Two sets of color-form compounds were used. For one set the colors were *red* and *green* and the forms were

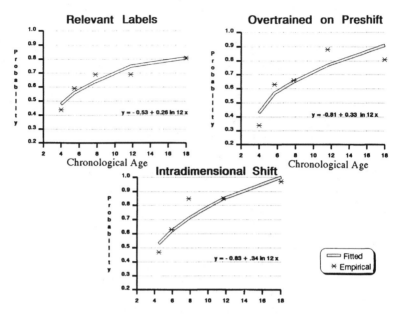

FIG. 3.3. Developmental trends fitted to the proportion of learners who made optional reversal shifts under three different training conditions.

square and *cross*. Each learner was trained on the preshift with one set and tested on the subsequent shift and test phases with the other set. This procedure is designed to determine whether the learner who was trained to choose the correct value on the relevant dimension during the preshift phase, will manifest a preference for the new set of values on the initially relevant dimension in the test phase. A learner who manifests a preference for the new values on the initially relevant dimension on 8 or more test trials is classified as having made an intradimensional shift.

This investigation was prompted by the challenge from some quarters that the age trends were restricted to the reversal shift procedure and would not be manifested if the intradimensional procedure were used. The optional intradimensional procedure shift was used with another sample of learners distributed over the same five age levels to determine whether there was an important difference between the two procedures (H. Kendler, Kendler, & Ward, 1972). The third graph of Fig. 3.3 shows the intradimensional shift produced a significant developmental trend and the log function fitted to the trend proved tenable. Moreover, when this function was later compared with the function fitted to an earlier optional reversal-shift experiment that used the color-form discriminanda the parameters proved to be almost identical (T. Kendler 1979b). Considering that the two studies were conducted by different experimenters, several years apart, and on entirely different samples; the two trends turned out to be remarkably similar.

Apparently manipulating the immediate training and transfer conditions known to affect selective encoding affected the parameters of the developmental function but left the form unchanged. All of these data taken together, attest to the generality of the developmental trend.

INTERPRETING THE DEVELOPMENTAL TREND

Thus what began as a series of experimental investigations, guided by a learning theory, began to take on a developmental cast. With this transition came the problems associated with using cross-sectional data—based on different individuals at the different age levels—as indicative of longitudinal, ontogenetic change. How these problems were dealt with is described in detail in T. Kendler (1979b) and summarized here.

Ontogenetic Change. One problem is that cross-sectional differences could be attributable to cohort differences, rather than age. For instance, the successive age samples could represent increasingly able individuals due to selection by the educational system. Whether cohort differences could explain the outcome was tested in the several ways.

One test simply omitted the university sample and fitted the log function to the remaining four age levels to determine how this would affect the developmental function in one of experimental conditions. The discriminanda in this condition differed in size and form and the learners were neither overtrained nor instructed to label the relevant features. This condition had the most subjects because it had served as the control for testing the effect of several experimental manipulations. The fitted function, with the university students omitted, turned out to be $y = -1.65 + 0.48 \ln x$, not much different than the fitted function with the university students included, which was $y = -1.59 + 0.47 \ln x$. When the restricted function was extrapolated to 18 years, the extrapolated probability was 0.93, compared well with the obtained probability, 0.91.

Although the developmental trend does not depend on the inclusion of university students, it is possible that the difference between the children at the various age levels are nevertheless due to cohort differences in intellect. All of the children who participated in these experiments were given the Peabody Picture Vocabulary Test (PPVT) immediately before the optional shift procedure began. The respective mean IQs for the four ordered age levels, which were 110, 107, 109, and 112, showed very little difference between the cohorts and no increasing trend at all.

A third test was performed that also bears on the more interesting question of how intelligence may be related to selective encoding. For this purpose, all children in each of the three stimulus conditions who were trained to criterion without any instructions to label the cues were divided into two approximately equal groups on the basis of whether their PPVT IQs were above or below 110. The means for the higher and lower IQ groups turned out to be 120.8 and 98.2, respectively. The overall proportion of reversal shifts for the each group, collapsed over age, were respectively .60 and .51; in the expected direction but not statistically significant. When the developmental trends for the higher and lower IQ groups were plotted separately, each developmental trend manifested a monotonic increase that was fitted with a tenable log function. There was, however, a difference between the two functions that suggested a considerable divergence in favor of the higher IQ group at the lowest age levels but the divergence diminished gradually until it disappeared completely at the highest age level. Because the statistical difference between the two fitted functions only approached significance the most that can be concluded is that, if IQ has any effect, it is primarily among the younger children. In any case, cohort differences in intelligence could not explain the increasing developmental trend.

Although the developmental trend is not to be accounted for by IQ differences there remains the possibility of a calendar time effect (Schaie, 1970). Since the learners at the different age levels were born and raised at different times the obtained trend could be due to some events associated with calendar rather than ontogenetic time. One way to determine which kind of time is operative is to compare the trends obtained from cross-sectional samples tested at different calendar times. If the age differences are replicated over widely spaced calendar-time intervals, then the developmental trends are not to be explained by events associated with calendar time. With respect to the developmental trends under consideration, the earliest trend (Kendler, Kendler, & Learnard, 1962) is based on data obtained between 1959 and 1960. Because it is simpler and more precise to compare the developmental trends in terms of fitted functions the log function was retroactively fitted to these data. The fit proved to be tenable (T. Kendler, 1979b). The most recent developmental trend (H. Kendler, Kendler, & Ward, 1972) is based on data collected between 1970 and 1971. The other trends presented in Figs. 3.2 and 3.3 are based on data collected in the 11 years between 1959 and 1970, long enough to cover a good part of the time span covered by each trend. This replication over different calendar times rules out the calendar-time explanation.

Gradual Change. Another problem arises because the developmental trend is measured by an increase in the *proportion* of learners who made reversal shifts. Such trends can be interpreted in accordance with alternative models. The most common model, usually applied to the developmental trends associated with Piagetian tasks (e.g., Winer, 1980), is deterministic and saltatory. In a deterministic model each individual is presumed to be in one stage or another and the response to the task diagnoses which stage he or she is in. The model is saltatory in that the transition between stages is discontinuous; development consists of a quantum-like leap from one stage to another. According to the deterministic model the developmental trend reflects the increasing number of individuals who function in the higher stage.

A less common but equally plausible model for interpreting such developmental trends assumes the development to be probabilistic and gradual. The development is probabilistic in that the ontogenetic change consists of an increasing disposition to perform at a higher level. The development is gradual in that this disposition is assumed to increase continuously over age. Hence the age-related increase in the proportion of reversal shifts is interpreted as an increase in the mean of a changing distribution of probabilities.

Testing which model applies to the reversal shift trends produced by cross-sectional data appears to require a longitudinal investigation that would follow the same children for many years; a discouraging prospect strewn with both practical and methodological difficulties. A more workable test was devised that consisted simply of administering a set of repeated measures—using comparable versions of the optional shift procedure—to each child at a given age level and counting the number of times each one made a reversal shift. A frequency distribution of the number of reversal shifts produced by children in the mid-age range can serve to distinguish between the two models.

The saltatory, deterministic model predicts a bimodal distribution at each age level in which each learner makes either mostly reversal or mostly nonreversal shifts. Developmental change should be manifested as a decrease over age in the proportion of children who respond in the lower mode and a concomitant increase in the proportion who respond in the higher mode. The continuous, probabilistic model predicts a unimodal distribution at each age level because the proportion of reversal shifts produced on the repeated measure tests should vary quantitatively and continuously around the mean for any given age. Developmental change should be manifested by a gradual increase over age in the mean of that distribution.

This repeated measures test was applied to the optional reversal shift procedure in two investigations. Both investigations presented each child with a series of four consecutive versions of the procedure spaced approximately 1 week apart. The discriminanda in both investigations differed in size and form. The only difference between the successive versions lay in which value—*large, small, circle,* or *triangle*—was correct in the preshift phase. The behavior measured was the number of reversal shifts made by each child on the four consecutive tests, which could vary from 0 to 4. In the first investigation (T. Kendler & Tabor-Hynds, 1974), the children were drawn from the second grade (mean CA = 8.0). The next investigation (Tabor & Kendler, 1981) was more ambitious. Three grade levels were represented, namely kindergarten, first, and third grade. Their mean ages were 5.5, 6.9 and 8.8, respectively.

The results of the two investigations were combined in Fig. 3.4 to present the frequency distributions of the proportion of children who made 0, 1, 2, 3, or 4 optional reversal shifts at each grade level. As can be plainly seen, each grade level produced a unimodal distribution. This result is consistent

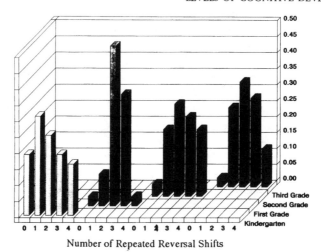

Number of Repeated Reversal Shifts

FIG. 3.4. Frequency distribution of the proportion of children within each
grade level who produced 0, 1, 2, 3, or 4 repeated optional reversal shifts.

with the model that interprets the empirical proportions as representing a
gradual increase in the mean of a changing distribution of probabilities and
inconsistent with the saltatory. deterministic model. Incidentally, Fig. 3.4 also
presents a clear example of how one could have a *quantitative* developmental change—increasing probability—that produces a *qualitative* difference—from nonselective to selective encoding.

Apparently the empirical developmental trends reflect a gradual ontogenetic increase in the probability of making a reversal shift. I should note
that there have been serious questions raised about the validity of such
developmental trends. Why then do these investigations produce such con-
sistency? To answer this question note first that the behavior being measured
is not stable; the trends refer to the probability that selective encoding will
occur and are therefore inherently unstable. They can easily be increased
or decreased by varying the stimulus of training conditions. Moreover the
probabilities change very gradually over a long time period. Given the probabilistic nature, the susceptibility to outside influence, and the very gradual
change, the trends will only become manifest when measured over a fairly
wide age range with sizable samples at each age level. Nevertheless the
trends are real and they need to be taken into account if we are to understand
the nature of selective encoding.

Explaining the Developmental Trends

There are two related facts to be explained. One fact is that two kinds of
encoding can be manifested in the same discrimination learning problem.
At the outset of the research, this fact was explained by the hypothesis that

two kinds of discrimination learning could be differentiated: mediated and unmediated. Unmediated learning entailed a relatively direct association between the features in the discriminanda and the correct choice; mediated learning entailed the interposition of a learned representational response. As the developmental data accumulated and as more became known about the biological basis of perception and about the evolution and development of the central nervous system, it began to make better sense to assume the existence of two different information processing modes that are mediated by different, hierarchically organized, neurological infrastructures. The infrahuman–human differences could be explained in terms of the later evolution of the higher-level infrastructures. The human ontogenetic trends could be explained as reflecting the maturational course of the relatively slow-to-mature higher level.

The levels-of-function theory that elaborates these two notions concerns the developmental changes in structure and function of the system that mediates between the input of the sensory information and the output of the choice responses, as manifested in simple discrimination learning tasks. Whereas the initial pretheory explicitly conceived of the mediating events (r–s) as hypothetical constructs that required no direct coordination to observable events (H. Kendler & Kendler, 1962), the levels theory is a behavioral theory formulated with a view to ultimate coordination with the evolution and development of the underlying neurological substrates.

The revision partitions the hypothetical mediating system into two separable components: an information processing (S) component and an executive (R) component. This chapter is primarily concerned with the information processing component, which contains the sensory and neural structures that give rise to the capacity to perceive and to interpret the significant features in the organism's environment. These capacities differ from one species to another, but within a species they presumably follow a preprogrammed developmental course based on the epigenetic combination of species-general genes and the individual's environment (Changeux, 1985).

In this version the two encoding modes are not mutually exclusive. The nonselective encoding mode continues to be necessary for the reception of *un*selected information that might later become important, such as when there is a change in the relevance from, say, one dimension to another. Rather, the selective encoding mode, because it sorts out the relevant from the irrelevant input, increases the capacity of the organism to control its own response. Consequently these two modes function quite harmoniously when the behavioral outcomes are compatible as in the preshift phase of the optional reversal shift, where selective encoding mode leads to the classification of the discriminanda in terms of the relevant dimension, and the nonselective mode leads to learning to choose the correct feature on the relevant dimension. However, there are circumstances where the behavior generated by these two levels can be incompatible as, for instance, in the test phase of the optional shift procedure where the selective mode produces a reversal shift and the nonselective mode produces a nonreversal shift.

When the behaviors associated with the two modes are incompatible, which mode will prevail is assumed to be a joint function of both extrinsic and intrinsic variables. Extrinsic variables refer to the relatively immediate environmental or experiential factors that influence behavior, such as the nature of the stimuli, the kind of instructions, and the amount or kind of training. The experiments showed that such extrinsic factors influenced the parameters of the fitted developmental function but had no effect on its basic form. Intrinsic factors refer to organismic characteristics such as the developmental status of the nervous system of the learner.

Developmental Change

The second fact to be explained is the gradual ontogenetic increase in the disposition for the selective encoding mode to prevail over the nonselective encoding mode. The earlier *S–R* mediational pretheory had assumed this change was attributable to the acquisition of appropriate representational responses. But further research showed that even the youngest children tested already had available well-learned verbal representations. Moreover, it seems unlikely that acquiring suitable representations for the elementary features of such basic dimensions as size, color, and form would produce such orderly, long-term, growth-like trends that extended all the way from early childhood to young adulthood. These considerations combined with the persistence of the developmental function in the face of changing circumstances all suggested that intrinsic determinants were at work here. To quote Hebb (1972):

> It is obvious that some of the changes of behavior following birth are due to physical growth, especially the increase of the infant's muscular strength. It is not so obvious that growth is also going on in the nervous system, and that learning is not the whole explanation of other changes that are observed. (p. 117)

Hence, to explain the systematic developmental increase in the disposition to make reversal shifts the revised theory looks to intrinsic factors such as maturation in the nervous system rather than to learning *per se*. The premise is that among humans the lower, nonselective level begins to develop very early and matures relatively quickly. The higher, selective encoding level begins to develop somewhat later and proceeds to mature much more slowly and gradually.

This assumption is consistent with the little that is known about maturation in the human cerebral cortex. Myelination is one measure of neural maturation. The last centers to myelinate in the cortex are the intra- or supramodal association areas (Flechsig, 1901). These areas begin to myelinate somewhat later than the primary projection areas but they continue to myelinate at a negatively accelerated rate well into and possibly beyond the second decade of life (Yakovlev & Lecours, 1967). Axonal myelination is positively related to impulse conduction velocity, to membrane excitability, and sometimes to the maximal frequency of impulses. The thickness of the myelin sheath at the first Ranvier node determines how many excitatory postsynaptic potentials are needed to generate a certain number of action potentials (Schulte, 1969). It is at least plausible that selective encoding is mediated by the higher centers in the brain and that these centers become functional at an early age but gradually become more efficient and responsive with increasing maturity. In the same vein, it is at least plausible that the disposition to encode selectively is a reflection of the degree of responsivity in the higher encoding level and that, among humans, one of the variables that determine this responsivity is the degree of maturation.

The introduction of purely hypothetical intrinsic factors like neuronal maturation is justified by a concern for the long-term direction of the science. For if we treat cognitive and cortical development as separate things we may never understand anything about either of them.

Species Differences in Selective Encoding

Chapter 2 reported that when infrahuman animals are tested on the optional shift procedure they are disposed to make nonreversal shifts. If the human ontogenetic trend can be explained as reflecting the maturational course of the relatively slow-to-mature higher level, then such infrahuman–human differences could reasonably be accounted for by the relatively late evolution of the necessary higher level structures. Before pursuing this point, I should note that whether or in what degree infrahuman animals have the capacity to encode selectively, as inferred from other procedures, continues to be controversial. There is a large body of data, based on many different experimental procedures, interpreted by some theorists to demonstrate selective attention in infrahuman animals. The experiments are too numerous and the procedures too diverse to be described here (see Sutherland & Mackintosh, 1971 for an excellent review). It is, however, fair to say that this issue remains controversial because the effects attributed to selective attention in animals are usually small, often unreliable, and explainable without assuming selective encoding (e.g., D'Amato & Jagoda, 1962; Mackintosh, 1975; Rescorla & Wagner, 1972). Moreover, resolving this issue in an all-or-none manner is not crucial if viewed from the perspective of the levels theory because the data derived from the optional shift procedure do not demonstrate that the infrahuman animals tested so far are incapable of selective encoding; they do imply that when the disposition to encode a certain set of features selectively or nonselectively are opposed, nonselectivity tends to prevail. The manifested difference in the disposition to encode selectively between human and infrahuman learners is assumed to be related to the difference between the degree to which the underlying neurological structures have evolved.

All in all, this formulation is consistent with two accepted generalities about evolution. Evolutionary changes are always made within the context of a design and architecture that already is in place. Neural substrates common to all mammals are expected to appear early rather than later in ontogeny because radical changes in early development would have too many effects on other developing structures.

CONCLUSIONS

Among humans, the probability of selectively encoding the cues on the relevant dimension increases with age in a gradual, quantifiable manner. These data can be explained by assuming that in human adults the information in the discriminanda is processed at two hierarchically organized, information processing levels: a lower nonselective level that processes all of the perceptible information and a higher selective level that selects only the relevant aspects for further processing. The developmental trends are explained if the higher level begins to develop later and proceeds toward maturity at a much slower rate than the lower level.

CHAPTER FOUR

Developmental Changes in Reasoning

Reasoning may . . . be very well defined as the substitution of parts and their implications or consequences for wholes. And the art of the reasoner will consist of two stages: First, sagacity, or the ability to discover what part . . . lies embedded in the whole . . . which is before him; Second, learning, or the ability to recall promptly (the part's) consequences, concomitants, or implications.
—William James (1948, p. 353)

When we began to investigate higher mental processes we surmised that abstraction and reasoning could be investigated separately. While discrimination learning was used to study abstraction, a different but equally simple procedure was used for studying reasoning. This procedure was adapted from the three-table maze Maier (1929) used to study reasoning in rats. Maier defined reasoning as the ability to combine the essentials of isolated experiences and he operationalized the "experiences" in an apparatus composed of three small tables joined together by three elevated pathways that met in the center. Each rat was permitted to explore all of the pathways and tables freely before being placed on one of the tables where food was available. The hungry animal was permitted to eat a small amount of food before being removed and immediately replaced on a second table to see whether it would then go directly to the table on which it had been feeding. Different start-goal table combinations were used for each trial. According to Maier, reasoning would be demonstrated by choosing the path that led to the food because such a choice required combining knowledge of where the food was with how to get there. Having found that the rats chose the

41

paths that led directly to the food significantly more often than chance would allow, Maier concluded rats showed some ability to reason.

HULL'S THEORY OF REASONING

The theory that guided the early research in this domain was based on ideas proposed by Hull (1930) in an influential article entitled "Knowledge and Purpose as Habit Mechanisms" that demonstrated how an $S–R$ learning theory might account for intelligent foresight. He defined foresight as the reaction to a possibly impending event. Such anticipatory actions present a dilemma for an $S–R$ learning theory because an event not yet in existence is not yet a stimulus and therefore cannot evoke a response. Hull resolved this dilemma by introducing the "pure stimulus act" which, like a mnemonic device, serves only to provide the stimulus for a subsequent response. The pure stimulus act later became known as a mediating response.

Hull conceived of this theoretical construct as enabling the organism to represent a chain of events in the external world by a chain of covert, mediating responses. He reasoned that a high grade organism possesses internal receptors that provide for a chain of covert, $s–r$ associations in which each link becomes associated with an ensuing, covert response. Once the first response is initiated the whole chain of covert responses can run off, even if the external events are interrupted. In this way, the world stamps its pattern on the organism and, in this sense, the organism "knows" the world. A sequence of representative, mediating responses provides a mechanism for foresight if the tempo of the inner response chain is faster than the outer world sequence it parallels. For example, if the last stimulus is noxious and produces flight, foresight will occur when the internal response sequence runs off quickly enough to initiate flight before the noxious event occurs.

Hull's Three-Segment Procedure for Testing Reasoning in Rats

Presently Hull (1952) used these ideas to provide a hypothetical account of the purported reasoning manifested by rats in Maier's three-table procedure. This account translated Maier's "separate experiences" into "separate ($S–R$) habit segments." Each habit segment was mapped onto a section of a hypothetical maze schematized in Fig. 4.1. This maze consisted of three separate segments, a major-goal segment (BG), a subgoal segment (AB), and a control segment (XY). Each segment was controlled for external cues, had a distinctively different floor surface, and each goal box had a distinctively different shape.

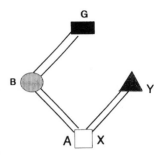

FIG. 4.1. Three segment maze for
testing reasoning in rats. From Hull
(1952).

To test for reasoning in this maze, the hypothetical rat learns on one
occasion to traverse the BG segment to obtain a large food reward (G). On
a second occasion the rat learns to traverse the AB segment for a small food
reward (B). Learning to traverse the XY segment for a similarly small food
reward (Y) occurs on a third occasion. Then the rat is placed in the start
box (A-X) to determine which path it will choose (ABG or XY) and how
smooth or rapid the response will be, particularly at the juncture between
the relevant subgoal and major-goal segments. To quote Hull (1952):

> It is perfectly obvious that normally intelligent humans would choose path
> ABG rather than path XY. How far down in the animal scale this capacity
> extends remains to be determined experimentally. We are at present far from
> knowing enough about individual and species differences to speak with any
> confidence on this matter from the theoretical point of view. However, the
> organism's performance of the sequence ABG, particularly at points A and B,
> may vary greatly: it may range from a smooth (rapid) unified act to a very
> slow and halting series of acts, depending on the capacity of the organism
> in question to join independently acquired behavior segments into novel
> wholes. This implies that the well unified type of response combination will
> be comparatively strong: that is, that the chance of the ABG choice will be
> around 100 percent, and that of the XY choice will be near zero percent.
> Such choices would be easy enough to distinguish either statistically or by
> inspection. But in the case of a feeble but genuine tendency for the ABG
> path to dominate (say 57%) a statistical method is indispensable. It follows
> that any experimental test for the presence of "insight" should provide a
> neutral alternative comparison or control response. The main point is that,
> except in an organism that possesses an extremely strong tendency to "insight,"
> we do not have the clear alternative of such a phenomenon versus the trial-
> and-error learning process, as has often been supposed; *rather, we have
> ordinary trial-and-error (possibly) supplemented more or less strongly or feebly
> by a distinct insight or intelligence factor.* (pp. 309–310; italics mine)

With this procedure Hull provided an objective method for pitting trial-
and-error learning against an insightful, rational mode of infrahuman prob-

lem solving. He also proposed that the capacity to perform insightfully is better conceived as a quantitatively varying disposition than as a competence one either has in full flower or lacks completely. And he purported to explain how his theory, augmented by the anticipatory goal response (r_g), could account for why a rat might behave insightfully in such a situation.

Hull's explanation assumed the major goal would evoke a major consummatory response, such as the flow of saliva. When the B–G segment is trained a fraction of the consummatory response (r_g) would become anticipatory and gradually move back from the major goal box (G) toward the relevant subgoal start-box (B) until it is evoked by B itself. When the AB habit is trained, B becomes the goal box and now comes to evoke both the major r_g as well as its own r_g. In the course of training on AB both r_gs gradually become anticipatory and move back toward A. Training on the XY habit evokes only its own r_g. In the test situation, when the rat is placed at A-X and required to choose between the two subgoal habits, it will make the ostensibly insightful A choice merely because there are more connections associated with A than with X.

However, Hull never actually used the three-segment procedure for testing reasoning, so we set out to test three implications of Hull's theory. First and foremost there was the overarching implication that higher mental processes could be explained by conditioning principles, if one utilizes the hypothetical mediating response mechanism. Hull's (1952) high hopes for this mechanism were expressed this way (p. 350):

> Further study of this major automatic device will presumably lead to the detailed behavioral understanding of thought and reasoning, which constitute the highest attainment of organic evolution.

Although this automatic device proved too fragile to bear the great weight Hull lay upon it, mediating representations do play an important role in providing rational solutions to the three segment problem. The second, more specific implication was that insightful problem solving depends on the organism's capacity to produce and transfer automatic, anticipatory goal reactions from one behavior segment to another. It seemed reasonable at the time to suppose that expanding our understanding of mediating responses could help explain the obvious phylogenetic and ontogenetic differences in problem solving ability. We expected carefully controlled experimental and comparative research to throw light on how this mechanism worked.

The third implication was more specifically related to the procedure illustrated in Fig. 4.1. Whenever Hull added a postulate to his theory, he proposed a number of testable deductions. This was no exception, but the deduction we set out to test was a critical one that Hull had not included in his list. If insightful behavior depended on the backward movement of r_g, then the insightful choice should be more likely when training on the major-goal segment precedes rather than follows training on the minor-goal segments.

Between 1956 and 1966 we conducted a series of experiments, mostly with children, using a variety of adaptations of Hull's procedure. Before that time, the three-segment procedure had never been used in an experiment, but since Maier had presumably demonstrated some capacity to reason in rats, I expected human children to do at least as well. The immediate purpose was to determine whether the probability of insightful solution would be affected by the order in which the separate habit segments are trained. The long range goal was to explore the variables that influence the production of appropriate mediating responses, a goal shared by many experimental psychologists at the time. We chose to study children because they presumably presented simpler instances of the mediating processes available to humans.

Adapting the Three-Segment Procedure to Children

This research required a portable apparatus that instantiated the three behavior segments but could be used with young children. The first apparatus actually resembled a small maze through which the children pulled the goal objects toward themselves by means of strings. Each of three subsequent experiments used a different apparatus that successively improved the controls and made the procedure more like a child's game. The last, most suitable apparatus is illustrated in Fig. 4.2. The procedure used with this apparatus is described in some detail to provide a sense of the problem the subjects faced as well as the logic of the inferential solution.

The three separately trained habit segments labeled BG, AB, and XY were instantiated by three distinctively colored, square panels, 17.5 cm on a side. The panels could be exposed to view singly or in combination by opening or closing the hinged doors in the front of each panel. The major goal object (G) consisted of a small, shiny, gold-colored charm. Each charm represented a character in a well-known fairy tale or nursery rhyme, such as little Bo-Peep, the cow that jumped over the moon, or the gingerbread man. Each BG training trial presented a different charm which the children seemed to enjoy identifying, with the experimenter's help when necessary. The sub-

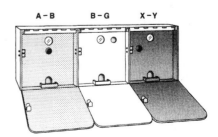

FIG. 4.2. Three-panel apparatus for testing inference in humans. From T. Kendler & Kendler (1967).

goals (B and Y) consisted of a small, steel ball bearing and a slightly larger, clear-glass marble, respectively.

The center panel provided the major goal (BG) segment. On its yellow, anodized surface was a circular opening into which the child could drop either subgoal. During BG training, the marble and the ball bearing were placed in front of the center panel. The object was to learn which of the two subgoals would cause the charm to be automatically propelled to a trough at the bottom from which it could be picked up and identified. Whether the marble or the ball bearing was the "right thing" was counter-balanced across subjects but for any one subject only one subgoal was correct. For example, if the marble was randomly designated as B for a given subject then dropping the marble into the opening would produce the charm, while dropping the ball bearing would produce nothing.

The two side panels, one red and the other blue, instantiated the AB and XY segments. In the center of each panel was a button that when pressed would automatically deliver either a marble or a ball bearing into a trough at the bottom of the respective panels. If, for example, the left panel was designated as AB and the marble was designated as B, then pressing the button on the left panel would deliver a marble to a trough at the bottom of the left panel. In this instance, the blue panel on the right would represent XY and pressing the button on this panel would deliver a ball bearing to the trough at the bottom of the right panel.

To describe the procedure, take the example where training begins with the subgoals and the marble serves as B. After the child was comfortably seated in front of the apparatus, the experimenter opened one side panel and said, "Press the button and see what happens." The child, who was usually amused when the marble dropped into the trough, was told to pick it up, look at it, and then return it to the experimenter. The experimenter, seated behind the apparatus and facing the child, could be seen to replace the marble in the apparatus to be available for a subsequent trial. The same procedure was repeated on the other side panel, which delivered the ball bearing.

After two such demonstration trials on each subgoal segment both side panels were opened. The child was shown one of the subgoals and told to press the button that would get one like it. This procedure was repeated with the marble and ball bearing presented in counterbalanced alternation until the child chose correctly on six successive trials. Even the youngest children in our samples, the 5-year-olds, learned very quickly how to obtain each subgoal. In fact the typical response at all tested age levels was to attain criterion without any errors.

During training on the major-goal segment, the two side panels were closed and the center panel was opened. A marble and a ball bearing were placed in front of the center panel and the child was told that, if he or she dropped "the right thing" into the hole, a fairy tale or nursery rhyme charm would drop into the trough at the bottom of the center panel. The charm could be picked up, identified, and played with briefly. Each subject was allowed as many trials as required to learn which subgoal was correct. Each correct choice produced a different charm. An incorrect choice produced nothing. The criterion was four successive correct choices, which most children attained in very few trials. Hardly any subjects made more than one error.

After training on all segments was completed the test trial was initiated by saying "Would you like to see another charm? Very well, this time I won't put out any little things but I will open all the doors. If you do what you are supposed to, you can make the charm come out. Go ahead." If the child had learned that only the left panel delivers the marble [A → B] and only the marble delivers the charm [B → G], then the inferential solution would be to press the button on the left panel to obtain the marble and then drop the marble into the opening in the center panel to obtain the charm [A → B → G].

Each child was first allowed 1 minute to respond on the test trial. If neither the A nor X button was pressed after the minute elapsed—many of the younger children did nothing but look confused or pained—the experimenter said, "Which button should you press to help you get the charm? Go ahead." After this broad hint almost all subjects pressed one of the buttons. The test trial was terminated when the subject either dropped one of the subgoals into the BG aperture or another minute had elapsed since the subgoal appeared. Such short time limits were instituted because, to our surprise, many of the younger children didn't solve the problem and became distressed as a consequence. This distress was quickly alleviated by showing them what to do.

Because there is a published review of the results of this entire research program (T. Kendler & Kendler, 1967) only the most pertinent findings of the last three experiments are presented here. Each experiment in this set used the apparatus and basic procedure described earlier. In the first of these experiments there were 128 kindergarten and 128 third-grade children drawn from Berkeley public schools (T. Kendler & Kendler, 1962). In the second experiment 64 kindergarten and 64 third-grade children drawn from Santa Barbara public schools participated (T. Kendler, Kendler, & Carrick, 1966). Each child was run individually and completed in one session. To assess possible IQ differences, the session began with the administration of the Peabody Picture Vocabulary Test. Within the two experiments there were no significant IQ differences between any of the experimental groups. As it turned out, the mean IQ for each experiment, all groups combined, was 108.

To determine how adults would perform, the subjects in the third experiment were 96 Barnard College students (T. Kendler & Kendler, 1967). These young women were told the procedure was designed for children and presented to adults in order to provide a standard against which to assess the children's performance. No intelligence test was administered to the college students since they doubtlessly differed from the public school samples in IQ as well as CA.

Each experiment consisted of a control group and an experimental group. The data of the control groups are first presented separately in order to describe the developmental changes in the spontaneous response of subjects to this problem.

Human Ontogenetic Trends

Hull's procedure explicitly provided two measures of insight. One measure was the proportion of subjects who made an initial, correct (A) choice. At the kindergarten level the respective proportions of control children who made initial correct choices in the Berkeley and Santa Barbara experiments were .50 and .53. These results were similar enough to attest to the reliability of the unexpected finding that the 5-year-olds' performance on this task was not significantly above chance. The third-grade control children did better; the respective proportion of initial correct choices at this level were .73 and .66, both significantly above chance. At the college level the proportion was .96.

To provide a more continuous developmental function, Fig. 4.3 presents the same data, plotted retrospectively, as a function of the Mental Age scores on the PPVT. To complete the picture the college students were arbitrarily assigned an MA of 18. The probability of an initial inferential choice was slightly below chance at the lowest end of the MA scale and increased gradually over a wide span. The form taken by this developmental function is reminiscent of the growth function obtained with the optional-shift procedure and is consistent with Hull's anticipation that performance in such problems may vary greatly, depending on the strength of a "distinct insight or intelligence factor."

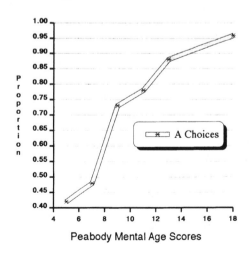

FIG. 4.3. Relates the proportion of initial correct (A) choices to the Mental Age scores.

The other measure proposed by Hull was the degree of smoothness at the juncture of the two separately acquired habit segments. Behavior at the juncture was measured by determining the proportion of subjects who made an initial correct choice then used the relevant subgoal (B) *directly* to obtain G. For example, the proportion of adults in the control group who made an initial correct choice and then, without any wrong moves, used the relevant subgoal to obtain G was .92. Such a solution was designated a *direct integration response* (DIR). The comparable proportion of kindergartners who made a DIR was .06 for each experiment. For the third graders the comparable proportions were .50 and .53, respectively.

To describe in more detail what happened on the test trial, over half (p = .56) of the 5-year-olds in both samples combined failed completely to solve the problem in the allotted time. Of these, a small group (p = .14) dropped the irrelevant subgoal (X) into the major goal (BG) panel; the remainder (p = .42) made no integration response at all. Many of these children tried to solve the problem by poking their fingers into the hole in the BG panel, indicating they understood they were to obtain the major goal but didn't know how to do so.

More to the point, of the .44 5-year-olds who succeeded in solving the problem only .06 did so directly. The remaining .38 obtained G only after making one or more previously trained but unnecessary responses. Some of these children made only one unnecessary response, such as pressing the incorrect button either before or after pressing the correct one. Others pressed one or the other button repeatedly before they finally used the relevant subgoal to obtain G. To my astonishment, a few children went through the entire training sequence. They pressed each button, picked up each subgoal and handed it to the experimenter, took each one back and set them in front of the BG panel before finally picking up the correct subgoal and using it to obtain G. Such responses, however inefficient, do constitute a solution but the process is closer to trial-and-error than to insight.

These results are consistent with two of Hull's assumptions: First, that there are two problem-solving modes, an insightful mode and a trial-and-error mode, and second, the tendency to respond in the insightful mode is a function of an underlying intellectual capacity. Hull's more specific assumption about how the mediating mechanism produced an initial A choice did not fare as well. His explanation assumed the A choice depends on the backward movement of the anticipatory goal response. If so, children trained initially on the major goal segments should produce more initial A choices on the test trial than children trained initially on the subgoal segments. Three different experiments were performed in the effort to provide optimal conditions for testing this deduction but none gave any indication of the predicted order effect. Each experiment involved two experimental groups; one group was trained in the A–B, B–G order; the other in the B–G, A–B order.

There was no difference between the two groups in any of these experiments (T. Kendler & Kendler, 1967). The evidence failed completely to support this critical implication of Hull's theory.

REASONING IN RATS?

When the very young children failed to manifest much insight in Hull's three-segment procedure one had to wonder about how rats would perform. Happily about this time other investigators were putting this question to experimental test.

Testing Rats on the Three-Segment Procedure

Unbeknown to me, when we began to use Hull's three-segment procedure to investigate reasoning in children, Koranakos (1959) was using the procedure with rats. The major goal in his experiment was a 2 gram food pellet; the two subgoals each were a 1/2 gram pellet. Each rat had 10 trials a day for 2 days on the major goal segment and on the next day 20 alternating trials on each subgoal segment. On the third day, the rat was allowed 10 test trials in which it could choose to approach either subgoal. Koranakos' intention was to test one of Hull's predictions about the conditions that would facilitate reasoning. These intentions were frustrated because the proportion of A and X choices were exactly equal. The rats gave no sign of any capacity to reason in Hull's three-segment procedure.

The question raised by Koranakos' results was subsequently pursued by Gough and his collaborators in a series of experiments designed to determine why rats seemed to be capable of reasoning in Maier's three-table procedure but not in Hull's three-segment maze (Gough, 1962). The first experiment replicated Koranakos' procedure but changed the way the maze was painted in order to enhance the difference between the two subgoals. The change had no effect; in the test situation the rats performed exactly at chance level.

Both Koronakos' and Gough's initial experiments trained the rats on the major subgoal first. The second experiment in Gough's laboratory tested the possibility that, during training on the relevant subgoal, the animal becomes frustrated because it cannot get to the anticipated large reward. The frustration might reduce the tendency to choose insightfully, so the experiment was repeated with a reversed order of training only to find that with rats, as we had found with humans, the order of training had no effect at all. As Gough put it, "Again 10 of the 20 animals turned in the predicted direction."

When it became evident that rats failed to show any capacity to reason in the three-segment procedure, Gough began to wonder how these negative results could be reconciled with the general impression in the literature that rats could reason. In the effort to explain this discrepancy he looked to

some experiments reported by Seward (1949) that were designed to repro-
duce Maier's three-table procedure with superior controls. Seward's apparatus was a T-maze that effectively eliminated the extramaze visual cues
present in the three-table procedure. In this T-maze one endbox was black,
the other white. As in the three-table procedure, the rats were allowed to
explore the entire maze for limited periods on several successive days with
no food present in either endbox. On the test day, each rat was individually
placed directly in one endbox where, for the first time, there was food in
the food cup. When the rat began to eat, it was lifted out and put in the
startbox. Eighty-eight percent of the rats went directly from the choice point
to the endbox where they had just been fed. The experiment was repeated
with the rats placed in both endboxes but only one contained food, with
essentially similar results. Like Maier's rats, these rats responded appropriately at above chance levels.

The most obvious difference between the Maier–Seward and the Hullian
procedure was that the former permitted free exploration of the entire maze
while Hull's procedure provided discrete training trials on each segment
separately. There are two ways in which this difference could matter. One way
had to do with the difference between preliminary free exploration and
discrete training trials. Seward's rats had 90 minutes free exploration, while
Gough's had 20 discrete reinforced trials on each subgoal. So Gough allowed
rats to freely explore between the startbox and the two subgoal boxes of the
Hullian maze for 90 minutes before the 40 reinforced trials. This time only 9
out of 20 rats chose correctly, indicating that free exploration versus discrete
training trials was not the important difference between the two procedures.

The other difference was that the opportunity to combine the various
segments was available in Seward's free exploration period and denied in
Gough's separate training phase. So Smith, one of Gough's colleagues,
allowed rats to explore the entire Hullian maze for 90 minutes before the test
trial. On the test trial they were prefed in the major goal box and then placed
in the startbox. All 20 animals turned to the side that led to the major goal box.

That the opportunity to combine the various segments during prior exploration was the telling difference between the Maier–Seward and Hullian
procedures was clinched by two other experiments cited by Gough. In these
experiments the rats were given *separate* free exploration in the subgoal
and major goal sections of the Hullian maze before the test trial. In neither
experiment did the rats show any preference for the relevant subgoal.

Conclusions About Reasoning in Rats

Gough surmised that in the Maier–Seward procedure the locomotor behavior
segments required to reach the goal have been contiguously associated during
the exploratory period. "Reasoning" in this case consists of choosing which of

two previously connected locomotor segments is appropriate to a newly introduced motivation–reinforcement contingency. If so, this behavior is similar to latent learning, as defined by the decrease in trials taken to learn a maze attributable to preliminary nonrewarded exploration (Tolman & Honzik, 1930). Although the explanation of latent learning has been a subject of dispute for a long time, Seward's results have since been confirmed many times.

More recently Maier's results with the three-table procedure were replicated (Herrman, Bahr, Bremner, & Ellen, 1982). This replication further substantiated the importance of the preliminary contiguous association between the to-be-combined pathways by showing that, when rats were allowed to explore the unbaited three tables and their interconnecting runways prior to the test trial, they chose correctly well above chance. If rats were not permitted this exploration prior to each test trial, their choice dropped to chance. Whether solution of the Maier–Seward problem measures the capacity for latent learning or reasoning will not be settled until we have better theories about such complex processes. The only point made here is that, whatever this process is called, it is available to rats.

Problem solving in Hull's procedure is different than in the Maier–Seward procedure in several ways. For one thing, the solutions require spontaneous integration of behavior segments that have *not* been previously integrated. For another, the process underlying such problem solving is readily available to mature humans and much less, if at all, available to rats. And among humans the probability that such solutions will occur increases ontogenetically. Lastly, the direct correct solution entails a logical inference.

The capacity to make this logical inference is certainly available to college students. As in the case of discriminative shifts, research with children and with rats found that the degree to which this higher level capacity is manifested depends on developmental level.

THE ROLE OF REPRESENTATION

The earliest explanation of these facts applied the developmental-mediation pretheory that had been used to explain the developmental changes in discrimination learning. In the three-segment problem, intelligent behavior was manifested by an initial correct (A) choice followed by a direct integration response (DIR). This behavior was assumed to depend on a hypothetical representational response (r_b) that abstracted the relevant connecting element (B) from the two different (subgoal and major goal) contexts in which it had appeared during the pretraining and thereby provided the basis for the logical inference.

This hypothesis was bolstered by the fact that, although approximately half of the kindergartners made an initial correct choice by chance, most of them failed to use the relevant subgoal produced by this choice to directly obtain the major goal. Instead they either handed the relevant subgoal back to the experimenter or pressed another button or both. While the conditional probability of a DIR, given an initial correct choice, was only .13, among the kindergartners it reached .76 for the third graders and .96 for the college students. Thus most of the kindergartners and some of the third graders failed to equate the relevant subgoal as it had appeared in the subgoal and major goal training. More concretely, for these children the marble (or ball bearing) that emerged from the side panel was one thing and the marble (or ball bearing) in front of the center panel was another. This suggested the ontogenetic and species differences in inferential problem solving were attributable to differences in the spontaneous production of a common representational response to the relevant subgoal (r_b) in the two different contexts.

The mediating representation was assumed to serve several functions. Because it was selective, r_b differentiated the relevant subgoal from its context in both the major and subgoal segments. Because it generated a common stimulus (s_b), r_b presumably served to associate the two segments in the order required for an initial inferential choice. Because it was covert, r_b could become anticipatory.

According to this formulation subjects who make DIRs spontaneously generate a common r_b during training, first during training on the A–B segment and then on the B–G segment. One possible common r_b could be a covert label for the relevant subgoal such as the word "marble." The r_b automatically generates a covert stimulus s_b. A possible s_b could be the proprioceptive or neural feedback produced by the verbal label. The s_b becomes the conditioned stimulus for both the A choice during subgoal training and the B choice during major goal training. The test trial evokes the mediating r_b–s_b link, which, in turn, evokes the A choice. The B consequently lands in its trough in the side panel. The sight of B was supposed to generate r_b–s_b link again, which then evokes the major goal response.

This explanation showed how a mediating mechanism, in conjunction with the laws of conditioning, could account for both the inferential A choice and the DIR that connects the previously separated segments. The ontogenetic increase in inferential solutions was attributed to an increase in the spontaneous production of a representational response that abstracted the relevant subgoal from its context thereby allowing the required associations to be learned. As an aside, note that this kind of mediation theory anticipated the succession of cognitive theories that were soon to dominate the field in that it divided the processes that mediate intelligent behavior into two main components, namely representation and memory.

These ideas were especially appealing because they related the developmental trends obtained with the three-segment procedure for measuring reasoning to the similar trends obtained with the discriminative shift procedure for measuring abstraction. Moreover, such an explanation lent itself to experimental tests.

Testing for the Representational Response

One experiment tested the hypothesis that the acquisition of a representational response to the relevant subgoal during training plays a role in inferential solutions by comparing the proportion of DIRs produced in a control and a switched subgoals condition (T. Kendler & Kendler, 1962). Two grade levels, kindergarten and third grade, were represented. The control groups at each grade level were trained and tested as previously described. The switched-subgoals groups were trained the same way but on the test trial the subgoals were surreptitiously interchanged so that a correct initial choice yielded the irrelevant subgoal and an incorrect initial choice yielded the relevant subgoal. The behavior measured was whether or not the subject made a DIR, meaning whether he or she picked up whichever subgoal was produced by initial choice and dropped it into the center panel without making any other previously trained responses.

This design provided the means for determining how a DIR is affected by two variables: Whether the correct choice is correct or incorrect, regardless of what subgoal it produced; and the physical presence of relevant subgoal, regardless of how it was obtained.

As depicted graphically in Fig. 4.4, among the kindergartners there were very few DIRs under either condition and neither variable significantly af-

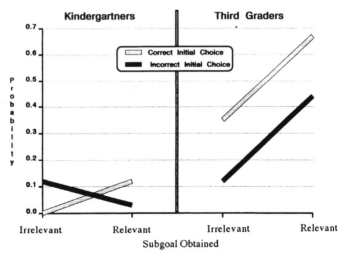

FIG. 4.4. Probability of a direct integration response as a joint function of the correctness of the initial choice and the relevance of the obtained subgoal.

fected the few DIRs that were produced. Among the third graders, however, both variables were operative. These children were significantly more likely to make a DIR if their initial choice was correct (light line) than incorrect (dark line), regardless of whether this choice produced the relevant or the irrelevant subgoal. This result suggests that at least some 8-year-olds made an intentional correct initial choice, based on the anticipation of obtaining B. The anticipation was strong enough to cause them to use the obtained subgoal to attempt to make a DIR even though it was irrelevant. This is evidence that covert representations of the relevant subgoal play a role in inferential problem solutions.

However, obtaining the correct subgoal, regardless of whether it was produced by an initial correct or incorrect choice, also significantly potentiated the probability of a DIR among the third graders. This result suggests that some third graders made an initial correct choice by chance but when they happened to get the relevant subgoal they were more likely to use it to obtain the major goal than when they obtained the irrelevant subgoal. In the language of mediation theory, some third graders were liable to generate the appropriate representational response in the presence of relevant subgoal but not in its absence.

The behavior of the third graders is consistent with the assumption that the inferential solution to the three-segment problem depends on a representational response to the connecting element. The appropriate representation is more likely to be produced by relatively mature children and more likely to occur when the relevant connecting element is visible than when it is not. As in a syllogism, this representation serves to abstract the connecting element from the different contexts in which it had previously appeared.

The behavior of both age levels extended the evidence for the existence of two levels of encoding from discrimination learning to inferential problem solving: a lower nonselective level that fails to differentiate the relevant from the irrelevant elements in the situation and a higher level that succeeds in doing so. At the same time these data expanded the meaning of "relevant element" from a dimension embedded in a compound to an object embedded in a context. This experiment provided evidence for the importance of selective encoding of the relevant common element in inferential solutions. The common element in our three-segment experiments was very obvious, at least to adults, but the problem could be made much more difficult by obscuring the common element. Surely one aspect of creative reasoning in the natural environment entails abstracting previously unrecognized but nevertheless common elements embedded in entirely different contexts.

At the time these data were considered as evidence for two problem-solving modes: an S–R mode that produces trial-and-error solutions, and a mediated S–r–s–R mode that produces inferential solutions. But, in retrospect, it seems to me that three rather than two problem-solving modes were manifested. One mode can be characterized in terms of the *S–R* schema where there is no mediating representation of the relevant connecting element. This mode is instantiated by the children—mostly kindergartners—whose initial choice produced the relevant subgoal but who did not use it directly to obtain G. There is no mediating representational response and whatever indirect solution that occurs results from trial-and-error.

The second mode is characterized by the production of a mediating representation evoked by the appearance of the relevant subgoal. The representation abstracts the relevant element from its context and enables the child to recall how B was used to obtain G. This mode calls for the ability to selectively encode the relevant common element but it does not necessarily require a logical inference. A common representational response to B plus simple recall will suffice. This mode is instantiated by the third graders in the switched-subgoal condition who made an initial X choice but obtained B and then remembered how to use it to obtain the major goal. There probably is a fair proportion of third graders in the control condition who might have appeared to be solving the problem inferentially but who actually made the initial A choice by chance. Once the B appeared they remembered how it could be used to obtain G.

The third mode also produces a relevant representation but entails an additional process that enables one to use this representation, in the absence of its referent, to infer that A is the logical initial choice. This mode is instantiated by the third graders in the switched-subgoal group, who presumably made intentional initial correct choices and obtained the incorrect subgoal but nevertheless used it to try to obtain G. The third mode would be instantiated in the control condition by those subjects who made an *intentional* initial correct choice and followed it directly with a DIR. Most adults performed in this mode as indicated by the fact that in the control condition .96 made correct initial choices and .96 of them followed with a DIR.

The developmental mediation theory can account for the representational response to the connecting element but the analysis into the three modes suggests that, while the representational response is necessary, it may not be sufficient to account for the kind of intentional, inferential solutions that were characteristic of the college students. Although not entirely obvious at the time this research was conducted, these were some of the earliest data to suggest there was more to inferential solutions than the representation of the relevant element and the invocation of memory.

Verbal Labels and Mediating Representational Responses

In the mediational pretheory the *r* became a representational response that could be idiosyncratic or universal, verbal or nonverbal, overt or covert, and central or peripheral. Moreover it gradually became clear that, if this theory were to account for the developmental differences observed in both discriminative transfer and inferential problem-solving experiments, some explanation must be added to the presumably universal laws of learning.

At first the developmental change was attributed to differences in the response repertoire. That is, the developmental changes were attributed to a transition from single link $(S-R)$ to mediated $(S-r-s-R)$ behavior, where r was a representational response to the features of the stimulus that happened to be relevant to the problem in hand. Some responses were presumed to provide more effective representations than others. Developmental differences were explained in terms of the availability of responses that lent themselves more or less readily to the representative function. Linguistic labels were deemed particularly suitable because they are representational and abstract in nature and they easily become covert and anticipatory (Luria & Yudovich, 1959; McGuigan, Culver, & Kendler, 1971; Vygotsky, 1962).

I shared with many other psychologists the notion that mediation in general depended on covert responses that generated feedback, thereby providing the stimulus for the next link in the chain of covert $s-r$ associations. Among humans linguistic labels seemed likely to be particularly important because they are so available, discriminable, and easily fractionated. Moreover, labels do not interfere with any other ongoing activity and they easily move forward in the behavior sequence. But, to emphasize my early commitment to the importance of learning, I also assumed that any response with the foregoing characteristics could, in principle, serve in the same capacity. If so, infrahuman animals and prelinguistic humans could be trained to produce representational responses, some of which may be better suited than others to particular tasks. This mediating response was assumed to obey the same automatic laws of learning as overt responses.

An obvious testable implication of this analysis was that training children to label the subgoals during training on the three-segment problem should increase the probability of inferential solutions. And the effect of this training should be inversely related to age. Two experiments were conducted to test this implication. The subjects in the first experiment (T. Kendler, Kendler, & Carrick, 1966) were children drawn from kindergarten and third-grade classes in the Santa Barbara public schools. Within each grade, the children were randomly assigned to either a no-label or a same-label condition. The no-label condition, described on p. 46, served as a control. Nowhere in the course of training were the subgoals labeled.

For the label condition the procedure was the same except that the child was required to label the subgoals during both the subgoal and major-goal training. At the outset of the subgoal training phase, the experimenter named each subgoal for the child. During subgoal training the child was shown the subgoal to be matched and instructed to name it before pressing the button on each trial. During major-goal training the experimenter put out the marble and ball bearing and the child was required, before making the actual choice, to name the one he or she intended to drop in the hole. For example, if a child labeled the glass marble as "purie" and the steel ball bearing as "steelie" during the subgoal training, the same labels were also used during the major goal training. Incidentally, these labels were picked up from the children during preliminary piloting.

The children easily learned to make the correct choices in both the subgoal and major-goal phases of the procedure under either the label or no-label condition. Most children at both grade levels reached criterion with no errors and experienced no difficulty producing appropriate linguistic labels. Apparently these natural language labels were already well established in the response repertoire of even the kindergartners. I expected that using a common label for B in the subgoal and major goal segments would potentiate both initial A choices and DIRs on the test trial for both grade levels but the effect would be greater for the younger children. However, the only statistically significant effect attributable to labeling was to increase the probability of a DIR among the kindergartners from .06 for the control group to .30 for same-label group. Contrary to expectation there was no increase at all in DIRs attributable to labeling for the third graders. Nor was there any significant effect of labeling on the initial A choice for either grade level.

Because these results only partially corroborated the theory guiding our research another similar experiment was performed under somewhat different conditions (T. Kendler & Kendler, 1967, pp. 182–183). In the first label experiment the children were trained first on the subgoal segments. The primary purpose of the second experiment was to determine whether the same-label training would potentiate initial A choices and DIRs among kindergarten children if they were trained first on the major-goal segment. The secondary purpose was to test, once again, the prediction derived from Hull's theory that there should be more inferential solutions if major-goal segment was trained first. Because old loyalties die hard I thought training first on the major-goal segment might be more conducive for the required associations to be formed.

The subjects were all kindergarten children. The experimental design was a 2 × 2 factorial with no-label versus same-label training as one main effect and B–G trained first versus last as the other. Perhaps Hull's theory about inferential behavior might apply to humans if verbal representations were substituted for consummatory goal responses. However, there was no effect attributable to the order-of-training on either initial A choices or on DIRs. The conclusion was obvious: Hull's theory about inferential behavior was no more tenable for humans than for rats. On the other hand, the potentiating effect of labeling on DIRs was replicated; the same-label condition ($p = .25$) produced slightly but reliably more DIRs than the no-label condition ($p = .12$). The null effect of labeling on initial A choices was also replicated. In fact, this time there were slightly less initial A choices in the same-label group than in the no-label group but, once again, the difference was not statistically significant.

The two label experiments together confirmed some implications of the developmental-mediation theory. They showed that: Children could be trained to make common representational responses; these representational responses potentiated DIRs; the potentiation was greater among the younger children. But the theory was only partially corroborated because it provided no explanation for why same-labels, shown to potentiate DIRs, had no similar effect on initial A choices.

In retrospect, the results of the label experiments, like the results of the switched-subgoal experiment, make sense if one distinguishes between three rather than two solution modes. The first one is a trial-and-error mode in which the initial choice is governed by chance and there is either no solution at all or an eventual solution after making previously learned but unnecessary responses. In the second mode, which can be called serendipitous, the initial choice is also a matter of chance. But if chance results in an A choice, B will be produced. The B, in turn, will elicit a DIR. A serendipitous solution requires a common representation for B in the A–B and B–G segments and a memory for how to use B to obtain G. In the third mode, which can be called inferential, the initial A choice is intentional. An inferential solution requires both a common representation for B and a logical inference of the A→B, B→G, hence A→G variety as well as the memory for how to obtain B. Thus a common representation may be necessary but not sufficient for an inferential solution.

The pertinent implication of this analysis is that representation of the relevant element and inferential reasoning may be separable processes. Verbal labels are likely to have a more direct effect on the tendency to produce appropriate representations than on the tendency to produce the appropriate inference. The effect would be to increase serendipitous solutions more than inferential solutions, which would explain how labels could increase DIRs more than initial A choices.

These experiments provided some of the early evidence for the need to differentiate two levels of executive control, as well as two levels of information processing. The two levels of executive control operate in two different modes that can be characterized as trial-and-error and rational. The encoding and executive components need to be separable in order to allow children to function at different levels in the different components, as in the case of the children who operate in the serendipitous mode. These children presumably selectively encoded the relevant information, but selective encoding was not, in itself, sufficient for generating the rational, inferential solution.

CONCLUSIONS

The probability of producing a rational, inferential solution to a simple problem that requires the integration of previously separate constituents depends on developmental status. While almost all adult humans solved this problem easily, rats proved incapable of doing so. Among humans, the probability of producing rational solutions increased with age. Experimental manipulations suggested that selective encoding of the relevant connecting element played a role but was not, by itself, sufficient to produce the rational inference.

CHAPTER FIVE

Automatic Learning and
Rational Hypothesis Testing

Man is born with a tendency to do more things than he has ready-made arrangements for in his nerve-centers. Most of the performances of other animals are automatic. But in him the number of them is so enormous that most of them must be the fruit of painful study. If practice did not make perfect, nor habit economize the expense of nervous and muscular energy, he would be in a sorry plight.

—William James (1892, p. 138)

The idea that humans can operate in either a rational or automatic mode is hardly novel. Nevertheless, this duality has been ignored in recent times, first by the behaviorists, who were so concerned with the automatic mode they tended to disregard the rational mode. Then the cognitivists reacted by emphasizing the rational mode at the expense of the automatic mode. Now the dust stirred up by the controversy between cognitivists and behaviorists has settled enough to clear the way for a renewed consideration of the two qualitatively different modes of behavioral control (e.g., Anderson, 1982; Norman & Shallice, 1980; Posner & Snyder, 1975; Shiffrin & Schneider, 1977).

The contribution of the levels theory lies in extending the dual mode notion to cognitive development by conceiving of the automatic and rational modes as governed by different levels of *executive* control that develop at different rates. The previous chapter showed that developmental differences in inferential problem solving, as measured by the three-segment procedure, can be explained by a bilevel, developmental theory of executive control. Presently it became clear that the same theory could explain a set of serendipitous findings about developmental trends in discrimination learning that

61

emerged from the use of the optional shift procedure to investigate selective encoding (T. Kendler, 1979a). These findings and their interpretation are summarized here.

DEVELOPMENTAL TRENDS IN LEARNING EFFICIENCY

They original purpose of the optional shift procedure (see Fig. 3.1) was to determine whether learners had selectively encoded the relevant dimension, as measured by behavior in the last, test phase. To use the procedure for this purpose, the test phase was preceded first with a preshift phase in which the discriminanda differed simultaneously on two dimensions but only one dimension was relevant. Training on the first phase was continued until the learner reached the criterion of ten successive correct choices. The incidental finding was that the ease of learning on the preshift phase was clearly related to the age of the learners. The shift phase followed immediately after criterion was attained on the preshift phase. In this phase only one pair of discrimanda was presented; consequently both dimensions become relevant but the reinforcement contingencies were reversed. Again training continued until the same criterion was attained. This phase was easier to learn because there was no irrelevant dimension, nevertheless the relationship between the ease of learning and age was manifested again.

To study this learning ontogeny more intensively, the learning data derived from a series of optional shift experiments conducted between 1966 and 1974 were combined to form a 3 (stimulus compounds) by 5 (age levels) design. The three stimulus compounds were size–form, size–color, and color–form. The five age levels were drawn respectively from nursery school (3–4-year-olds), kindergarten (5–6-year-olds), second grade (7–9-year-olds), sixth grade (11–12-year-olds), and university undergraduates (arbitrarily designated as 18-year-olds). Each learner had been trained to criterion on only one stimulus compound.

Figure 5.1 presents the geometric mean of errors + 1 to criterion as a function of age on the initial and shift discriminations for each stimulus condition. Using the geometric mean served to reduce the very large difference in variability between the age levels by contracting the upper end of the error scale. The result was a very orderly decrease in errors over age on both phases, replicated in each stimulus condition. When simple logarithmic, exponential, and power functions were fitted to the empirical data, a power function of the form $y = ax^{-b}$ provided the best fit to each of the six curves. The fits were good enough to account for at least 98% of the variance in each instance. These curves reflect a gradual, decelerated, ontogenetic increase in learning efficiency between early childhood and young adulthood that applies to both the preshift and shift phases of the procedure.

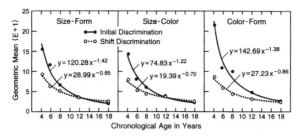

FIG. 5.1. Developmental trends fitted to the (geometric) mean number of errors to criterion under three different stimulus conditions. From T. Kendler (1979a).

A BILEVEL EXPLANATION
OF THE LEARNING ONTOGENY

This ontogenetic increase in learning efficiency can be explained by assuming that simple discrimination-learning problems can be solved in either a trial-and-error or a rational mode. The trial-and-error mode is identified with continuity theory, where learning depends on a gradual increase in the strength of the association between the correct stimulus and the choice response. Young children are assumed to be disposed to learn in the automatic, associative mode.

The rational mode of problem solving, as applied to discrimination learning, is assumed to solve the problem by means of a successive hypothesis-testing process. Adults are assumed to be disposed to solve the problem in the rational, hypothesis-testing mode. The empirical ontogeny of learning efficiency is explained by assuming that the tendency for the hypothesis-testing mode to prevail increases gradually as children mature. This theory produced the following testable implications.

Adult Performance and Hypothesis-Testing Theory

One implication is that young adults are disposed to solve the problem presented by the optional shift procedure in the rational mode. There is no widely accepted theory of rational problem solving but one can consider how a learner, who operates in the rational mode, would solve a simple problem in which one is only required to learn which one of four possible stimulus features is correct. The formulation proposed by Krechevsky is too vague for this purpose but Trabasso and Bower (1968) proposed and tested a simple mathematical model of rational discrimination learning that provided several predictions applicable to the optional shift procedure. Their model assumed the learner presented with a discrimination learning problem alternates between a search and test mode. In the search mode the learner decides which attributes to sample and how to classify them. The selected attributes are referred to as the focus sample of hypotheses. After selecting a focus sample, the learner enters the test mode and, on the next trial, tests the hypotheses in that sample. When a response is not reinforced this signals an error, causing one to return to the search mode and select a new focus sample consistent with the information on the previous error trial. The learner continues to alternate between search, sample, and test operations until a solution is reached which produces an errorless run. Thus, learning in the rational mode results in a quantum leap from a presolution to a solution state. In contrast, learning in the associative mode results in a gradual increase in the probability of the correct choice.

To illustrate how the Trabasso–Bower model applies to the preshift discrimination, suppose that on the first trial one is required to choose between *small-triangle* (+) and *large-circle* (−). Suppose one chooses *large-circle*, which signals an error causing one to enter the search mode. The search mode produces a focus sample of tenable hypotheses consistent with the information supplied by the last error. The tenable hypotheses would be "small," "triangle," or the compound "small-triangle." Suppose that on the next trial the discriminanda consist of *large-triangle* (+) versus *small-circle* (−). Since there is no *small-triangle*, the tenable focus-sample is narrowed down to "small" and "triangle." But the learner can only guess whether *small* or *triangle* is correct. Hence, the probability of arriving at the correct solution after the first error is one out of two or .5. This probability is referred to as the learning rate, symbolized by c.

According to this model there is a constant learning rate for each problem that equals the ratio of correct to possible hypotheses. In the present instance this ratio is .5. This learning rate provided the means for testing the applicability of the hypothesis-testing model to adult performance in the preshift discrimination because the proportion of learners who attain solution after each error should be a constant proportion (.5) of the learners who remain.

Strictly speaking, the Trabasso–Bower model requires the elimination of learners who make no errors because learning is assumed to occur only after an error. There is, however, little justification for eliminating the sizable group of adults who made no errors at all. Instead, the probability of producing zero errors was arrived at in the spirit of the hypothesis-testing rationale. Because there are two discriminanda the probability of a correct choice on the first trial equals .5. Because the tenable focus sample, say *small* and *triangle*, contains only two features the correct choice will lead to the solution state with a .5 probability. Hence, the joint probability that a learner will be correct on the first trial and will also select the correct hypothesis equals $c/2$ or .25.

All theories of hypothesis testing assume that once the individual arrives at the correct hypothesis there will be no further errors. This feature of hypothesis testing has been referred to as the win-stay-rule (Levine, 1959,

1966). Given these assumptions, the model predicts that the proportion of learners who attain criterion on the preshift discrimination after 0, 1, 2, or 3 errors should be .250, .375, .188, .094 respectively, leaving only .093 to make 4 or more errors. These theoretical proportions were used to compute the predicted frequency distributions of errors-to-criterion in the preshift phase of the optional shift. Figure 5.2 compares the predicted with the empirical frequency distributions for the adults in the sample. The fit of the two distributions, for each stimulus-compound condition taken separately ($N = 48$), is fairly good. The fit for all conditions combined ($N = 144$) is almost perfect.

The next application of the hypothesis testing model was to the shift phase that follows immediately after learning the preshift phase. The shift phase uses only one pair of discriminanda and reverses the reinforcement contingency. Since there is no warning about the changed contingency the first choice should be an error. As expected, all adults made an error on the first trial of the shift phase.

After the first error, a hypothesis tester should reenter the search mode and select a new focus sample consistent with the information on the first error trial. Using the example in Fig. 3.1, the resulting focus sample of hypotheses would be *large* and *circle*. Because either or both hypotheses are correct on the shift phase, there should be no further errors. Actually, .58 of the adults, all stimulus conditions groups combined, did make but one error. However there were adults who made more than one perseverative error, defined as the number of consecutive errors made prior to the first correct response. As many as .32 made two perseverative errors, and .10 made three or more. The

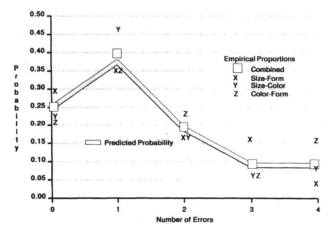

FIG. 5.2. Compares the predicted and obtained frequency distributions of the number of errors produced by the adults prior to attaining criterion on the preshift phase, for each stimulus condition taken separately and for all conditions combined.

perseverative errors could reflect a weak degree of associative learning as a result of the ten rewarded criterion trials. Or they could be attributable to a rational intention to test a few more times whether a hypothesis that worked so well had suddenly stopped working. In either case, a better measure of hypothesis testing in the shift discrimination would be whether the learner stayed with the correct hypothesis once the perseverative errors ended. Let such behavior be referred to as win-staying. Win-staying in the shift phase would be a manifestation of the quantum leap from a presolution to a solution state that characterizes the rational, hypothesis testing process. The win-stay measure is useful because it provides an estimate of the proportion of learners who operate in the hypothesis testing mode during the shift phase. For instance, the proportion of adults who made no errors beyond their last perseverative error (win-stayed) in the *size-form*, *size-color*, and *color-form* conditions, were .91, .84, and .94.

The premise that the great majority of adults are disposed to solve the problem in a rational, hypothesis testing mode is supported by these data.

CHILDREN'S PERFORMANCE
AND INCREMENTAL LEARNING

Given that hypothesis testers obey the win-stay rule, solution consists of a quantum leap from a presolution to a solution state. Such a leap is often referred to as either saltatory or one-trial learning. If the win-stay rule applies, the learning curve prior to solution should be flat, or—to use the technical term—stationary. In practice, stationarity is tested by averaging the learning curves of a group of learners to determine whether the transition from a presolution to a solution state is saltatory, as the hypothesis testing model predicts, or gradual, as the associative model predicts. Adult learning in these simple problems was too rapid to test for stationarity. But there is ample evidence that adult learning curves for more difficult problems are likely to be stationary prior to solution (e.g., Bower & Trabasso, 1964).

In the associative mode reinforcement serves to automatically and gradually strengthen the tendency of the correct cue to evoke the choice behavior. Consequently, learning curves should be gradual. Because the dual-mode hypothesis assumes the associative mode is likely to prevail among the youngest children, the testable implication is that their learning curves should be gradual rather than stationary.

Stationarity can be measured in a variety of ways, but the least biased method depends on constructing Vincentized learning curves (Suppes & Ginsberg, 1963). Vincentized curves are based on the averaged proportion of correct responses over percentiles of trials. Therefore this kind of learning curve has the virtue of equating the weight contributed by the fast and slow learners. Figure 5.3 presents the Vincentized learning curves for all three

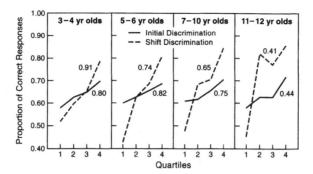

FIG. 5.3. Vincentized learning curves for the preshift and shift phases produced by each preadult level in the sample. From T. Kendler (1979a).

stimulus conditions combined. To construct these curves the number of trials for each learner prior to the last error were divided into quartiles. The four data points represent the proportion of correct choices in the four successive quartiles for each preadult age level for both the preshift and shift phases.

The first graph in Fig. 5.3 shows that among the 3–4-year-olds the learning curve increased monotonically in both phases. The shift learning curve is steeper due to the negative transfer produced by reversing the reinforcement contingencies. Each curve in Fig. 5.3 is based on the performance of all learners who satisfied the minimum requirement for dividing their performance into four quartiles. To satisfy this requirement a learner had to have at least four learning trials prior to the last error, which amounts to a minimum of five precriterion trials. Those who learned in fewer than five trials were necessarily excluded from this analysis. The proportions of learners who satisfied the requirement, and were therefore represented in the learning curves, appear beside each curve in the figure. Not many of the youngest children were excluded because the great majority required more than four trials to reach criterion for both the preshift and shift phases of the procedure. Hence, the first set of learning curves is consistent with the assumption that very young children tend to learn in the gradual, associative mode.

The remaining graphs show that some older children also learned gradually. Note, however, that the proportion of children represented in the learning curves decreased monotonically with age. This decrease reflects the fact that the number of children who learned in less than five trials increased monotonically with age, presumably because more of them were likely to hypothesis test. Because nonstationarity should apply only to the relatively slow, incremental learners, it is appropriate, though adventitious, that the rapid learners should be eliminated from this test. These data are therefore consistent with the premise that there is some disposition at each age level for children to learn in the gradual, associative mode, but this disposition decreases ontogenetically.

Ontogenetic Increases in Hypothesis Testing

The next set of data tested the premise that the disposition to solve the problem in the rational mode increases as children mature. This test required a technique for diagnosing hypothesis testing. Win-staying in the shift phase met the requirement. Unfortunately this technique does not apply to the preshift discrimination because the presence of the *ir*relevant visual dimension allows the learner to make a correct choice based on an incorrect hypothesis. For instance, one can choose *small-triangle* based on the hypothesis that *small* is correct when the correct hypothesis is *triangle*. However, in the shift discrimination there is no *ir*relevant visual dimension. Consequently the first correct choice should validate any reasonable hypothesis the learner holds.

Figure 5.4 shows that hardly any 3–4-year-olds win-stayed in each stimulus condition. Moreover, except for the slight reversal in the size–form condition, there was a steady increase in win-staying over age in every stimulus condition that extended all the way into adulthood. The authenticity of this ontogeny is verified by several published experiments that used the blank-trials method designed by Levine (1966) to study hypothesis testing in children. This method consists of a simultaneous discrimination between pairs of stimuli that differ on more than one visual dimension. Only one value on one dimension is correct, the remaining dimensions are irrelevant. During the training phase the learner is informed about whether he or she is correct or incorrect after each choice.

The training trials are followed by a set of blank trials, so-called because no further information about correctness is given. The discriminanda on the blank trials are arranged in a manner that enables the experimenter to use the pattern of choices to discern the hypothesis that guided the learner's choice. Eimas (1969b), Ingalls and Dickerson (1969), and Gholson, Levine, and Phillips (1972) applied the blank-trials method to children in experiments that, taken together, covered an age range from kindergarten to college level. Although each experiment was designed for a different purpose, they all found that solutions based on rational hypothesis testing increased systematically with age.

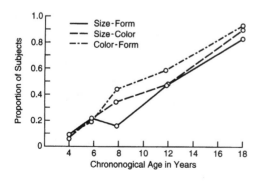

FIG. 5.4. Developmental trends in the proportion of learners who hypothesis-tested in the shift phase under each stimulus condition. From T. Kendler (1979a).

Thus, whether hypothesis testing is inferred from the application of the win-stay rule, or from manifesting a consistent hypothesis testing pattern in the blank trials procedure, the evidence is consistent with the premise that rational problem solving increases gradually between early childhood and young adulthood.

Bimodal Frequency Distribution of Errors

Another testable implication of the theory concerns the frequency distribution of errors in the preshift discrimination for all ages combined. If there are two learning modes represented in the total sample of learners, and one mode is much more efficient than the other, then the total frequency distribution should be decomposable into two distributions. One distribution should consist of hypothesis testers and the other of incremental learners. Each distribution should be characteristic of the respective learning mode.

A definitive test of this implication requires a substantial sample with a fairly even mix of the two populations. Combining the error scores on the preshift discrimination of the entire sample for all age levels and stimulus conditions met this requirement. The considerable variability in this distribution was reduced by using log (errors + 1); the same scores used to quantify the learning ontogenies presented in Fig. 5.1. The frequency distribution was rendered more compact by grouping the transformed error scores into eight equal class intervals. The eight class intervals, expressed in total errors were: 0, 1–2, 3–6, 7–14, 15–30, 31–62, 63–126, and 127–254.

The resulting empirical frequency distribution of errors to criterion, for the total sample, is represented by the solid frequency polygon in Fig. 5.5. This distribution looked sufficiently bimodal to encourage partition into the two theoretical components also represented in the figure. The partitions were produced as follows. The first step used the win-stay measure to estimate the proportion of learners in the total sample who solved the problem in the hypothesis testing mode. Since .39 of the total sample win-stayed in the shift phase this value served as the estimated proportion of hypothesis

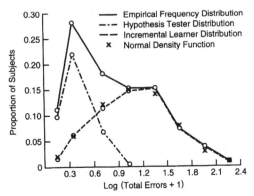

FIG. 5.5. Frequency distribution of the transformed error scores in the preshift phase, for the entire sample, partitioned into hypothesis testers and associative learners. From T. Kendler (1979a).

testers. The next step applied the Trabasso–Bower model again to construct the predicted frequency distribution of errors among the hypothesis testers. Hence, if all learners were hypothesis testers the proportion in the first four class intervals would be .25, .56, .18, and .01, respectively. Multiplying these proportions by .39 produced the theoretical hypothesis tester distribution.

The theoretical frequency distribution of errors for associative learners was produced by simply subtracting the theoretical proportion of hypothesis testers from the total empirical proportion of learners in each class interval. The remainder was used to construct the associative learner distribution. The neat way the two estimated frequency distributions fitted into the total empirical frequency distributions provides further support for the premise that two qualitatively different problem-solving modes can be distinguished. For instance, according to the hypothesis testing model, the mode of the hypothesis testers' distribution should be in the second class interval since .56 of the learners who win-stayed should be contained therein. That the left-hand mode of the total empirical distribution falls in the predicted class interval constitutes one source of confirmation. This part of the analysis also confirms the estimate of the proportion of hypothesis testers in the total sample. If the estimate had been too high, the peak of the hypothesis tester distribution could have exceeded the obtained peak. If it had been too low, the incremental learner component could have been bimodal. That the distribution takes this form supports the applicability of hypothesis testing theory to the higher level.

At the same time one could hardly avoid noticing that the incremental-learner distribution turned out to look like a normal curve. When a normal density function (marked by **X**'s in Fig. 5.5) was fitted to this distribution the fit was very close. Although not predicted, this particular outcome fits well into the scheme of things. If this partition were arbitrary, one would scarcely expect it to yield a normally distributed residue. Moreover, the different character of these two distributions highlights an interesting difference between the two problem-solving modes. When the win-stay rule is applied, the number of errors is governed by chance; specifically the chance that the learner discovers which feature is correct on any given trial. The data indicated, for example, that most if not all of the differences between adults was explained simply by the probability of guessing correctly. Consequently, among hypothesis testers, the frequency distribution of errors depends entirely on chance rather than on individual differences in capacity or experience. This does not imply that such variables have no effect on the disposition to solve the problem in the hypothesis-testing mode. But, once the win-stay-lose-shift rule is activated, individual variability is masked. On the other hand, one can reasonably suppose that individual differences in capacity, experience, or motivation contribute significantly to the performance of the associative learner and that these differences are randomly

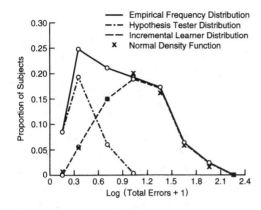

FIG. 5.6. Frequency distribution of the transformed errors on the pre-shift phase, for the mid-age levels (5–12-year-olds) only, partitioned into hypothesis testers and associative learners. From T. Kendler (1979a).

distributed in the sampled population. If so, the distribution of total errors for this group should take the form of a normal distribution with a relatively high degree of variability.

Besides postulating two qualitatively different problem-solving modes, the theory also postulates that the probability of solving the problem in the rational mode increases *gradually* over age. Because it is possible that the partition of the total sample was largely based on the difference between the adults and the 4-year-olds, the gradual change premise was tested by applying the same analysis with these two age levels excluded. As Fig. 5.6 shows, the partition into hypothesis testers and incremental learners is just as effective for the middle range of ages as for the total sample.

Some corroboration of the analysis into two components has been produced by Block, Erickson, and McHoes (1973). They set out to test how well a theoretical learning function derived from the Bower–Trabasso (1964) hypothesis-testing model would fit the cumulative frequency distributions of total errors made on a discrimination-learning task by children at two age levels: 7–8-year-olds and 10–12-year-olds. The best fit was obtained under the assumption that the children at each age level could be classified into two groups on the basis of their learning rate, with the faster learners more numerous in the older group. They concluded that a theory of concept learning in children must allow for categorical differences among learners and for developmental differences through changes in the proportion of learners falling into each of the categories.

Relationship Between Encoding and Learning Modes

Chapter 3 presented evidence that information can be processed in either a lower-level selective mode or a higher-level nonselective mode. Which encoding mode prevailed can be diagnosed by whether the individual learner made a reversal or a nonreversal shift in the test phase of the optional shift procedure. This chapter has shown that simple discrimination-learning problems can be solved in either a lower-level associative mode or a higher-level hypothesis-testing mode. Which problem-solving mode prevailed can be diagnosed by whether or not the individual win-stayed in the shift phase of the procedure. The question that arises next is how are the different information processing and learning modes related? For instance, do learners who encode in the higher, selective mode necessarily learn in the higher, hypothesis testing mode? Are the two information-processing and problem-solving modes different aspects of the same process or are they different processes? The optional shift procedure provides one way to answer such questions by computing the empirical contingencies between the various diagnostic categories.

A dual component system with two levels in each component gives rise to four possible contingencies. Figure 5.7 presents the proportion of individuals in the total sample—all age levels and stimulus conditions combined—represented in each contingency. Slightly less than a third of the total sample (.31) encoded *non*selectively and solved the problem associatively. These individuals performed at the same, lower level on both measures. A similar proportion (.30) encoded selectively and solved the problem rationally. These individuals performed at the same, higher level on both measures. Thus a majority (.61) performed within the same level. However, a substantial proportion of the sample (.39) responded at one encoding level and solved the problem at the other executive level. These crossovers imply that the process controlling selective encoding is not necessarily the same as the process controlling rational hypothesis testing. The other outcome to note was that the crossovers tended to be lopsided. The crossover from the higher encoding mode to the lower executive mode (.28) was much more likely than vice versa (.11). In fact, the learners who encoded in the selective mode (.30) were almost as likely to solve the problem in the associative mode as in the hypothesis testing mode.

Figure 5.8, which plots the two types of crossovers developmentally, shows that the same relationship was produced at every age level except adulthood. A substantial proportion of children at each age level who encoded selectively did *not* hypothesis test, implying that encoding at the higher level is not a sufficient condition for solving the problem at the higher executive level. This is similar to the suggestion produced by the research on inferential problem solving reviewed in chapter 4. On the other hand,

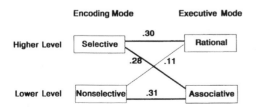

FIG. 5.7. Empirical contingencies between the encoding and executive modes for the entire sample.

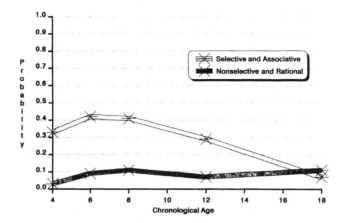

FIG. 5.8. Compares the two types of crossovers at each age level.

Fig. 5.8 also shows that hardly any of the individuals at each age level who encoded nonselectively hypothesis tested. Given some error of measurement, the very low proportion represented in this crossover, suggests that while selective encoding is not a sufficient condition for hypothesis testing, it may be necessary.

Figure 5.9 compares the overall ontogeny of selective encoding with the ontogeny of hypothesis testing. At every age level below adulthood, more learners encoded selectively (made reversal shifts) than hypothesis tested (used the win-stay rule). This outcome suggests that selective encoding develops earlier than rational problem solving, which was also suggested by the data on inferential problem solving.

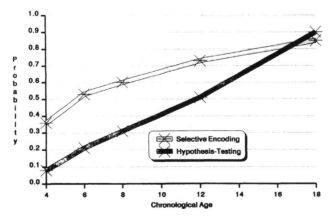

FIG. 5.9. Compares the developmental increase in the proportion of selective encoders and hypothesis testers.

The empirical relationships summarized in the last three figures indicate a need to distinguish between the processes that govern selective encoding and hypothesis testing. To say the same thing in the language of current cognitive theories, representation of the relevant information and rational hypothesis testing are separable processes. As for the levels theory, this evidence is consistent with the distinction between the information processing and executive components.

CONCLUSIONS

As measured by performance in discrimination learning, there is an orderly, ontogenetic increase in problem-solving efficiency among humans. The evidence brought to bear showed that this ontogeny can be explained by assuming two problem-solving modes: a lower-level, less efficient, automatic, associative mode that develops relatively early and a higher-level, more efficient, rational mode that develops later.

The associative mode gradually improves performance on the task. The rational mode produces a quantum leap from a presolution to a solution state through the operation of hypothesis testing. The ontogenetic increase in problem-solving efficiency results from a gradual increase in the probability that the rational mode will prevail. The evidence also suggests that, while selective encoding may be necessary for rational problem solving, it is not sufficient.

CHAPTER SIX

Explaining Learning Sets

A rule, in the sense to be discussed here, is a prescribed guide for conduct or action . . . The guidelines may be prescribed by being formally adopted or explicitly formulated, or the prescription may simply be implicit in the correction and training that is given. . . .
—Encyclopedia of Philosophy (V. 7, p. 231)

Learning sets were first reported by Harlow (1949), who trained naive, adolescent, rhesus monkeys day after day on a very long series of successive, object-discrimination problems to find out what they would learn about learning. Each problem presented a choice between a single pair of three-dimensional objects that differed in multiple ways. Each pair of objects, which could vary in texture, height, brightness, color, or form, was exposed to the monkey, side by side, in the Wisconsin General Test Apparatus illustrated in Fig. 6.1. A food reward was hidden under one object while the other was left unbaited.

Instead of training the animals to criterion, each problem was presented for a predetermined number of trials. When this number was reached the monkey was shifted to another problem with a different pair of objects that also differed in multiple ways, then to a third problem, and so on, until the number of different problems reached 344. Within each problem only one object was correct and the left–right position of this object varied from trial to trial in a predetermined balanced order. The stimulus pairs were equated for difficulty and their serial order was randomly determined. For each monkey the first 32 problems were each run for fifty trials; the next 200 problems for six trials; and the last 112 problems for an average of nine trials.

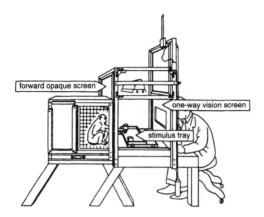

FIG. 6.1. Wisconsin General Test
Apparatus. From Harlow (1949).

To analyze the effect of this training, the 344 problems were sorted into
eight successive problem blocks and the averaged learning curve for the
first six trials in each block was compared as in Fig. 6.2. The first trial in
each block was correct 50% of the time by prearrangement; whichever object
the monkey chose was randomly designated as correct on half the problems
and incorrect on the other half. The percent correct on the remaining trials
were free to vary. The successive learning curves showed a steady increase
in learning efficiency as the number of problems increased. By the last block
of problems, the monkeys made the correct choice 95% of the time after
just one trial on each problem. Harlow characterized this increased efficiency
as learning-to-learn and labeled the end product a "learning set." The ability
of monkeys to acquire learning sets has since been widely replicated.

　　Learning sets are not limited to monkeys; they can be formed by other
animals (Warren, 1965), including human children, who manifest the same

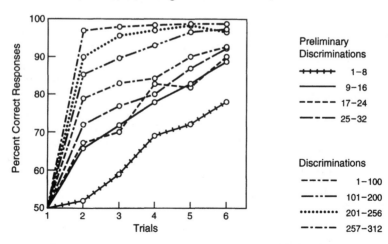

FIG. 6.2. Discrimination-learning curves on successive blocks of problems.
From Harlow (1949).

trends but are likely to reach maximum efficiency in less trials than monkeys (Harlow, 1949; Levinson & Reese, 1967). Nor are learning sets limited to object-discrimination problems. Monkeys and children can acquire other kinds of learning sets, such as learning to choose the position that was correct on the first trial, the stimulus object that was incorrect on the first trial, or the odd member of a triad consisting of two identical objects and one that is different. But this discussion is mostly limited to the simplest case, the object discrimination learning set, to show how it can be explained by the premises of the levels theory.

DUAL PROBLEM-SOLVING MODES

Learning set research requires a sharp distinction between the learning *within* each block of problems (*intra*problem learning) and the transfer *between* the successive blocks (*inter*problem learning). *Intra*problem learning, as reflected in each separate learning curve of Fig. 6.2, describes how each block of problems was learned. For instance, *intra*problem learning in the first (1 to 8) block was gradual and slow. Specifically, the increase in correct choices was monotonic and by the sixth trial the percent correct exceeded chance by approximately 25%. In contrast, *intra*problem learning in the last block (257 to 312) was rapid and saltatory. Practically all choices were correct by the second trial and there was a quantum leap between trial 1 and 2 from chance to almost 100% correct.

The difference between the *intra*problem learning on the first and last block of problems can be explained as follows. Learning in the first block is gradual and slow because the monkeys begin to learn the early problems in the incremental, associative mode. Learning in the last block is rapid and saltatory because these problems are solved in the rational, hypothesis-testing mode. According to the hypothesis-testing model discussed in chapter 5 whatever choice a monkey makes on the first trial provides enough information to make the saltatory leap into the solution state regardless of whether the first choice is correct or incorrect. If the first choice is correct, the monkey should win-stay with that choice for the remainder of the trials; if incorrect the monkey should enter the search mode and produce a focus sample of tenable hypotheses compatible with the information provided by the first choice. Since there are only two objects and one of them was incorrect, the only tenable hypothesis concerns the other object, so the second choice should be correct. With such simple problems a rational solution should produce a quantum leap into the solution state after the first trial.

If all the monkeys solved each problem in the rational mode, the averaged learning curve presented in Fig. 6.2 should make a saltatory leap from 50% on trial 1 to 100% on trial 2 and this high level of performance should be maintained on the trials 3 through 6. Because the last block of trials (257–312) does jump from 50% to almost 100% by trial 2, it is reasonable to suppose that by the completion of training all learners were performing in the hypothesis testing mode. Thus, according to the dual-mode premise, the monkeys begin learning-set training by solving the discrimination problems in the relatively inefficient, associative mode. After training on a great many successive, different problems they wind up solving the problems in the relatively efficient, rational mode.

Consider now the *inter*problem learning manifested in the successive changes in the learning curves between the first and last problem blocks. If there were a single learning mode that gradually becomes more efficient with increased training, then the increased percent of correct responses in the successive curves should be spread proportionally over trials 2 to 6. Instead of such a proportionally distributed set of changes, by far the greatest part of the change occurs between trials 1 and 2. A dual-mode theory of problem solving provides a more plausible explanation of the concentration of improvement between trials 1 and 2 by postulating that training on successive problems increases the probability that problems will be solved in the rational mode. Solution in the rational mode is likely to produce the observed saltatory jump between the first and second trial that can be seen in Fig. 6.2. The effect of training on successive problems should increase the proportion of problems solved by the second trial.

The implication of this explanation is that most problems in the first block are solved in the gradual, associative mode and most problems in the last block are solved in the saltatory, rational mode. Between the first and last problem blocks, each learning curve represents a composite of problems solved in the associative mode and problems solved in the rational mode. And the mix changes gradually as the number of successive problems increases.

If so, it should be possible to partition the empirical learning curves for each block of trials between the first and the last into the associative and rational components. To produce the partitions, one could identify the problems solved in the rational mode as those solved by the second trial. One could then use this performance criterion to partition the problems into two components. The rational component would consist of problems solved by trial 2 and the remaining problems would constitute the associative component.

Once the two components are separated, calculating the percent of correct choices on trials 1 through 6 on the associative component becomes possible. The two sets of percentages can be used to reconstruct the two learning curves, one for the rational component and one for the associative component, for each block of problems. The learning curves for the rational component would, by definition, jump from 50% to 100% on trial 2 and remain at 100% for trials 3 to 6. The learning curves for the associative component are, however, free to vary. In the nature of things, the number of problems solved in the associative mode would dwindle as the learning set increased.

Therefore, the curves for each successive block of problems would become more irregular. With that proviso, the prediction would be that each curve in the associative partition should show a gradual increase in the percent of correct choices between trials 1 and 6 similar to the gradual increase manifested in the first block of problems. That is, each learning curve in the associative learning component should increase slowly and gradually and the form of the curves should be similar.

The trial-by-trial data required for such a test are not available to me and I know of no published data that decomposes the intraproblem data into two such components, but looking at the data in Fig. 6.2 it seems likely that the curves between the first and the last set of problems could be so decomposed and that they would take the predicted form. Although that remains to be seen, the point is that this explanation is, in principle, testable. Meanwhile there are other related data to be considered.

ALTERNATIVE EXPLANATIONS OF LEARNING SET

Harlow's Explanation

There have, of course, been other theories that sought to explain learning set. Harlow's explanation (1949; Harlow & Hicks, 1957), like that of Lashley and Krechevsky, was grounded in the observation that choice behavior of the animals prior to learning was often systematic. A monkey could choose one position or the incorrect object for many consecutive trials. Harlow referred to such systematic response tendencies as "error factors" and proposed that both *inter*problem and *intra*problem learning consisted of nothing more than their inhibition or suppression.

He identified four error factors: stimulus perseveration, differential cue, response shift, and position habit. The *intra*problem learning manifested in learning sets was assumed to consist of the gradual inhibition of whatever error factors the monkey brought to the each problem. *Inter*problem learning, the learning within each problem, he explained by assuming that with each new problem the error factors reemerged and therefore needed to be inhibited again. Learning set was supposedly based on the gradually increasing transfer of this inhibition from problem to problem.

This theory led Harlow's students and other primate researchers to perform a variety of error-factor analyses on their discrimination learning data but they all remained inconclusive. To cite Levine (1975), one of Harlow's prominent students:

> Perhaps the most obvious feature of this budding tradition was that no two articles contained the same analyses. The use of . . . (other kinds of learning sets), for example, called for special factors. . . . Even the four factors . . . (proposed by Harlow) . . . are unrelated to each other. This small domain, therefore, quickly developed a chaotic appearance. (p. 59)

Relating Learning Sets to Hypotheses

As a graduate student in Harlow's laboratory, Levine tried to bring order into the chaos by redefining and increasing the error factors. He organized the factors in a theoretical framework and produced a method of measurement that flowed from the framework as a natural consequence. Levine's first model (1959) renamed Harlow's error factors "hypotheses" (H's) after Krechevsky's earlier use. Also, instead of considering only incorrect systematic responses that needed to be eliminated, he added correct systematic responses that could be acquired as a result of learning-set training. For example, he named the correct systematic response acquired in object learning sets as a Win-stay-Lose-shift (object) H because the reference was to the object rather than to any abstracted feature.

To regularize research on learning sets he listed eight other pertinent H's and provided a method for determining which H was in control from the pattern of choices manifested in the first three trials of each learning-set problem. In this way each H was operationally defined by a particular, identifiable, pattern of choices and labeled by the inferred controlling factor. For instance, a Position-preference H was defined as 3 choices in a row to the same position and a Stimulus-preference H as 3 choices in a row to the same stimulus. The win-stay-lose-shift H (object), was defined as either a $- + +$ or a $+ + +$ pattern of choices. These definitions permitted the strength of each hypothesis to be measured by the percent of times it appeared during the course of learning-set training.

Levine's model made learning sets amenable to associative-learning theory by treating the whole pattern of responses, rather than each individual choice, as the dependent variable. These whole patterns were then assumed to be susceptible to the traditional effects of reinforcement and extinction. Accordingly, the acquisition of an object learning set consisted of the gradual strengthening of the Win-stay-lose-shift H(object) and the gradual weakening of the other H's.

Note that Levine's first model assumed there was nothing unique about the Win-stay-lose-shift H; it had the same status as Stimulus or Position preference H's. But not long after, he shifted the focus of his research from monkeys to human adults and changed his conception of H's from directly observable response patterns to mediating processes. The revised model (Levine, 1963) also differentiated two distinctly different kinds of hypotheses: Response-set H's and Predictions H's. To cite Levine's (1975) own retrospective account of this differentiation:

> What is important is the shift that occurred in the use of the term 'hypothesis.' In treating the monkey's response, an H was a preference, or a habit, or a Response-set (e.g., a position preference). In dealing with the human, however, an H could also be a *Prediction* about nature, and S was assumed to respond in a way that would maximize his rewards if his Prediction were correct. Response-sets were conceived of as automatic and rigid, the response

pattern appearing regardless of the feedback. Predictions manifested a more flexible system, with the prediction and its concomitant responses sensitively contingent upon feedback. (p. 146)

Using a modified procedure better adapted for human subjects, but still based on the pattern analysis of a small number of consecutive trials, Levine (1963) showed that college students used only Prediction *H's*; they never manifested Response-set *H's*. In contrast, he noted that Response-set *H's* are widespread among rats (Krechevsky, 1932a), monkeys (Harlow, 1950; Levine, 1959) and chimpanzees (Schusterman, 1961). Response sets are also prevalent among young children (Gholson, Levine, & Phillips, 1972).

The distinction between Response sets and Prediction *H's* in Levine's revised model comes close to the distinction between associative and rational problem solving, except for one important difference. As for the similarities, Prediction *H's* and rational problem solutions are analogous in that they are both based on the production of tenable hypotheses which the reinforcement contingencies either confirm or disconfirm. In Levine's model the invocation of Prediction *H's* is deemed characteristic of adult humans.

Levine's Response sets, which are more likely to be found among children and nonhuman animals, are analogous to associative habits that produce repetitions of incorrect choices attributable to innate preferences or previous learning. In Levine's formulation Response sets were, however, regarded as totally insensitive to feedback, whereas in the dual-mode theory rewards are assumed to automatically strengthen and nonrewards automatically weaken associative habits. But this difference is probably more attributable to methodology than to principle. Because learning-set procedures require the use of many problems, efficiency requires keeping the number of trials per problem be as few as possible. Only a few responses are required to identify Prediction *H's*; in contrast associative learning may take many trials before gradually becoming manifest, more than the few trials Levine's methods allowed. Levine seemed to have observed that, within the few trials per problem he used to define Response sets, no manifest learning appeared. But one cannot safely conclude from such data that the so-called Response sets are totally insensitive to feedback since the fact is that, given enough trials on object discrimination-learning problem, nonhuman animals and young children do learn to make the correct choice. With this proviso in mind, Levine's differentiation between prediction *H's* and Response sets could be an earlier version of the differentiation between associative and rational modes of operation.

DISTINGUISHING BETWEEN ASSOCIATIVE AND RATIONAL MODES

Bessemer and Stollnitz (1971) carried Levine's ideas further by explicitly distinguishing two general factors that differ qualitatively in their mode of operation. They named these factors "habits" and "hypotheses." Habits, which encompassed both Harlow's error factors and Levine's Response set *H's*, were defined as relatively stable approach and avoidance tendencies directly elicited by the immediate stimulus situation. The key word here is *stable* for reasons that will become evident. The stable habits were attributed to innate tendencies or previous learning history. In other words, habits are the product of learning in the associative mode.

The second class of factors were named hypotheses, after Levine's usage. Hypotheses, such the win-stay-lose-shift (object) *H*, were defined as relatively transient response tendencies determined partly by present events and partly by short-term memories of intertrial contingencies. Hypotheses, in other words, are the product of problem solving in the rational mode.

Bessemer and Stollnitz not only independently came to the conclusion that discrimination-learning problems can be solved in two different modes, they also provided additional supporting evidence. One of Bessemer's experiments (1967) demonstrated that monkeys who had acquired a win-stay-lose-shift (object) *H* remembered the learning set well but soon forgot the individual correct choices. He first presented learning-set-experienced monkeys with a series of three-trial problems and then tested for retention of the correct choice on the same problems 2–5 days, 2 weeks, and 26 weeks later, respectively. The respective performance on the *first* retention trial over these three intervals was .55, .58, and .57, only slightly better than chance. The poor retention of the correct choices contrasted sharply with the retention of the learning set itself, where there was a decline of only 2% on the *second* trial performance over the same time intervals.

The stability of a well-trained discrimination-learning habit involving a single pair of objects is well established. But, because in learning-set training many successive problems are presented, further evidence is required to determine whether *many* stable habits can also be acquired successively. Strong (1959) demonstrated that rhesus monkeys trained to criterion can achieve a high degree of retention of the rewarded choices on many different, successively trained discrimination problems. He trained experimentally naive, rhesus monkeys to a criterion of 90% correct on 72 problems in six separate blocks of 12 problems each. Recall tests of sample problems showed essentially no retention loss for up to 7 months after training was completed.

If, as Harlow surmised, learning sets were teaching monkeys how to learn, then learning-set-sophisticated monkeys should also remember what they had learned. Bessemer's experiment showed that learning-set-sophisticated monkeys rapidly forget most of the specific associations they might appear to have learned during the course of typical learning-set training, where each problem is presented for a only a few successive training trials. Experiments like these demonstrate that well-trained habits are well remembered, well-trained learning sets are also well remembered, but the various hypotheses that are confirmed in a series of learning-set problems are soon forgotten.

Learning set is the label Harlow bestowed on the interproblem learning when he supposed it to be merely a matter of gradually learning to inhibit certain errors. We now know this is not the whole story. Interproblem learning is explained in the Bessemer–Stollnitz model as a passage from an associative to a hypothesis mode. But what are the monkeys learning that makes this passage possible? The answer that suggests itself is that they are learning a rule, where a *rule* is defined as a prescribed guide for conduct that reflects the regularity in some set of events. The regularity in the case of learning sets lies in the reinforcement contingencies. The win-stay-lose-shift (object) rule, for instance, serves as a guide for generating hypotheses that produce solutions to a class of problems, the class in which one should choose the object that yielded the reward on the previous trial and avoid the object that did not. Because there are only two possible hypotheses only one trial is required to determine which one is tenable. Although rules may be explicit, as in learning the rules of a board game, they may also be implicit, as when a young child learns the rule governing the inflection of regular verbs. A learning set refers to an implicit rule, no access to consciousness is necessarily implied. Nevertheless, rules acquired in learning-set problems are more abstract, efficient, and rational than habits. The rules are more abstract in that they refer to a class of problems rather than a single set of discriminanda, more efficient in that they provide for generating simple hypotheses that produce one-trial learning, and more rational in that they make more intelligent use of empirical regularities. Learning sets are presumably produced by the rational mode.

Learning-set research demonstrates that monkeys can learn some simple, implicit rules. They can learn a win-stay-lose-shift (object) rule, a choose-the-odd-object rule, and rules that refer to position rather than to objects. Learning to use any one of these rules can require hundreds of instances to which the rule applies. But when the rule is applied it lends itself to saltatory, one-trial learning. While the win-stay-lose-shift rule applies to choices that follow the first trial, this rule provides no guide for the first choice on each new problem. Indeed the rule's utility depends on that property because it can apply to any pair of objects. Distinguishing between the rule and the specific choice response can also explain why monkeys can learn simple rules like win-stay-lose-shift (object) when the number of trials on each problem are as few as three. After it became known that only a few trials per problem were necessary, the typical procedure for learning-set-training research was to present only a few trials per problem throughout training. That three trials are sufficient makes sense if one is learning a rule that applies to formulating a correct hypothesis after the first trial, that is tested on the second trial, and confirmed on the third.

Bessemer's retention research used only three training trials on each problem. Memory for the correct hypotheses for a block of problems faded almost completely within a day because a few trials were not enough to strengthen the arbitrary association between the particular rewarded objects and the choice response. One could say the rule-generated hypotheses are held briefly in working memory, but without more rehearsal they are not transferred to long-term memory store. The rule itself is well-remembered because the typical learning-set procedure is presented for as many different problems as are necessary for the monkey to attain some fairly rigorous criterion such as 90% correct choices on trial 2. The typical way to represent the course of learning set training is to plot the percent of correct choices on trial 2 as a function of the number of problems presented. Figure 6.3, for example, plots the trial 2 choices in the Harlow (1959) experiment cited earlier. Note that plotting the acquisition of a learning set in this manner yields a gradual learning curve in which the learning is measured in terms of problems just as the acquisition of a habit is measured in terms of trials.

Many experiments have shown that monkeys require only a few trials per problem, while they require hundreds of different problems, to learn the win-stay-lose-shift rule (Miles, 1965). Apparently the memory for both rules and habits is a function of the amount of repetition, albeit what is repeated differs. To remember a habit requires many repetitions of the same discriminanda. To remember a rule requires many repetitions of the same class of problems. The monkeys remembered the rule well because they had ample practice in applying them.

Relations Between the Rational and Associative Modes

According to the levels theory the higher-level rational mode does not replace the lower-level associative mode. Rather the two modes continue to function cooperatively in parallel as long as the behavior they control is compatible. Consequently, sufficient repetition of the appropriate response to a set of discriminanda can convert an easily forgotten rational solution into a well-re-

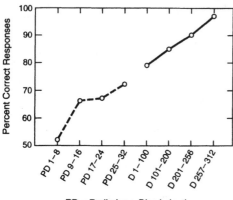

PD = Preliminary Discriminations
D = Discriminations

FIG. 6.3. Discrimination learning-set curve based on trial 2 responses. From Harlow (1949).

membered habit. What began as a problem is presently taken care of automatically until circumstances change and the automatic behavior is no longer appropriate. As proposed by Wundt a century ago, if or when the automatic behavior is no longer appropriate a new problem is generated, which reactivates the rational mode.

A testable implication of this formulation is that, if the rational mode is to be effective in solving a new problem, it must be capable of inhibiting any incompatible behavioral tendencies produced by the lower automatic mode. Bessemer (1967) also provided evidence that the learning sets are capable of inhibiting but do not eradicate incompatible habits. This evidence comes from learning-set-sophisticated monkeys' choices on the first trials of a series of win-stay-lose-shift (object) problems. In learning-set research the usual procedure is to arrange for a 50% correct initial choice on each acquisition problem, by randomly rewarding whatever discriminandum was chosen on trial 1 for half of the problems and nonrewarding the other half for each subject. The effect is that, on half of the problems, the correct choice will accord with any preferences the monkeys may have had. On the other half of the problems the correct choice will oppose any such preference. When there is no rational basis for making a choice such a preference is presumably based on habits attributable to innate predispositions or to previous learning.

The original purpose of Bessemer's experiment was to test for the retention of the correct choice in each problem by presenting learning-set-sophisticated monkeys with a new block of eight problems for 6 trials each and subsequently measuring retention of the first correct choices on the same problems one day later. The retention test presented the same block of problems, in the same order, for 6 retention trials. Memory for the correct choice is best measured by trial 1 in each problem because by trial 2 this memory and the application of the win-stay-lose-shift rule are conflated. An unexpected finding emerged when the problems were sorted into two sets, according to whether the first choice on a given problem was rewarded or unrewarded. In effect these problems were sorted according to whether the previous day's training was with or against preference.

The left graph of Fig. 6.4 compares performance on the problems trained with and against preference the first time this set of problems was presented. The trial 1 response was not plotted because the procedure dictated that half of the choices had to be correct. By trial 2 these sophisticated monkeys were highly likely to make the correct choice regardless of whether they were trained with or against preference and they continued to be mostly correct on trials 3 through 6. Clearly if there were preferences manifested on trial 1 they were either eradicated or inhibited on the remaining 5 trials.

The right graph of Fig. 6.4 plots the choice behavior on the retention test given 24 hours later. The pertinent result is that recall on trial 1 was much better for animals trained with than against preference. Apparently, on trial 1 of the

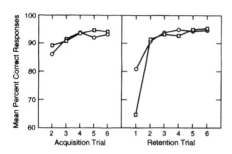

FIG. 6.4. Effect of initial preference on retention of learning sets. From Bessemer and Stollnitz (1971).

second day the initial preference manifested on the first day reappeared suggesting that monkeys do have a tendency to prefer one discriminandum over another and that this preference is temporarily overridden rather than eradicated when the appropriate rule is brought to bear on trials 2 through 6. The results of the retention test affirms this presumption because, regardless of whether they were once again trained with or against their preference, by trial 2 there was no difference between the two sets.

This outcome suggests that the rule-governed solution only temporarily inhibited the habit. When the rule was not applicable the habit reemerged, but only on the first trial. By the second trial of the retention test, the sophisticated monkey reinvoked the rule and continued to choose correctly for the remaining trials. These data are consistent with the premise that the two modes can operate in parallel. But, if they lead to incompatible outcomes, other things being equal, the rational mode will inhibit the behavioral expression of the lower mode.

Another more clear-cut demonstration of the higher mode's capacity to inhibit the lower mode's expression is provided by another, different learning-set experiment. Riopelle and Chinn (1961) trained rhesus monkeys to choose the object in one position on the first trial of each problem without interfering seriously with their object-discrimination performance on later trials. These animals could respond on the basis of a well-trained, automatic habit to, say, choose the left object on the first trial of each problem, and use the win-stay rule to choose the appropriate object, regardless of its position, on the subsequent trials.

In short, learning-set research not only supports the premise that two problem-solving modes can be distinguished but it also provides evidence that the two modes operate in parallel and that when their behavioral expression conflicts the higher mode prevails.

THE DEVELOPMENT OF LEARNING SETS

Phylogenetic Development

Harlow firmly believed his learning-set experiments tapped an ecologically valid mechanism for increasing the capacity of monkeys to adapt to the changing conditions they find in their natural environment. He was also certain that learning sets acquired by man have accounted for his ability to adapt and survive. In 1949, when he reported that rhesus monkeys could acquire object-quality learning sets, he included some data on "another primate species" trained on the same problems. The species referred to was children, 17 in all, between 2 and 5 years of age whose IQs ranged from 109 to 151. The only data he cited to support the extrapolation to mankind were derived from these 17 children trained to an unspecified criterion on a series of 6-trial problems of the sort used with the monkeys, except that beads and toys substituted for food rewards. Of these children, 13 gradually acquired a learning set and they did so in many less trials than the rhesus monkeys. The other 4 children seemed to be on the way when the experiment was ended after 84 problems had been presented.

Harlow was cautious about interpreting the difference between the children and the monkeys as indicative of a capacity difference, preferring instead to emphasize that the same basic mechanisms were operating in both species. To other investigators, however, this difference suggested that learning-set training could provide an objective method for comparing intelligence across species. A number of studies using learning set procedures for such comparative purposes appeared in the literature. Warren (1965) summarized some of this literature by comparing discrimination-learning-set formation, measured by trial 2 performance, as compiled from five different experiments (Fig. 6.5). In each experiment the animals were trained on 6-trial, win-stay-lose-shift (object) problems.

The combined results show the rhesus monkeys acquired learning sets much more quickly than the squirrel monkeys, marmosets, and cats. The performance of the rodents (rats and squirrels) was the poorest of all. On the basis of these and the other experiments Warren (1965) concluded:

> In general the available data suggest that the phylogenetic development of the capacity for learning-set formation in mammals is best described as a continuous (ogive-type) function, with no sharp discontinuities between adjacent taxa, but with marked quantitative difference between the extremes of the distribution . . . How long this tidy phylogenetic sequence in learning-set proficiency will endure. is a matter of conjecture. (pp. 262–263)

The conclusions were tentative because equating conditions across different species is exceedingly difficult, if not impossible. There is also the claim that no valid conclusions about evolutionary development can be derived from such comparisons because they do not follow a true ancestral lineage. A rebuttal of this criticism is that ancestry is not the only defining feature of evolution. It may be more appropriate to study the evolution of intelligence by using the increase in adaptive complexity of a given structural or functional unit in organisms, which may or may not be directly related in the ancestral sense. As noted by Gottlieb (1984), the functional perspective

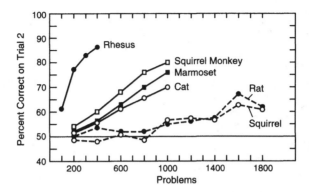

FIG. 6.5. Discrimination-learning-set formation by primates, carnivores, and rodents. From Warren (1965).

does not deny ancestry in terms of clades, where a clade is defined as a group of organisms descended from a common ancestor. Rather, this other perspective also allows for classification by function in terms of grades (Huxley, 1957), where a grade is a particular level in an ascending series of improvements on any given structural or functional unit that results in increases in complexity, (differentiation), centralization, plasticity, and independence of the immediate environment (Rensch, 1959). The evolving structural and functional unit implicit in the typical scale used by comparative psychologists is the central nervous system. From this perspective to order animals in terms of the complexity of the central nervous system is crude but not erroneous.

Ontogenetic Development

Chapter 5 showed that, when human beings are presented with a single discrimination problem, two problem-solving modes can be distinguished: an incremental, associative mode and a rational, hypothesis-testing mode. The procedure used was the optional shift and the hypothesis-testing mode was operationally differentiated from the associative mode by the use of a win-stay rule in the shift phase of the procedure. The probability of win-staying was shown to increase systematically with age.

The learning-set research discussed in this chapter has shown that certain mammals can learn to use a win-stay-lose-shift rule. Such learning can require the prior presentation of many successive problems to which the rule applies. Because such learning sets are learnable it might appear that the developmental changes in hypothesis testing among humans is based entirely on learning. Such a conclusion is, however, unwarranted because it erroneously presupposes that learning and maturation are mutually exclusive. Rather learning and maturation can, and usually do, work together to determine the course of ontogenetic development. One cannot experimentally differentiate between maturation and prior experience in humans in order to study how they interrelate, but some insight into this relationship can be gleaned from an experiment with laboratory-born rhesus monkeys (Harlow, Harlow, Rueping, & Mason, 1960).

The monkeys in this experiment were assigned at birth to one of five basic groups according to the age at which they began training. The respective ages measured in days were 60, 90, 120, 150, and 360. The monkeys, 63 in all, were separated from their mothers within 9 hours after birth and subsequently raised under highly controlled conditions with no experience in discrimination learning until they reached their assigned starting age level. Each animal was first trained on a conventional, single-pair, discrimination-learning problem to a criterion of 10 correct responses in 11 trials. They all attained criterion, although the number of errors they made varied inversely with age.

After attaining criterion on the single-pair problem, each monkey began training on an object-discrimination learning set. All subjects were trained on four 6-trial problems each day until the 360-day group had completed 400 problems and the other groups had completed 600. Figure 6.6 compares the rate at which the several groups of monkeys acquired the learning set, as measured by the percent of correct choices on trial 2. The steeper the slope of the learning curve, the faster the rate.

The two lowest curves show the learning curves for the two youngest groups to be almost flat. Although these very young monkeys were able to learn a single-pair discrimination problem to criterion, there is little evidence that they learned the win-stay-lose-shift rule after 600 trials. Only slight improvement was manifested by the two intermediate-age groups, who performed better than the youngest groups but had not yet attained a high level of learning when training ended. If monkeys at the intermediate ages could acquire a learning set, they apparently would do so relatively slowly.

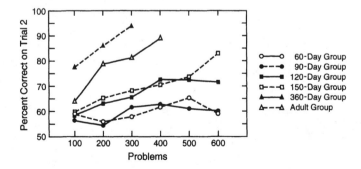

FIG. 6.6. Trial 2 performance as a measure of learning-set formation in rhesus monkeys who began training at different ages. From Harlow, Harlow, Rueping, and Mason (1960).

The 360-day group attained a a high level of performance but at a slower rate than an adult group that was included for comparison.

These data indicate that for rhesus monkeys the capacity to acquire a win-stay-lose-shift (object) learning set increases as the animals mature. There is no way to rule out completely the possibility that this developmental change is attributable to some form of experience, other than training on the win-stay-lose-shift rule. But learning-set research has established there is little positive transfer between the learning of rules that do not share a common property. Learning the win-stay-lose-shift rule, for instance, does not make it easier to learn the oddity rule and vice versa. If there is no general transfer of rule learning and the animals had no prior formal experience with the win-stay-lose-shift rule it is reasonable to conclude that the capacity to acquire a learning set rule is influenced by maturation. At any rate, Harlow et al. (1960) boldly concluded that:

> It becomes progressively more apparent that interproblem learning as measured by learning-set formation differs sharply from simple intraproblem learning. Although learning-set capacity is certainly dependent upon maturation and doubtless grows in an orderly manner, it is also true that no animal acquires this capability without extensive practice. (p. 120)

Levinson and Reese (1967) later investigated the relationship between age and the capacity to acquire the win-stay-lose-shift (object) learning set among humans. They trained preschool children, fifth graders, college students, and elderly individuals (68–85-year-olds) on a series of 10 4-trial problems per day until they completed 5 consecutive problems with no more than one error on trials 2, 3, and 4. Between early childhood and young adulthood there was an increasing capacity to acquire the learning set. The median number of problems required to attain criterion was 20.4 for the preschoolers, 10.8 for the fifth graders, and 6.7 for the college students. The elderly subjects were extremely variable but their median performance was much poorer than any of the other age groups. These results indicate that between early childhood and young adulthood the ease of acquiring a learning set is an increasing function of age for humans as well as for rhesus monkeys. These developmental trends, considered in the light of the levels theory, provide converging evidence that the capacity to solve discrimination-learning problems in the hypothesis-testing mode increases gradually between early childhood and young adulthood.

In the optional shift procedure the capacity to function in the hypothesis-testing mode is measured by the spontaneous probability of win-staying in the shift-discrimination; the greater the probability the greater is the capacity. In learning-set training, this capacity is measured by the ease with which the lose-shift-win-stay rule is learned. Both measures attest that the capacity to function in the hypothesis-testing mode increases with age among humans. While the learning-set research shows that the acquisition of particular rules is dependent on learning, the developmental differences in the acquisition of the appropriate learning set show that the rate at which these rules are learned is age-related.

All of these data taken together suggest a gradual, developmental increase in the capacity to function in the hypothesis-testing mode. This increasing capacity is at least partly attributable to maturation.

CONCLUSIONS

Learning-set research provides further evidence that discrimination-learning problems can be solved in either an associative or hypothesis-testing mode. The two modes function in parallel but when they evoke incompatible behaviors the hypothesis-testing mode has the capacity to inhibit the behavior evoked by the associative mode. In addition, this research showed that: First, the capacity to function in the hypothesis-testing mode is available to rhesus monkeys. Second, their capacity to solve problems in this mode is a combined function of practice and maturity. Third, solutions arrived at in the hypothesis-testing mode are more efficient but they are quickly forgotten; solutions arrived at in the associative mode require more trials but they are well-remembered.

Besides confirming the existence of these two modes, learning-set research provides evidence that each mode is adapted to serve a different purpose. If a problem presents itself often enough, the repetition will automatically produce a gradual increase in the disposition to choose correctly. Because automatic responses are likely to be reliable, rapid, and effortless they are useful in situations where the same choice remains appropriate on frequent occasions or over long time intervals. The higher mode produces an intentional, rational choice based on a rule-guided, hypothesis-testing strategy that makes use of at least some of the available information gleaned from previous experience. Such solutions are particularly useful when a new problem for which there is no suitable automatic response is encountered.

As for developmental changes in the capacity to perform in the higher mode, most of the learning-set research was done with adolescent or adult monkeys, thereby demonstrating that this species are capable of learning to perform in the higher executive mode. But in the case of both monkeys and humans, the ease with which learning sets are acquired is an increasing function of age.

CHAPTER SEVEN

A Model of
Lower Level Operation

God is in the details.

—Attributed to Albert Einstein.

I have been using discrimination learning to explore the fundamentally different conceptions of problem solving expressed in the continuity–noncontinuity controversy. The result is an organic resolution that integrates the two ostensibly conflicting conceptions in a single theory about the psychological system that mediates discrimination learning. Like the central nervous system, the psychological system has a structural, functional, and operational aspect. The structure delineates and relates the component parts of the system. The function describes what these components do and the operations specify how they do it.

The structure of the proposed psychological system consists of an information processing and an executive component. Each component is organized into different levels. This structure is modeled after the central nervous system, which is also differentiated into a mostly afferent (information processing) and a mostly efferent (executive) component, with each component organized into different levels. Using the central nervous system as a substantive model provides an analogy between the hypothetical entities of the elusive psychological system and the more tangible entities of the nervous system. The analogy makes the intangible psychological system more comprehensible and suggests relationships between the hypothetical entities (Nagel, 1961). Keeping to this substantive model also enhances the possibility of a more generalized neuropsychological theory that integrates the biological and psychological facts.

92

The overall function of each component in the psychological system is straightforward. The information-processing component encodes the information provided by the discriminanda into usable form. The executive component uses the output of the information-processing component to determine which discriminandum to choose. Although the functions of the levels within each component are related, they operate in different modes. How the information is encoded and how the choice is made depends on which level is in control.

The operational aspect of the system describes how each level works, what it does in order to execute its function. The difference between the levels have so far been described in general terms by asserting that the lower level operates according to continuity principles; encoding is nonselective and choice behavior is based on gradual, automatic, associative learning. The higher level operates on noncontinuity principles; encoding is selective and problem solving is saltatory, rational, and intentional. Sooner or later such a theory needs to specify more precisely how these hypothetical levels perform the functions attributed to them. This chapter discusses a formal model of lower level operation that adds some of this requisite precision to the theory.

Although the levels theory, as a whole, uses the nervous system as a substantive model, the more specific model of lower level operation is formal rather than substantive. Unlike a substantive model, a formal model uses an abstract, logical set of relations as an analogy. A complete theory establishes correspondences between the theoretical and empirical notions. A formal model provides the rules for relating the elements of the theory to each other and to the logically derived, empirical consequences (Nagel, 1961). The formal model discussed in this chapter consists of a set of postulates expressed in a mathematical form capable of generating logical, testable implications about discrimination learning and transfer behavior. Because a mathematical model of continuity theory can take different forms, the discussion begins by distinguishing the theory from the proposed model.

THE CONTINUITY THEORY
OF DISCRIMINATION LEARNING

When Spence (1936) formulated his continuity theory he intended to propose a set of principles subject to amendment, addition, and ultimate specification. His basic thesis was that:

> Discrimination learning . . . involves . . . the relative strengthening of the excitatory tendency of a certain component of the stimulus complex as compared to other elements until it attains sufficient strength to determine the response. By the conditions of the experiment the relevant stimulus component is always reinforced and never frustrated, whereas irrelevant components receive both reinforcement and frustration. (p. 430)

He proposed the first mathematical model to show, in detail, how some important facts about discrimination learning in rats could be explained by continuity theory, without having to resort to either selective attention or hypothesis testing. Other models based on continuity theory have since been proposed to explain additional facts (e.g., Hull, 1943; Spence, 1937; Spiker, 1970). Although these models differ in particulars, they all assume the learner begins each task with a pre-established set of tendencies to approach or avoid each discriminable feature in the compounded discriminanda. The pre-established tendencies derive either from innate preferences or previous experience. During training the strength of each tendency is gradually modified according to the following principles:

1. *Principle of reinforcement.* If a response is followed by a reward, the excitatory tendency to approach each discriminable feature in the chosen discriminandum is strengthened by a certain amount.

2. *Principle of inhibition.* If a response is not followed by a reward, the inhibitory tendency to avoid each discriminable feature in the chosen discriminandum is strengthened by a certain amount.

Principles 1 and 2 account for how subjects learn to choose the correct discriminandum and/or avoid the incorrect one.

3. *Principle of stimulus generalization.* In the case of continuous dimensions, there is a generalization of acquired excitatory and/or inhibitory tendencies to other values on the same dimension in the form of a gradient around the respective positive and negative features. This principle accounts for why more salient stimuli are learned relatively easily.

In addition to these general principles there are two other basic assumptions:

4. The total excitatory strength of a stimulus compound is equal to the sum of the excitatory tendencies of the component stimuli.

5. When a choice is made, the discriminandum having the greatest total excitatory strength will prevail.

A mathematical model of such a theory specifies how each premise is implemented, thereby increasing the capacity of the theory to generate more precise, detailed, logically derived predictions.

INTRINSIC CUE-DOMINANCE (ICD) MODEL

The various models of discrimination learning associated with continuity theory were formulated at different times for different purposes. Spence's 1936 model, for instance, did not include the generalization assumption, which he added to continuity theory in 1937. Moreover, his specific assumptions about how the excitatory and inhibitory tendencies increment were admittedly arbitrary. At that time, his primary purpose was to show that continuity theory could explain the facts adduced by Lashley to reveal selective attention and insight in rats. He left it for others to provide a better model when more facts are available. The Intrinsic Cue-Dominance (ICD) Model (T. Kendler, 1971; T. Kendler, Basden, & Bruckner, 1970; Rust & T. Kendler, 1987) proposed to expand the application of continuity theory to lower level behavior as measured by discriminative shift procedures. The special purpose was to explain how, without invoking selective attention, one dimension in a compound can exert more control over choice behavior than another.

Distinguishing Intrinsic From Acquired Dimensional Dominance

Long ago Aristotle observed that, given simultaneous stimulation, the stronger dimension always extrudes the weaker. Brilliant color differences can extrude, say, very small size differences. Pavlov (1927) showed experimentally that, if a conditioned stimulus is compounded of two dimensions, the cues on one dimension can completely overshadow the other. Let such overshadowing or extruding be referred to as dimensional dominance. Dimensional dominance has been established in a variety of species, including pigeons (Reynolds, 1961), rats (Lawrence, 1950), monkeys (D'Amato & Fazzaro, 1966), human children (Suchman & Trabasso, 1966) and human adults (Trabasso & Bower, 1968).

Because dimensional dominance seems to imply selective attention to the dominant dimension, its universality has been taken as evidence for the universality of selective encoding and against continuity theory. However, relating dimensional dominance to selective attention conflates two distinctive forms of dimensional dominance: intrinsic and acquired. With this distinction in mind, the ICD model can show that dimensional dominance, properly interpreted, supports rather than denies the applicability of continuity theory to lower level learning and lends further credence to the levels theory.

The difference between intrinsic and acquired dimensional dominance is easier to convey if the terms are defined. As Harnad (1987) noted, *dimension* refers to one of many physical continua—such as luminance, size, wavelength, or orientation—along which compounded discriminanda can be differentiated, analyzed, or categorized. *Cue* refers to a particular value on a dimension that can serve as the basis for the perception of some real world attribute, feature, or property—such as bright, large, green, or vertical. Compounded discriminanda are composed of two or more dimensions. *Dimensional dominance* refers to the tendency for the cues on one of the compounded dimensions to exert more weight on choice behavior than the cues on the other dimensions.

Two forms of dimensional dominance, namely intrinsic and acquired, can be distinguished. *Acquired* dominance is instantiated when: (a) At least one dimension in the discriminanda is relevant and another is irrelevant to the reinforcement contingencies. (b) The relevant dimension exerts more weight on choice behavior than the irrelevant dimension or dimensions. For example, suppose the discriminanda differ in size and brightness but only the size cues are relevant, acquired dominance would be instantiated if the size cues were dominant. The levels theory assumes this form of dominance is controlled by the higher encoding level, to which continuity theory does *not* apply.

Intrinsic dominance is instantiated when: (a) The difference between the cues on one dimension is more intrinsically distinctive than the cues on the other dimension. (b) Both dimensions are relevant to the reinforcement contingencies. (c) The cues on the more distinctive dimension exert more weight on choice behavior than the cues on the less distinctive dimension. Thus intrinsic dominance is determined by the nature of the stimuli. The levels theory assumes this form of dominance, which is manifested in infrahuman animals as well as in humans, is a function of a lower level encoding process whose effects on learning can be explained by continuity theory.

This explanation begins by noting that the distinctiveness of the difference between any two values on a given dimension is an increasing function of their psychophysical difference. The difference between, say, black and white is more distinctive than the difference between two similar grays. The psychophysical difference, as the term implies, is a joint function of psychological and physical determinants. The physical determinant refers to differences measured on a physical dimension such as luminance, area, or wavelengths. The psychological determinant refers to the innate sensitivity of the organism to these differences, as measured on a psychological dimension such as brightness, size, or color. Such sensitivity is determined by the sensory receptive system and can vary widely between dimensions within a species, and between species within a dimension most likely as a result of evolutionary adaptations. Some species of bats who hunt at night are, for instance, exquisitely sensitive to small differences in sounds so high pitched they are beyond what humans can hear or even conceive. High pitched sounds are best for the sonar system these bats use to navigate in the dark (Dawkins, 1986). Humans have the capacity to discriminate miniscule differences in voice-onset time thereby enabling us to distinguish between voiced and voiceless consonants, like *b* and *p* (Eimas, Siqueland, Juszyk, & Vigorito, 1971). Such subtle auditory discriminations make spoken languages possible.

Let the term intrinsic dimensional *salience* refer to the psychophysical difference between the cues on a given dimension. Intrinsic salience is fixed by nature not nurture (Zeaman & Hanley, 1983). Say we are training infrahuman animals to choose between a pair of discriminanda compounded of size and form. And we have established that, although the difference between the cues on both dimensions are perceptible, the size difference is more intrinsically salient than the form difference. Intrinsic dominance would be manifested if the size cues exerted greater control than the form cues on the choice behavior of the animals. The question is why should this be? To explain intrinsic dimensional dominance by claiming that the more salient cues invoke more selective attention is merely a restatement of the fact. The ICD model was designed to determine whether, by invoking the principle of stimulus generalization, continuity theory could explain intrinsic dominance, without resorting to a vaguely defined selective-attention construct.

Stimulus generalization refers to the transfer of a learned response from one stimulus to other similar stimuli on the same dimension. The form usually taken by stimulus generalization is illustrated in a protypical experiment performed by Guttman and Kalish (1956). They conditioned five groups of pigeons to peck at a disk illuminated with a monochromatic light of a given wavelength (hue). Each group was trained on a different wavelength. The pretraining was followed by a generalization test that illuminated the key with other varying wavelengths. As illustrated in Fig. 7.1, the tendency for different stimuli on the same dimension to evoke the learned response fell along a gradient that decreased gradually as the similarity to the training stimulus decreased. Decreasing stimulus-generalization gradients have been replicated many times in other species using different stimulus dimensions. A decreasing stimulus generalization gradient is a clearly adaptive response to the variety found in nature. There may well be a neural basis for stimulus generalization. For example, the degree of behavioral stimulus generalization for tone frequency can be predicted accurately from the pattern of response of single nerve cells in the auditory cortex (Thompson, 1965).

While stimulus generalization is useful for transferring learned responses to similar stimuli, this mechanism could impede discrimination learning. Suppose an animal is learning to choose the larger of two objects. Every correct choice would directly increase the tendency to choose *large*. If the generalization gradient encompasses the incorrect, *smaller* size, then the

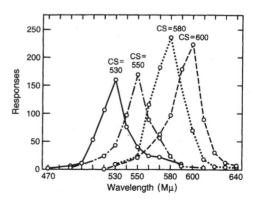

FIG. 7.1. Illustrative mean stimulus generalization gradients. From Guttman and Kalish (1956).

tendency to evoke the incorrect choice would, at the same time, be indirectly strengthened. How much the incorrect choice is strengthened would depend on the degree of generalization between the two sizes. A large degree of generalization could considerably strengthen the tendency to make the incorrect as well as the correct choice. Since each rewarded trial increases the tendency to respond to both the correct and incorrect stimulus, the greater the generalization, the more it will interfere with discrimination learning. In this way stimulus generalization can explain the fact that lower level discrimination learning can be expedited by increasing the physical difference between the correct and incorrect stimuli (Bush & Mosteller, 1951; Hull, 1943; Shepp & Zeaman, 1966; Spence, 1937, 1960).

Note that intrinsic dimensional salience—as measured by the physical difference between the cues on a common dimension—and stimulus generalization are inversely related. The more salient the dimensional difference, the less the stimulus generalization, and consequently the more rapid the learning. The inverse relationship between intrinsic salience and stimulus generalization provides for an adaptive balance. Natural selection can be expected to potentiate sensitivity along dimensions where fine distinctions are useful. In this case stimulus generalization is narrow and learning to respond differently to values on such dimensions is relatively easy. Where fine distinctions are less useful, sensitivity is attenuated, stimulus generalization is greater, and learning to make differential responses is relatively difficult. Rats, for instance, require hundreds of trials to learn to choose between an illuminated triangle and circle (T. Kendler, Basden, & Bruckner, 1970). Presumably, there is a great deal of generalization between these two forms because learning to respond to sharp distinctions between forms are of little or no use to this species. On the other hand, the same species learns to choose between two positions very rapidly, presumably because learning to make subtle, spatial distinctions are useful ecologically. If these rats were tested for dimensional dominance on form-position compounds, position would be so dominant it could completely mask any learning on form. This would be an example of intrinsic dimensional dominance.

The ICD model shows how incorporating stimulus generalization enables continuity theory to explain in detail a number of facts about discrimination learning, including the facts about intrinsic dimensional dominance, without invoking selective attention.

FORMAL PREMISES OF THE INTRINSIC CUE-DOMINANCE (ICD) MODEL

The ICD model assumes that lower level discrimination learning is a non-selective, incremental process that operates according to the following summarized premises.

1. Let E refer to the excitatory tendency to choose a given value on a particular dimension and let E_{max} refer to the maximum, direct strength E can attain. Each rewarded trial (n) directly increases the E of *each* cue in the rewarded discriminandum by an amount (Θ) proportional to the difference between E_{max} and E_n. Hence

$$E_{n+1} = E_n + \Theta(E_{max} - E_n) \tag{1}$$

Suppose a subject was learning to choose between *small triangle* (+) and *large circle* (−). As the number of rewarded trials increased, E_{small} and $E_{triangle}$ would each increase asymptotically as they each approached E_{max}.

Even the simplest form of discrimination learning is complex enough to be determined by several variables besides stimulus salience. Some of this complexity is encompassed in the model which takes account of any previous training or innate preferences by allowing the Es to vary at the outset of training. The effect of individual and species differences in learning capacity are encompassed by allowing the rate of increase (Θ) to vary accordingly. The effect of motivational variables, such as drive strength or magnitude of reward, could be expressed as variations in the asymptote (E_{max}).

2. Each rewarded response also produces an indirect, generalized increase in E for each cue in the *non*rewarded discriminandum (e.g., *small* and *circle*). Let the maximum generalized E be expressed as a proportion (A) of E_{max}. Hence

$$E_{n+1} = E_n + \Theta[(A \times E_{max}) - E_n] \tag{2}$$

where A is a value positively related to the psychophysical similarity between the correct and incorrect cues on a given dimension.

Thus, while each rewarded choice directly increases the E for each correct cue in the compound, it also gradually increases the E for each incorrect cue in proportion to the similarity between the two cues.

3. To take cognizance of inhibitory as well as excitatory transmission in the central nervous system, let I refer to the tendency to inhibit the approach to a given cue. Each nonrewarded trial (m) strengthens the I for each cue in the *in*correct discriminandum in the following manner:

$$I_{m+1} = I_m + \varphi(I_{max} - I_m) \tag{3}$$

where φ is different from Θ and I_{max} is different than E_{max} to allow the parameters associated with rewarded choices to be different than the parameters associated with nonrewarded choices.

Thus each nonrewarded trial gradually increases the I for each incorrect cue until its asymptote is reached. Hence learning can occur as a result of reward or nonreward or both.

4. Because generalization applies to inhibition, as well as to excitation, each nonrewarded choice produces an indirect, generalized increase in I for each cue in the *correct* stimulus compound. Hence

$$I_{m+1} = I_m + \varphi[(B \times I_{max}) - I_m] \tag{4}$$

where B is a value that varies between zero and one. B is allowed to differ from A in case the generalization gradient of inhibition and excitation should differ.

5. To relate E and I, let the effective excitatory tendency (E^*) for each cue equal the algebraic difference between the E accumulated on the correct trials and the I accumulated on the incorrect trials. For example

$$E^*_{triangle} = E_{triangle} - I_{triangle} \tag{5}$$

The E^* for a given cue may, therefore, be positive or negative depending on whether the associated E is greater or less than the associated I.

6. This premise stipulates how the E^*'s associated with each cue in a compound combine. Given a discriminandum composed of two or more separable (noninteractive) dimensions the E^*'s summate algebraically. For example

$$E^*_{small\ triangle} = E^*_{small} + E^*_{triangle} \tag{6}$$

To keep matters as simple as possible, this combination rule is limited to compounds made up of noninteractive stimulus dimensions, such as color, position, form, and size. A more comprehensive theory would require an interaction term to encompass interactive dimensions, such as height and width. At this stage of theorizing it seems sensible to limit theoretical complexity by using discriminanda that minimize interaction effects.

7. Which discriminandum will be preferred on any given trial is a function of the algebraic difference (d) between the summed E^*'s. For example

$$d_{st-lc} = E^*_{small\ triangle} - E^*_{large\ circle} \tag{7}$$

where d_{st-lc} refers to the difference between the respective E's for *small triangle* and *large circle*. Note that d may take either a positive or negative value. If $E^*_{small\ triangle}$ is greater than $E^*_{large\ circle}$, then *small triangle* will be preferred. How strong that preference will be depends on the magnitude of d.

8. The final premise relates the probability (p), of choosing one discriminandum over another, to d in the form

$$p = 1/(1 + e^{-cd}) \tag{8}$$

where e, the base of natural logarithms represents the constant 2.7187... and c is a numerical parameter. The relevant properties of this expression are that $p = .50$ when $d = 0$ and the lower asymptote of p approaches zero, while its upper asymptote approaches one.

SIMULATED APPLICATIONS OF THE ICD MODEL

The simulations illustrate how the model explains some basic facts about discrimination learning, including the facts about intrinsic dimensional dominance. To produce the simulations a set of computer programs enabled a computer to learn a variety of simultaneous, visual, discrimination-learning problems in accordance with the premises of the model. The discriminanda, represented in the program by numbers, were always presented in pairs that differed on one or more visual dimensions and on position. Position (left or right) was, however, always represented as irrelevant to the reinforcement contingencies. The output of the program was the successive, trial-by-trial change in the hypothetical constructs E^*, d, and p. Plotting these changes illustrates graphically how the model describes the learning process and what it predicts about observable behavior under specified experimental conditions.

In all of the simulations both learning rate parameters (Θ and ϕ), were set at .10, both motivational parameters (E_{max} and I_{max}) were set at 100 and the c parameter was set at .020. These settings were chosen simply to provide clear illustrations. To simplify matters further the stimulus generalization parameters associated with reward (A) and nonreward (B) were also assumed to be equivalent.

Unless otherwise designated, each simulation began with setting all E^*'s to zero, and was followed by a consecutive series of discrimination-learning trials in the same order used in the optional shift research. On each trial the computer made a choice in accordance with the premises of the model. After each trial the program first computed the effect of the choice on E, I, and E^*. Next, depending on which discriminanda would be represented on the following trial, the program first computed d for each represented dimension, then the combined d for the two compounded discriminanda, which it finally used to compute p. The p, with the aid of a random number generator, settled the next choice. The criterion of learning was set at 10 successive trials in which p reached or exceeded .80.

INTRINSIC DIMENSIONAL SALIENCE EQUATED

One Relevant Dimension

The first set of simulations applied the model to the simplest condition. As illustrated in Fig. 7.2, the discriminanda were represented as differing on only one relevant visual dimension, say *form*. Position was irrelevant, as always. The intrinsic salience of the difference between the values on the form and position dimensions were equated ($A = B = .25$). Two phases were programmed: a pretraining phase, where the *circle* choices were rewarded,

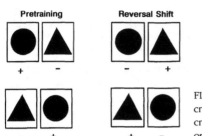

FIG. 7.2. Illustrative paired discriminanda in a simultaneous discrimination learning problem with one relevant visual dimension.

followed immediately by a reversal shift, where the *triangle* choices were rewarded.

Figures 7.3 a, b, and c, which follow in sequence, respectively present the simulated, trial-by-trial changes in the hypothetical constructs E^*, d, and p, as training proceeded, first during the pretraining and then during the reversal shift.

Effective Excitatory Tendency (E*)

E^* measures the tendency to approach *each* discriminable cue in the compound. Figure 7.3a illustrates the simulated changes in E^* as a function of the number of training trials during each training phase. At the outset of the pretraining phase each E^* was set to zero. Because *circle* choices were always rewarded E^*_{circle} soon took on a *positive* value that increased gradually

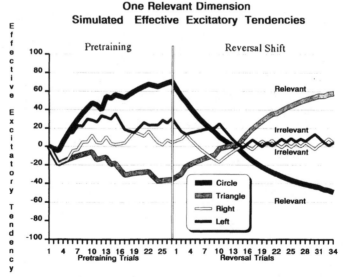

FIG. 7.3a. Simulated trial-by-trial changes in the effective excitatory tendency (E^*) associated with each cue during the pretraining and reversal shift phases, when form was relevant, position was *ir*relevant, and the two dimensions were equally salient.

as the trials accumulated. The increase was somewhat irregular due to the generalized inhibition produced by the occasional incorrect choices.

Because *triangle* choices were never rewarded $E^*_{triangle}$ soon took on a *negative* value and became increasingly negative as the trials mounted. The increasing negativity was also irregular due to the generalized excitation produced by the correct choices. These changes illustrate how the simulated tendency to approach the correct cue and avoid the incorrect cue increased over the course of the pretraining phase.

Figure 7.3a also shows that the E^*'s for the form cues were not the only E^*'s affected by the training because the discriminanda also differed in position (*left* or *right*) from trial to trial. Position, however, was *ir*relevant and *ir*relevant cues are, by definition, rewarded on roughly half of the trials and nonrewarded on the other half. Consequently E^*_{left} increased whenever *circle*(+) happened to be on the left and the computer happened to make a correct choice. As a corollary, E^*_{left} also decreased whenever *triangle* happened to be on the left and the computer happened to make an incorrect choice. The same, of course, held for E^*_{right}. Consequently, E^*_{right} and E^*_{left} fluctuated noisily from trial to trial, each in its own way.

Criterion was attained on the preshift phase by trial 27, which ended the pretraining and initiated the reversal phase. During the reversal phase *triangle* became correct and *circle* incorrect while *position* continued to be *ir*relevant. Due to the reversed reinforcement contingencies, E^*_{circle} began to decrease and gradually became negative and $E^*_{triangle}$ increased and gradually became positive. Meanwhile E^*_{left} and E^*_{right} continued to fluctuate around zero. Criterion was attained on the reversal shift phase by trial 34.

Differential Excitatory Tendency (d)

While E^* represents the hypothetical tendency to approach or avoid each cue in the discriminanda, which value on each dimension tends to be preferred is represented by d, the differences between the associated E^*s. Which compounded discriminandum tends to be preferred is determined by the combined difference (d) between the respective E^*'s on each dimension. Consequently, learning to make the correct choice is more directly represented by the trial-by-trial changes in d than in E^*.

Pretraining Phase. The changes in d were computed for each dimension separately and for the compound-as-a-whole by subtracting the E^* for the given incorrect value from the E^* for the given correct value. Thus, during the pretraining phase d_{form} was computed by subtracting $E^*_{triangle}$ from E^*_{circle} on every trial. Computing $d_{position}$ was more complicated because the correct position varied from trial to trial. This computation subtracted the E^* for the position that would be correct on the next trial from the E^* that would be incorrect. Lastly, $d_{compound}$ was computed by summing the d's for the component dimensions.

Figure 7.3b presents the simulated changes in d for each dimension separately and for the compound as a whole. During the pretraining each trial increased d_{form} regardless of whether the choice was correct or incorrect. Hence d_{form} increased gradually with little fluctuation. This relatively smooth increase represents a hypothetical learning curve that abstracts the increasing tendency to prefer the correct value on the relevant dimension from the noise produced by the presence of the *irrelevant* position dimension.

The lighter thin line in the same figure shows that during pretraining the d's for the *irrelevant, position* dimension fluctuated around zero because the *irrelevant* cues were reinforced on roughly half of the trials and nonreinforced on the other half. Whenever $d_{position}$ was positive, the preference for the correct discriminandum increased slightly and whenever it was negative the preference for the correct choice decreased slightly.

The tendency to prefer the correct over the incorrect discriminandum on a given trial depends on the algebraic sum of the d's associated with each dimension in the compound. In this simulation $d_{compound}$ was computed by summing d_{form} and $d_{position}$. Hence $d_{compound}$, represented in Fig. 7.3b by the jagged thick curve, reveals an overall increase in the tendency to prefer the correct compound accompanied by a great deal of intertrial variability. The variability was mostly due to the intermittent reinforcement associated with the cues on the *irrelevant* dimension.

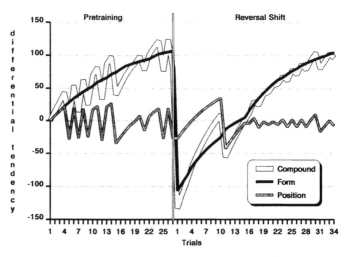

FIG. 7.3b. Simulated changes in the differential tendency (d) in favor of the correct value on each represented dimension, and on the compounds they form.

This simulation shows how the empirical learning curve can be parsed into two constituents. One constituent is the increasing preference for the correct value on the relevant dimension which increases relatively steadily during the course of training. The other constituent is the intertrial variability, or noise, due to the relationship of the *ir*relevant cues to reward and nonreward.

Reversal Training Phase. In the reversal phase the reinforcement contingencies were reversed. The d_{form} became negative at the outset of this phase because of the preference for *circle* over *triangle* established in the pretraining phase. This preference, however, gradually decreased with each training trial until its direction was reversed. Meanwhile, $d_{position}$ continued to fluctuate around zero because *position* continued to be *ir*relevant. Presently d_{form}, and hence $d_{compound}$, increased enough to produce the criterion run.

Probability of a Correct Choice (p)

The d construct represents *learning*, defined as the strength of the disposition to favor one cue or one compound over another. This disposition could be manifested in measurable behavior in a number of ways, such as the response latency, the resistance to extinction, or the probability of making a correct choice. The last premise in the model relates this disposition to *performance* by assuming that the probability of a correct choice ($p_{correct}$) on any given trial is a logistic function of $d_{compound}$. Using a random number generator in conjunction with this assumption made it possible to simulate how $p_{correct}$ changed during the pretraining and reversal shift phases (Fig. 7.3c).

FIG. 7.3c. Simulated changes in the probability of a correct choice (*p*) in the same condition.

Learners in live experiments are usually trained to some arbitrary criterion, say 9 or 10 successive, correct choices. The criterion is designed to be stringent enough to safely assume the probability of a correct choice is well above chance. But, because the simulations allowed for computing the probability directly, criterion was designated as 10 successive trials in which $p_{correct}$ reached or exceeded .80. Figure 7.3c shows that, in the pretraining phase, $p_{correct}$ increased gradually, but very noisily. In the reversal phase $p_{correct}$ dropped sharply almost to zero and consequently required more trials to complete the criterion run than in the pretraining phase, which began with $p_{correct}$ equal to .50.

Explained Facts

This simulation demonstrates how the model explains two rudimentary facts about lower level discrimination learning. One fact is that animals and young children can learn to approach the correct value and avoid the incorrect value on the relevant dimension. The other is that learning to reverse these tendencies is possible but usually requires more trials than the pretraining.

In the more general sense, this simulation also illustrates how the model explains two truisms, namely that behavior is variable but practice makes (almost) perfect. In a more specific sense, the simulation illustrates how the model explains two established but ostensibly contradictory facts about discrimination learning. One fact is that lower level learning curves, averaged over a group of learners, usually show a smooth increase in the probability of a correct choice as training trials accumulate. The other fact is that *individual*, trial-by-trial, learning curves are usually very irregular.

Averaging over trials smooths out the learning curve because the irregularity is partly attributable to the intertrial variability produced by the *ir*relevant dimensions and partly to the variability inherent in p. Both sources of variability should be distributed randomly over individuals—or, within individuals, over trials—and should consequently cancel out when averaged either way.

In sum, this simulation shows how the model explains both discrimination and reversal shift learning, as well as the characteristic irregularity in individual performance and the smoothness of averaged performance.

Multiple Relevant Dimensions

The first simulation in this next set applied the model to discriminanda with two relevant dimensions by training the computer to choose between a *small-triangle* (−) and a *large-circle* (+). Both visual dimensions, *size* and *form*, were relevant while *position* remained *ir*relevant. The salience of all represented dimensions was again equated at $A = B = .25$ and there was no reversal shift. To simplify matters, from now on only the simulated learning, represented by changes in d, and in performance, represented by the changes p, are presented.

Simulated Learning Process

Figure 7.4 plots the simulated changes in d for each dimension separately and for the compound as a whole. During training, d_{form} and d_{size} increased in an identical manner because *size* and *form* were both redundant and equally salient. Meanwhile, $d_{position}$ fluctuated around zero, sometimes potentiating and sometimes attenuating the preference for the correct discriminandum.

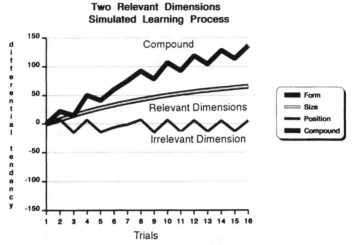

FIG. 7.4. Simulated changes in d when there were two relevant visual dimensions, position remained irrelevant, and all represented dimensions were equally salient.

When discriminanda are multidimensional, the d's for the represented dimensions summate algebraically. Hence $d_{compound}$ increased more noisily but more rapidly and attained a higher asymptote than either d_{form} or d_{size} taken separately. The noise was the contribution of the *ir*relevant dimension.

Simulated Performance

Figure 7.5 presents the simulated effect of increasing the number of relevant dimensions by comparing $p_{correct}$, when the computer was trained with only one dimension relevant—as in the first simulation—with the present simulation, where there were two relevant dimensions. The number of *ir*relevant dimensions in both conditions was held constant at one. Criterion was attained in fewer trials when the number of relevant dimensions was increased from one to two.

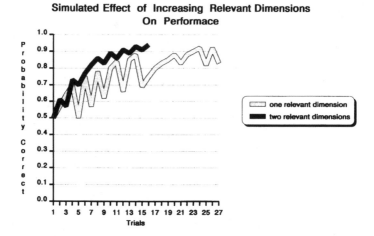

FIG. 7.5. Simulated effect of increasing the number of relevant dimensions from 1 to 2 on the probability of a correct choice.

Explained Facts

One fact explained by this simulation is that the efficiency of lower level discrimination learning increases as the number of relevant dimensions increases (Eninger, 1952; Hara & Warren, 1961; Warren, 1953). This phenomenon is referred to as dimensional additivity. Another testable implication of the model is that adding relevant dimensions should also increase the ultimate attainable level of performance.

What would be the simulated effect of further increasing the number of relevant dimension? The answer required a brief departure from the format to simulate the effect on number of trials to learn when the number of relevant dimensions was varied from one to ten. All the other parameters remained unchanged and the number of *irrelevant* dimensions was held constant at one. The result was the orderly decrease in trials to criterion, as a function of the number of relevant dimensions, presented in Fig. 7.6.

This simulation demonstrates that an associative, incremental learning theory can predict very rapid, even one-trial learning, if the number of relevant dimensions sufficiently outweighs the number of irrelevant dimensions. This capacity is significant theoretically because it demonstrates that the occurrence of one-trial learning among infrahuman animals, under certain conditions, is not necessarily antithetical to incremental associative learning. After all, it is reasonable to suppose that in nature the important discriminations entail many relevant dimensions. The fact explained here is that increasing the number of relevant dimensions produces faster learning but, as also shown in Fig. 7.6, the facilitative effect decreases gradually with each increase (Bourne & Restle, 1959).

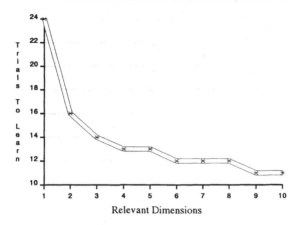

FIG. 7.6. Simulated effect of additional increases in the number of relevant dimensions on learning efficiency.

Multiple Irrelevant Dimensions

The next set of simulations tested the effect of increasing the number of *ir*relevant dimensions from one to two by training the computer to choose between discriminanda that differed in both *size* and *form*, but this time only the *form* cues were relevant, leaving both *size* and *position ir*relevant.

Simulated Learning Process

Figure 7.7 plots the changes in d for each cue and for the compound as-a-whole separately. Under these conditions d_{form} increased steadily while both d_{size} and $d_{position}$ fluctuated noisily around zero. The $d_{compound}$ also increased as training proceeded while fluctuating very widely around d_{form}.

The wide fluctuations in $d_{compound}$ were mostly attributable to the combined fluctuations of the *ir*relevant size and position cues. Because the d's combine algebraically, the fluctuations of the *ir*relevant cues attenuated each other every time one was negative and the other positive. On these trials the noise was relatively low. But, on the other trials, when one *ir*relevant cue was positive and the other negative, the noise was potentiated. Consequently the effect of adding an *ir*relevant dimension was to increase the intertrial variability.

Simulated Performance

Figure 7.8 compares the simulated effect of increasing the number of *ir*relevant dimensions by comparing the learning curves when the computer was trained with one versus two irrelevant dimensions. Increasing the number of *ir*relevant dimensions increased the trials required to attain criterion

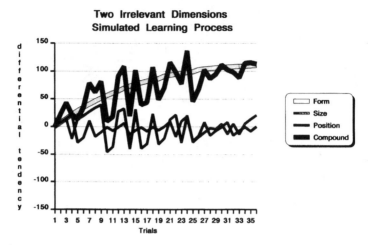

FIG. 7.7. Simulated changes in *d* when there is one relevant visual (form) dimension, two *ir*relevant (size and color) dimensions, and all represented dimensions are equally salient.

but did not alter the asymptote of $p_{correct}$. The decrease in learning efficiency produced by adding an irrelevant dimension was due to the increased noise.

Explained Fact

Bourne and Restle (1959) demonstrated that adding *ir*relevant cues interferes with learning in a range of conditions. Another testable implication is that adding irrelevant cues should not, however, decrease the ultimate level of performance.

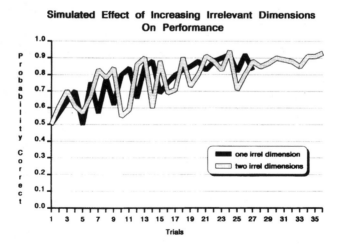

FIG. 7.8. Comparing the simulated probability of a correct choice with one versus two *ir*relevant dimensions.

Intrinsic Dimensional Salience

Continuity theory assumes intrinsic salience affects discrimination learning by inversely affecting the degree of generalization between the two values on each represented dimension. A large difference between the two values would be *more* perceptually salient and would produce *less* stimulus generalization than a small difference. Salience is represented in the ICD model by the A and B parameters. These parameters modulate the maximum attainable differential tendency (d_{max}) which, in turn, determines the rate at which p increases over the course of training and the asymptote it attains.

In this simulation the computer was trained under two conditions on the simple problem in which the two discriminanda again differed on only one relevant (form) and one (size) irrelevant dimension. In one condition the relevant, form dimension was assigned a high degree ($A = .10$) and in the other a low degree of intrinsic salience ($A = .80$). In both conditions the irrelevant, position dimension was assigned an intermediate degree of intrinsic salience ($A = .25$).

Simulated Performance. Figure 7.9 presents the simulated effect of varying the salience of the relevant dimension on performance as measured by the probability of a correct choice. Because the salience differential was very large, the effect was marked. The high salience condition produced much faster learning. Moreover, the ultimate level of performance attained was also higher.

Explained Facts. That increasing the intrinsic salience of the relevant dimension facilitates discrimination learning in infrahuman animals is a repeatedly confirmed fact. This fact has also been shown to apply to children (Smiley, 1973; Smiley & Weir, 1966).

INTRINSIC DIMENSIONAL DOMINANCE

Most of the foregoing simulations concerned well-established, fundamental facts about lower level learning which can be explained by other models (e.g., Bourne & Restle, 1959; Bush & Mosteller, 1951; Spiker, 1970; Zeaman & House, 1963). The real challenge posed by the ICD model is to explain lower level learning in a way that disentangles the intrinsic and acquired versions of dimensional dominance. Dimensional dominance is instantiated when the compounded discriminanda are composed of two or more relevant dimensions and one dimension exerts more control over choice behavior than the other. Take, for example, a pair of discriminanda where size and form are both relevant and redundant (Fig. 7.10). If the form dimension exerts the greater weight, then the dimensional dominance of *form* over *size* would be instantiated. Dimensional dominance can take two forms: intrinsic and acquired. If

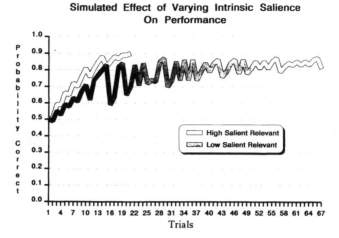

FIG. 7.9. Simulated trial-by-trial changes in *p* produced by varying the intrinsic salience of the relevant dimension.

the dominance is attributable to relevance then acquired dominance is instantiated. If the dominance is attributable to differential intrinsic salience— as measured by the relative magnitude of the psychophysical difference between the cues on the represented dimensions—then intrinsic dominance is instantiated. The ICD model applies only to intrinsic dominance.

Opposed-Cues Procedure

Investigating dimensional dominance, however, presents problems because the weights exerted by the various dimensions represented in the discriminanda are not directly observable and therefore cannot be measured directly. For instance, when an organism is learning to choose between, *large circle* to *small triangle* all we can observe is which compound is chosen. There is no way to directly determine whether the choice is based on *form*, on *size*, or on both. More precisely, if the discriminanda are com-

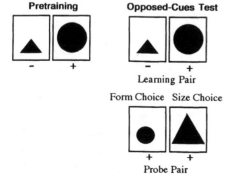

FIG. 7.10. Examples of discriminanda in an opposed-cues test for measuring intrinsic dimensional dominance.

posed of two or more relevant and redundant dimensions there is no way to directly measure the relative weight exerted by each dimension. The usual way to get around this difficulty is to use discriminative transfer tests to provide indirect measures of dimensional dominance. Discriminative transfer tests assess how training on a prior discrimination-learning problem affects performance on another subsequent problem. Historically, transfer tests have been used to infer something of practical or theoretical consequence about learning that cannot be assessed directly. An articulated model of learning provides the rationale for such transfer tests and delineates the controls required to justify the inference.

A widely used transfer test, known as the opposed-cues procedure, consists of a pretraining and a test phase. The pretraining phase presents a problem in which there are at least two relevant and redundant dimensions. The test phase, introduced after criterion is reached on the pretraining phase, is designed to determine which dimension dominated the pretraining and by how much.

Figure 7.10 illustrates the two phases of the opposed-cues procedure used in this simulation. During the pretraining phase only one pair of discriminanda—*large triangle* (+) and *small circle* (–)—was presented and *position* was switched from trial to trial. Consequently *size* and *form* were both relevant and redundant; only *position* was irrelevant. This pair of stimuli is designated as the *learning pair* and the trials on which they were presented are designated as the *learning trials*.

Following attainment of criterion on the pretraining phase, the test phase was introduced during which 10 opposed-cues probe-trials were interspersed between approximately 10 learning trials. On the learning trials only the *learning pair* was presented and only responses to the *large circle* continued to be rewarded. On the interspersed probe trials the *probe pair—small circle* (+) and *large triangle* (+)—was presented and either choice was rewarded. The probe pair opposed the cues in that they required a choice between the previously correct, *large* size and the previously correct, *circular* form. This pair of discriminanda is referred to as the probe pair because they probe which dimension will dominate choice behavior. In this case a majority of *large*-triangle choices on the probe trials would connote the dominance of the size cues, while a majority of small-*circle* choices would connote the dominance of the form cues.

Simulating the Opposed-Cues Procedure

Equated Intrinsic Salience

To illustrate how the model explains intrinsic dominance we begin with the simplest case, where there are two relevant visual dimensions, for example, *form* and *size*. According to the ICD model the intrinsic salience of each dimension is represented by d. The relative salience of the two relevant dimensions is represented in the model by the difference between the ds associated with each dimension. As the simulations in this set illustrate, dimensional dominance, in turn, is determined by the difference between the ds associated with each dimension. The direction of the dominance is determined by which dimension has the greater d; the degree of the dominance is determined by size of the differential.

The first simulation in this set applied the model to illustrate how the opposed-cues procedure measures dimensional dominance. For this purpose the A and B parameters for each represented dimension were set equal at .25. If the model is valid no intrinsic dominance should be manifested.

Simulated Learning Process. Figure 7.11a presents the simulated changes in d for each dimension during the pretraining and test phases of the procedure. The relative weight exerted by the two relevant dimensions is measured by the relative contribution of d_{form} and d_{size} to $d_{compound}$. Because d_{form} and d_{size} started pretraining from the same initial value and were equally salient, the weight contributed by the two dimensions to $d_{compound}$ was equal throughout this phase.

If d could be measured directly in live subjects there·would be no need for a test phase. Until there is a more direct measure available, we depend on the test phase to provide an indirect measure of the relative weight exerted by the two relevant dimensions on learning. The trouble with the

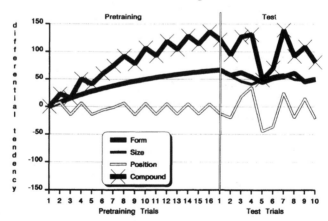

FIG. 7.11a. Simulated changes in d in an opposed-cues test for intrinsic dominance, when the two relevant dimensions were equally salient. The weight contributed by the two dimensions was equal in the pretraining phase and remained close to equal in the test phase.

indirect measure lies in the potential confounding produced by the obligatory introduction of the probe pair, where each choice must either be rewarded or nonrewarded. Therefore, each probe trial must inevitably have some effect on the subsequent trials. We chose to reward either choice on the probe trials in our live experiments. This confound could be avoided by using only the first probe trial, but any single probe trial is too subject to chance factors. We chose to use 10 probe trials in our research and to alternate the probe trials with learning trials to help reduce the confounding.

The potential confounding is illustrated in the simulated changes in d on each of the 10 probe trials during the test phase, as plotted on the right side of Fig. 7.11a. One effect of the probe trials was to markedly increase the noise associated with the *ir*relevant dimension which, in turn, markedly increased the intertrial variability for the compound as a whole. How much did the confounding affect the measure of relative weight exerted by the size and form cues? If there were no confounding the course of d_{form} and d_{size} should have remained identical. In this simulation the two d's did not behave in exactly the same way on the test trials; nevertheless the similarity remained considerable. The computed mean for the 10 probe trials was similar enough—55.0 for d_{form} and 53.4 for d_{size}—to indicate that the confounding, in this case, was minimal.

Simulated Performance. Figure 7.11b plots the simulated changes in performance on the learning and on the probe pairs separately. The simulated probability of a correct choice on the learning pair ($p_{correct}$) indicates

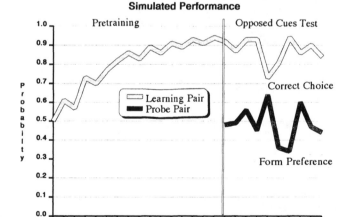

FIG. 7.11b. Simulated performance on the opposed-cues test when the two relevant dimensions were equally salient. Equal dominance was manifested by the tendency for form preference to hover around chance.

how performance was affected during each phase of the procedure. The $p_{correct}$ gradually attained a high, stable level by the end of the pretraining phase but became considerably more variable during the test phase due to the introduction of the probe trials. Nevertheless, the mean $p_{correct}$ averaged over the 10 interspersed learning pair trials (.88) remained high.

Consider now the behavior on the interspersed probe trials. When the two dimensions are equally salient the weight exerted by the size and form dimension should be equal. Therefore neither dimension should be preferred consistently. As expected, the simulated probability of preferring *form* over *size* (p_{form}) fluctuated noisily around chance. The mean p_{form} for the 10 probe trials was .48 showing that scarcely any preference for either dimension emerged when the intrinsic salience was equated.

When intrinsic salience is equated the model would predict that no significant intrinsic dominance should be manifested. There is no explained fact cited here because there is, to my knowledge, no pertinent experiment, probably because of the technical difficulty involved in equating dimensional salience.

Disparate Intrinsic Salience

To simulate the effect of disparate intrinsic salience, a high degree of salience ($A = B = .05$) was assigned to the form cues and a much lower degree ($A = B = .50$) was assigned to the size cues. The position cues were assigned an intermediate value ($A = B = .25$). All other determining variables were held constant.

Simulated Learning Process. Figure 7.12a shows that d_{form} increased more rapidly and approached a higher asymptote than d_{size} in the pretraining phase. This differential in favor of d_{form} began early and gradually increased until criterion was attained. The differential explains why the more salient dimension contributes more to learning than the less salient dimension.

In the test phase, introducing the probe trials again increased the intertrial variability for both the relevant and the irrelevant dimensions. But the differential in favor of d_{form} was maintained, despite the increase in intertrial variability.

Simulated Performance. Figure 7.12b presents the simulated performance on both phases of the procedure. Consider first the performance on the learning pair. In the pretraining phase, where only the learning pair was presented, $p_{correct}$ reached a high, fairly stable level. In the test phase $p_{correct}$ became more variable; nevertheless the mean averaged over the 10 interspersed learning pair trials was .87.

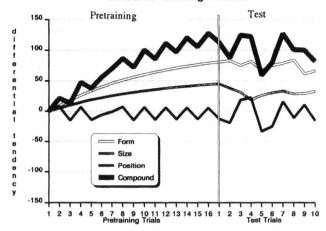

FIG. 7.12a. Simulated changes in *d* in an opposed-cues test for intrinsic dominance, where the form dimension was represented as more salient than the size dimension. The form dimension weighed in more heavily than the size dimension in both the pretraining and test phases.

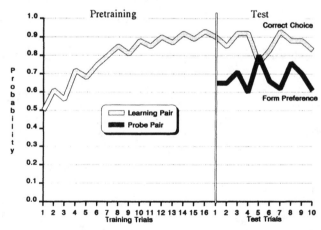

FIG. 7.12b. Simulated performance on the opposed-cues test when the two relevant dimensions were differentially salient. The more salient dimension dominated choice behavior during both the learning and test phases.

117

Consider now the behavior on the interspersed probe trials. Because the form dimension was considerably more intrinsically salient than the size dimension, p_{form} was above chance on each of the 10 probe trials. The mean p_{form} averaged over the 10 probe trials was .68.

Explained Facts. This simulation shows how the model explains the empirical fact that, when rats (T. Kendler, Basden, & Bruckner, 1970) and pigeons (Miles & Jenkins, 1973) are trained on the opposed-cues procedure, the more salient dimension dominates their choice behavior. Another fact the model explains is that increasing the physical difference between the cues on a given dimension increases their intrinsic dominance in infrahuman animals (Basden & Kendler, 1976; Miles & Jenkins, 1973) and in young children (Smiley, 1972). In addition to establishing the existence of intrinsic dimensional dominance these experiments demonstrated that intrinsic dimensional salience is not a property of the dimension *per se* but inheres rather in the difference between the given values on that dimension. As we shall see presently this is one of the signal differences between intrinsic and acquired dimensional dominance.

CONCLUSIONS

A model that assumes encoding is nonselective and learning is associative can explain the basic facts about lower level discrimination learning, including the facts about intrinsic dimensional dominance, without invoking selective attention. The manifestation of intrinsic dimensional dominance in discrimination learning is explained by invoking the mechanism of stimulus generalization. Stimulus generalization refers to the tendency for responses associated with a given value on a dimension to generalize to other values on the same dimension. The degree of generalization is typically inversely related to the psychophysical difference between the two stimuli. Thus the greater the psychophysical difference between the values on the dimension, the more salient is the perceived difference and the smaller is the degree of generalization. In this formulation the weight exerted by the dimension is not determined by its perceived vividness *per se*, it is determined by the degree of stimulus generalization between the respective values. In other words, intrinsic dimensional salience and intrinsic dimensional dominance are both determined by the psychophysical difference between the values on the given dimension.

The ICD model demonstrates how lower level discrimination learning, including the effects of intrinsic dimensional salience, can be explained by continuity theory without invoking selective attention.

CHAPTER EIGHT

Acquired and Intrinsic Dominance

To understand the problem of mind it is essential that we first separate lower from higher behavior and not make the mistake of seeing mental processes everywhere.

—Hebb (1972)

Continuity theory can explain a number of the facts about lower level discrimination-learning without invoking selective attention. This claim denies neither the existence nor the importance of the capacity to render the relevant aspects of the incoming information more important than the *ir*relevant. As William James (1892) observed:

> One of the most extraordinary facts of our life is that, although we are besieged at every moment by impressions from our whole sensory surface, we notice so very small a part of them. The sum total of our impressions never enters into our experience, consciously so called, which runs through this sum total like a tiny rill through a broad flowery mead, Yet the physical impressions which do not count are there as much as those which do, and affect our sense organs just as energetically. Why they fail to pierce the mind is a mystery, which is only named and not explained when we invoke *die Enge des Bewusstseins*, 'the narrowness of consciousness' as its ground. (p. 192)

But, while selective attention is a core concept for contemporary cognitive psychology, how it works remains elusive; named but not explained. Perhaps some of this mystery could be dispelled if we understood how selection operates in simple discrimination-learning. Selective attention in discrimination-learning is measured by first training learners to choose between binary

119

compounds arranged so that one dimension is relevant and the other is *ir*relevant to the reinforcement contingencies. When criterion is reached a transfer-of-training test is administered to determine which dimension dominates choice behavior. Dimensional dominance is instantiated if the relevant dimension is dominant (e.g., Sutherland & Mackintosh, 1971; Zeaman & House, 1963). Two forms of dimensional dominance can be distinguished. *Intrinsic* dominance is produced by intrinsic salience. *Acquired* dominance is produced by relevance. Acquired dominance is a manifestation of selective encoding.

Measuring Acquired Dominance

Intrinsic dominance can be measured by a simple opposed-cues procedure. Acquired dominance can be measured by a more complex version of the opposed-cues procedure known as the optional shift. This procedure also begins with requiring the learner to choose between discriminanda composed of two visual dimensions but one dimension is relevant and the other is *ir*relevant to the reinforcement contingencies. The training is followed by a subsequent phase that puts the two dimensions into opposition in order to determine which one dominates choice behavior. If the relevant dimension dominates, and intrinsic salience is controlled, then acquired dominance is instantiated.

The procedure is referred to as the optional shift, because it gives the learner the option of learning with or without selective encoding. The simplicity of the task provides the means for investigating both the phylogenetic and ontogenetic development of selective encoding since it can be used for infrahuman animals as well as humans over a wide range of ages. Another advantage is that it provides a measure of individual as well as group performance. (A note for the cognoscente: The optional shift also controls for the confounding effects of intermittent reinforcement during the transfer phase.)

The optional shift procedure, described in detail in chapter 2, is briefly reviewed here to refresh the reader's memory. As illustrated in Fig. 8.1, there are three phases: a preshift, a shift, and an opposed-cues test. Our example again uses discriminanda compounded of size and form.

The preshift phase alternates two pair of discriminanda. Each pair differs simultaneously on two visual dimensions, but the reinforcement contingencies are arranged so that only one of these dimensions is relevant to the reinforcement contingencies. The paired discriminanda are presented in a random-type alternation until criterion is attained. In the example, *triangle* is correct and *circle* is incorrect, regardless of their size. Hence, training on the preshift phase establishes that *form* is relevant and *size* is *ir*relevant. Position, as always, continues to be *ir*relevant. A learner who encodes selectively can be said to have learned to attend to the forms and ignore the

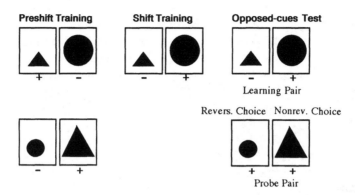

FIG. 8.1. Illustrating the three phases of the optional shift procedure when the discriminanda differ in size and form.

sizes of the discriminanda. The same idea is expressed more precisely by saying acquired dominance is manifested if the cues on the relevant dimension have acquired more weight than the cues on the irrelevant dimension.

When criterion is attained on the preshift, the shift phase is introduced without any warning. On this phase only one pair of discriminanda, the learning pair, is presented and the reinforcement contingencies are reversed. In the example the reinforcement shifts from *small-triangle* in the preshift phase to *large-circle* in the shift phase. Because only one pair of discriminanda is presented in the shift phase, both visual dimensions become relevant and redundant. The question is whether the value (*circle*)—on the initially relevant (*form*) dimension—will exert greater weight on learning in the shift phase than the value (*large*)—on the previously *ir*relevant (*size*) dimension.

When criterion is attained on the shift phase, the opposed-cues test phase is introduced without any warning. During this phase *both* pair of discriminanda are again alternated in the same random-type order as in the preshift phase. There is no further change in reinforcement contingencies on the learning pair. The other pair now becomes the probe pair, so named because how the learner responds to this pair indicates whether the relevant dimension has acquired more weight than the *ir*relevant dimension. The learning and probe pairs are presented in random-type alternation for as many trials as it takes to obtain ten responses to the probe pair. There is no further change in the reinforcement contingencies on the learning pair. On the probe pair any choice is rewarded. Acquired dimensional dominance is instantiated if the initially *in*correct cue on the initially relevant dimension dominates the learner's choice in the probe trials.

The problem presented by the optional shift procedure can be solved with or without selective encoding. Consequently, how learners respond can be approached from two perspectives. From the perspective of the model, the procedure provides another test of validity. From the perspective of the levels theory, the procedure provides both an operational definition and a tool for diagnosing acquired dimensional dominance. The discussion that follows considers the matter from both perspectives, beginning with the perspective of the ICD model of lower level discrimination-learning.

**SIMULATED APPLICATIONS OF THE ICD MODEL
TO THE OPTIONAL SHIFT PROCEDURE**

Equated Intrinsic Salience

All of the following simulations, like those in chapter 7, made the simplifying assumption that A and B are equal. The first set of simulations presents the hypothetical case where intrinsic salience is equated by setting both A and B for each of the three represented dimensions equal at .25. The remaining parameters for this simulation and those that follow were set at the same values as in the simulations presented in chapter 7 (p. 101).

The emphasis in these simulations is on the relative weight exerted by the relevant and irrelevant visual dimensions. According to the model, this relative weight is measured by the relative magnitude of the associated ds. To make the required comparisons, let d_{rel} represent the preference for the correct value on the *initially* relevant dimension, and let d_{irrel} represent the preference for correct value on the *initially* irrelevant dimension. For instance in the illustrative procedure (Fig. 8.1) d_{rel} would refer to the tendency to prefer the correct value on the form dimension, and d_{irrel} would refer to the tendency to prefer the correct value on the size dimension in each phase of the procedure.

Simulated Learning Process

Figure 8.2a simulates the trial-by-trial changes in the differential tendency (d) associated with each dimension in each phase of the procedure.

Preshift Phase. In the preshift phase (first panel of Fig. 8.2a), the d for the relevant dimension (d_{rel}) increased monotonically until criterion was attained. The d for the *irrelevant* visual dimension (d_{irrel}) represents the tendency to prefer whichever value on the *size* happened to be rewarded on the given trial. Consequently, d_{irrel} fluctuated noisily around zero. Since position was also irrelevant $d_{position}$ also fluctuated noisily around zero in its own way. Criterion was attained when d_{rel} exceeded the combined ds for the irrelevant position and size dimensions enough to produce the criterion run.

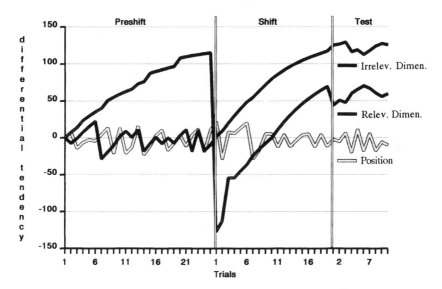

FIG. 8.2a. Tracing the simulated changes in the differential tendency associated with each dimension during the three phases of the optional shift procedure when all represented dimensions were equally salient.

This simulation shows that almost from the outset of training on the preshift phase, the relevant dimension exerted more weight on choice behavior than either of the irrelevant dimensions and this differential increased steadily throughout the preshift phase.

Shift Phase. During the shift phase (center panel of Fig. 8.2a) only one pair of discriminanda was presented. Both visual dimensions became relevant and redundant and the reinforcement contingencies were reversed. Only position remained irrelevant. In this phase d_{rel} represents the tendency to prefer the newly correct value on the initially relevant dimension; d_{irrel} represents the tendency to prefer the newly correct value on the initially *ir*relevant dimension.

The pertinent observation in the shift phase is the relative weight exerted by the relevant and *ir*relevant dimension. At the outset of the shift d_{rel} was strongly negative because the reinforcement contingencies had been reversed, while d_{irrel} was close to zero because this dimension had been irrelevant in the preshift phase. Consequently, at first the relevant dimension continued to exert the greater weight on choice behavior, albeit in the negative direction. However, since in this phase both dimensions became relevant, as training proceeded d_{irrel} gradually increased and d_{rel} gradually became less negative. Note that when d_{rel} crossed zero, near the middle of the shift phase, the *ir*relevant dimension was clearly exerting the greater weight. Although the difference between the weight exerted by the two dimensions was narrowing when criterion was attained, the *ir*relevant dimension outweighed the relevant dimension throughout the shift phase.

Partly because there were two relevant and only one *ir*relevant dimensions, criterion was attained before either d_{rel} or d_{irrel} became asymptotic. Had the training continued the difference between the two *d*s would have continued to decrease. But, as this simulation demonstrates, the model implies that, if the intrinsic salience is equated, the differential should never significantly favor the initially relevant dimension.

Test Phase. During the test phase both pairs of discriminanda were again alternated. The learning pair continued to be reinforced as in the shift phase, while any choice was reinforced on the probe pair. The last panel in Fig. 8.2a shows that, although introducing the probe pair increased the noise on both visual dimensions, the advantage of d_{irrel} over d_{rel} was maintained throughout the test phase.

This simulation demonstrates that, if intrinsic salience is equated, then the weight of the *ir*relevant dimension during the test phase should continue to be at least as great, or more likely, greater than the weight of the relevant dimension.

Simulated Performance

The differential tendencies for each represented dimension are theoretical constructs that cannot, at least at present, be directly measured in live learners. The usefulness of such constructs depends on their capacity to explain or predict observable performance. One performance measure predicted by the model is the probability of choosing one compounded discriminandum over another. Figure 8.2b presents the simulated trial-by-trial probability of a correct choice ($p_{correct}$) on whichever pair happened to be presented in each phase of the procedure.

Preshift Phase. In the preshift phase, where the two pairs of discriminanda were alternated, the simulated $p_{correct}$ (light gray curve) increased gradually but noisily. This learning curve is quite noisy because the number of *ir*relevant dimensions exceeded the number of relevant dimensions.

Shift Phase. During the shift phase there are two simulated performance measures. One measure, represented by the light-gray curve in the mid-panel of Fig. 8.2b, traces the simulated probability of a correct choice on the learning pair ($p_{correct}$), which was presented on each trial during this phase.

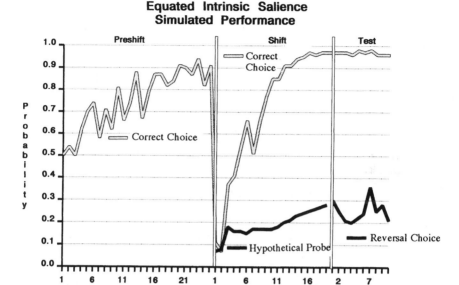

FIG. 8.2b. Tracing the simulated changes in the probability of a correct and a reversal choice in the same condition.

Note that $p_{correct}$ in the shift phase increased faster and approached a higher asymptote than in the preshift phase, despite the reversed reinforcement contingencies. This was because the number of relevant dimensions exceeded the number of irrelevant dimensions in the shift phase while the opposite was true in the preshift phase.

Turning now to the probe pair on which the learner can make either a reversal or a nonreversal choice. One choice is labeled *reversal* because it is the reverse of what had been the correct response on this pair in the preshift phase. Thus if, as in our example, the correct choice during the preshift phase were *large-triangle*, the reversal choice during the shift phase would be *small-circle*. The other possible choice is referred to as *nonreversal* merely to distinguish it from a reversal choice. Which choice is likely on any given trial depends on which dimension is dominant, as determined by the relative weight exerted on choice behavior. If the relevant dimension is dominant a reversal choice is more probable; if the irrelevant dimension is dominant a nonreversal choice is more probable. Let $p_{reversal}$ represent the probability of a reversal choice.

During the shift phase (center panel of Fig. 8.2b) $p_{reversal}$ is hypothetical because it represents the computed probability of making a reversal choice *as if the probe pair were presented after every learning trial,* although this pair of discriminanda was never presented at all in this phase of the simulation. As such, the hypothetical $p_{reversal}$ is a pure measure of the predicted, trial-by-trial transfer from the learning pair to the probe pair. In this simulation the hypothetical $p_{reversal}$, represented by the darker-gray curve in the mid-panel of Fig. 8.2b, was almost nil at the outset of the shift, increased gradually as the shift trials increased, but remained below .30 at criterion. That $p_{reversal}$ was below chance indicated that the initially *ir*relevant visual dimension was dominant throughout the shift phase. No acquired dominance of the relevant dimension was manifested.

Predicted Facts. The purely hypothetical probe applied to every trial is only possible in simulations. But in live experiments one can insert actual probe trials at well-separated intervals during the shift phase and measure the proportion of reversal choices made by a group of learners. Rust and Kendler (1987) used this procedure to test the capacity of the ICD model to predict the choice behavior of a group of 4-year-old, nursery-school children on the shift phase. The children were trained on the size-form discriminanda; these discriminanda were the closest we came to equating the intrinsic salience of the relevant and *ir*relevant dimensions.

The probe pair was inserted on the first, fourth, and ninth trials, and after that on every ninth trial throughout the shift phase until criterion was attained and 30 overtraining trials were completed. The most pertinent outcome was that the mean $p_{reversal}$ on the interspersed probe trials was very low at the beginning of the shift phase, increased gradually as training on the learning pair proceeded until it leveled off near .5 as criterion was approached. No further change was manifested on the probe trials during the overtraining. No acquired dimensional dominance was manifested. We were able to use the ICD model to fit parameters to these data that matched the empirical performance on both the learning and probe pairs rather well.

Test Phase. In most live applications of the optional shift procedure, as well as in the present simulations, no probe trials are introduced during the shift phase. Instead the test phase, initiated after criterion is attained on the shift phase, provides an opposed-cues test of dimensional dominance. In the test phase the learning and probe pairs are presented in random-type alternation until 10 probe trials are completed. The learning trials continue to be rewarded as in the shift phase while on the probe trials either choice is rewarded. Thus this phase provides two performance measures: $p_{correct}$ on the learning trials and $p_{reversal}$ on the alternating probe trials. The last panel of Fig. 8.2b plots the simulated outcome on these two performance measures.

The light gray curve represents the simulated $p_{correct}$ on the learning pair. Although it would seem that introducing the probe pair in the test phase would cause $p_{correct}$ to decrease slightly and become more variable, the simu-lated $p_{correct}$ remained as high and as steady as it was before the test phase began. Turning now to the $p_{reversal}$ on the 10 interspersed probe trials (dark gray curve), we see this probability oscillated around the computed value attained toward the end of the shift phase. The probability of a reversal choice on each of the 10 probe trials remained well below chance.

Explained Fact. The simulation illustrates why the model predicts that, when intrinsic salience is equated, $p_{reversal}$ should not significantly exceed chance. This prediction was verified in another experiment with 3- and 4-year-old children that used the standard optional shift procedure with the same size-form discriminanda (T. Kendler, 1974). The mean $p_{reversal}$ in the test phase was .39, indicating that, on the average, this sample of very young children behaved in accordance with the model.

FROM THE PERSPECTIVE OF THE LEVELS THEORY

To recapitulate briefly, the levels theory assumes the system that governs discrimination learning can be differentiated into two levels. At the lower level information processing is nonselective and learning is associative. At the more cognitive, higher level information processing is selective and problem solving is rational. The two levels of function are regulated by different neurological infrastructures. While these infrastructures are, at present, purely hypothetical, the lower level is assumed to develop, and hence become functional, earlier than the higher level both phylogenetically and ontogenetically.

With respect to information processing, the lower level encodes, in parallel, all of the perceptible information. If the higher level is functional, it selects only the relevant portion of the information for further processing. While on most occasions these two processes supplement each other, circumstances can arise in which the behaviors they would produce are incompatible. Under such circumstances whichever level provides the strongest input to the executive component will determine which behavior is evoked. The relative strengths of the inputs are assumed to be a joint function of past experience, present circumstance, and the developmental status of the higher level substrates.

The optional shift provides a procedure for producing incompatibility between the two levels. The incompatibility is created by first establishing one dimension as relevant and the other as irrelevant in the preshift phase and then reversing the reinforcement on the relevant dimension in the shift phase. How the learner responds to the probe trials in the test phase discloses whether the initial relevance or the subsequent reversal has the greater effect on behavior. The previous simulation showed that, if the lower, nonselective process is in control and the intrinsic salience is equated, the irrelevant dimension should exert more weight, as measured by the tendency for nonreversal choices to prevail. On the other hand, if the higher selective process is in control, then the relevant dimension should exert more weight, as measured by the tendency for reversal choices to prevail. Given the appropriate controls, how the learner responds to the probe trials in the test phase discloses which kind of encoding prevailed.

Eight or more reversal choices out of the 10 probe trials constitute a preponderance of reversal choices significant at the 5% level of confidence. Hence counting the number of reversal choices made by each learner in the test phase allows for classifying the performance of every individual as constituting either a reversal or a nonreversal shift. A performance that produced 8 or more reversal choices on the 10 probe trials would be classified as a reversal shift, while a performance that produced less than 8 reversal choices would be classified as a nonreversal shift. Accordingly, if intrinsic dimensional salience is equated, a reversal shift indicates that the higher, selective level of encoding prevailed over the lower, nonselective level. A nonreversal choice indicates that the lower, nonselective level prevailed. For instance, in this simulation the computer produced only 2 reversal choices out of the 10 probes, which would properly classify the computer's performance as a nonreversal shift.

From the perspective of the levels theory the implication is that, if the intrinsic salience of the relevant and irrelevant dimension is equated, adult humans should be disposed to make reversal shifts. Infrahuman animals should be disposed to make nonreversal shifts, and among humans, the probability of reversal shifts should increase with age. Although there are a number of experiments that confirm such developmental differences, I know of none that actually equated perceptual salience. However, the next set of simulations illustrate what should be expected when intrinsic salience is not equated.

DISPARATE INTRINSIC SALIENCE

This set of simulations explores the effect of disparate intrinsic salience on behavior in the optional shift, in order to clarify the distinction between intrinsic and acquired dimensional dominance, test the capacity of the ICD model to explain some additional established facts, clear up some confusion in the literature, and delineate how the procedure can be used appropriately to diagnose selective encoding. For these purposes two conditions that differ only with respect to the relative intrinsic salience of the two visual dimensions were compared. In one condition the initially relevant (e.g., *form*) dimension was more salient; let this be referred to as the Relevant-Dimension-Salient (RDS) condition. In the other condition the initially *ir*relevant dimension (e.g., *size*) was more salient; let this be referred to as the Irrelevant-Dimension-Salient (IDS) condition.

For this simulation one visual dimension was assigned a high degree ($A = B = .10$) and the other a low degree of intrinsic salience ($A = B = .80$). The salience of the position dimension remained at an intermediate value ($A = B = .25$). The remaining parameters were left unchanged. One simulation in this set (the RDS condition) assigned the higher salience to the relevant dimension. The other simulation (the IDS condition) assigned the higher salience to the *ir*relevant dimension. To make the necessary comparisons, the simulated outcomes of the two conditions are presented in a side-by-side graphic format for each phase of the procedure taken separately.

Preshift Phase

Comparing Simulated Learning Processes

Figure 8.3a compares the simulated learning in the preshift phase of the optional shift under the two conditions, as represented by the trial-by-trial changes in *d* associated with each dimension. One can see at a glance that

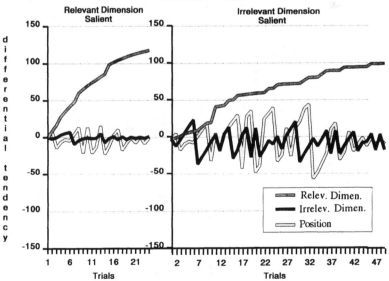

FIG. 8.3a. Comparing the changes in the simulated differential tendency associated with each represented dimension during the preshift phase under two conditions. In one condition the relevant dimension was relatively salient; in the other the *ir*relevant dimension was relatively salient.

d_{rel} increased faster and d_{irrel} was less noisy in the RDS than in the IDS condition.

Comparing Simulated Performance

When the simulated performance in the two conditions was compared (Fig. 8.3b) the probability of a correct choice in the RDS condition increased faster, was less variable, and reached a higher asymptote than in the IDS condition.

Explained Facts

Three experiments compared the effect of premeasured intrinsic salience. Rats served as learners in two of the experiments; in the third the learners were young children. Each rat experiment first used a version of the simple opposed-cues procedure (p. 112) to determine the relative intrinsic salience of the two visual dimensions. Then the animals were trained on the optional shift procedure using the premeasured dimensions in a counterbalanced design. Half the rats were trained on the RDS condition; the other half were trained on the IDS condition.

The discriminanda used in the first rat study (T. Kendler, 1971; T. Kendler, Kendler, & Silfen, 1964) differed in size (7.0 vs. 3.8 cm. on a side) and

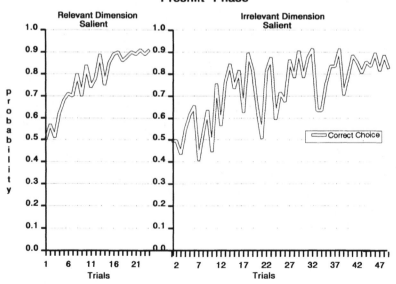

FIG. 8.3b. Comparing the simulated changes in the probability of a correct choice during the preshift phase under the same two conditions.

brightness (*black* vs. *white*). In the preliminary, simple opposed-cues test the brightness difference proved to be somewhat more intrinsically salient than the size difference. In the main experiment another group of rats from the same strain were trained on the optional shift procedure using the same size-brightness discriminanda. To counterbalance the effect of intrinsic salience the animals were randomly assigned to either the RDS or the IDS condition. Learning on the preshift phase was significantly faster in the RDS condition.

The second experiment, which used hooded rats (T. Kendler, Basden, & Bruckner, 1970), was specifically designed to test the ICD model. The discriminanda differed in color (red vs. green) and form (circle vs. triangle). The preliminary opposed-cues procedure to measure intrinsic salience found the color differences to be very much more salient than the form differences for this strain. (Subsequent brightness tests showed the green to be brighter than the red. Doubtless the rats were responding to the brightness rather than the hue differences.) The main experiment trained another group of hooded rats on the optional shift procedure in a counterbalanced design. Because the intrinsic salience differential was huge, the preshift phase in the RDS condition was learned over 10 times more rapidly than in the IDS condition. Moreover, we had to use a relatively low criterion of 75% correct because training the rats in the IDS condition to a more stringent criterion proved to be practically impossible even after thousands of trials. This outcome is consistent with the prediction that learning should not only be slower, but should also asymptote at a lower value in the IDS condition.

The third experiment used the optional shift procedure in a counterbalanced design with first- and third-grade children (Smiley, 1972). The discriminanda differed in color and form. Intrinsic salience was defined in this experiment by the physical difference between the stimuli on the two dimensions. There were two degrees of color differences and two degrees of form differences. At both grade levels and for both the color and form dimensions the RDS condition required significantly fewer trials than the IDS condition to reach criterion on the preshift phase.

As the model predicts, the relative intrinsic salience of the relevant and *ir*relevant dimensions can affect both the ease and asymptote of lower level learning. The greater the salience differential, the more pronounced is the effect.

Shift Phase

Consider next the implications of the model for learning and performance on the shift phase of the procedure, where only one pair of discriminanda is presented and the reinforcement contingencies on that pair are reversed.

Comparing Simulated Learning Processes

Figure 8.4a compares the simulated learning in the shift phase under the two conditions. Because the reinforcement contingencies were reversed at the outset of the shift phase, d_{rel} in both conditions became markedly negative. As for d_{irrel} both curves began the shift phase near chance because the irrelevant dimension had been reinforced and nonreinforced about equally often in the preshift phase. As retraining on the shift proceeded both d_{rel} and d_{irrel} increased gradually because both dimensions had become relevant and redundant. Meanwhile the $d_{position}$ oscillated noisily around zero because position remained irrelevant in both conditions.

So much for the learning, as noted earlier, the pertinent observation in the shift phase is the effect on the relative weight exerted by the relevant and *ir*relevant dimension in the two conditions. In the RDS condition d_{rel} rose more sharply and approached a higher asymptote than d_{irrel} because the relevant dimension was more intrinsically salient. Presently the two curves crossed. This crossover indicates that the *ir*relevant dimension exerted the greater weight at the beginning of the shift, but as training progressed the balance gradually shifted in favor of the relevant dimension. By the time criterion was reached, the relevant dimension in the RDS condition dominated the irrelevant dimension *simply because it was more intrinsically salient.*

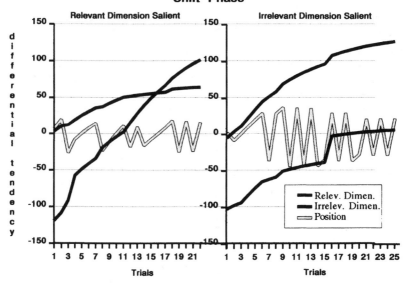

Disparate Intrinsic Salience
Comparing Simulated Learning Process
Shift Phase

FIG. 8.4a. Comparing the simulated changes in the differential tendency associated with each dimension during the shift phase under the same two conditions.

In the IDS condition the relationship between d_{rel} and d_{irrel} was markedly different. Because the relevant dimension had a relatively low intrinsic salience, d_{rel} remained below d_{irrel} throughout the shift phase. Consequently the irrelevant dimension dominated from the beginning to the end of the shift phase. The implication is that no amount of overtraining in the shift phase would overcome the dominance of the *ir*relevant dimension in the IDS condition.

Comparing Simulated Performance (Learning Pair)

The shift phase (Fig. 8.4b) provides two performance measures in each condition. Compare first the simulated probability of a correct choice on the learning pair, represented by light gray curves. One thing to note is that, although the learning curve for the IDS condition was relatively noisy, the number of trials required to attain criterion under the two conditions was not very different because, in this phase, both visual dimensions were relevant.

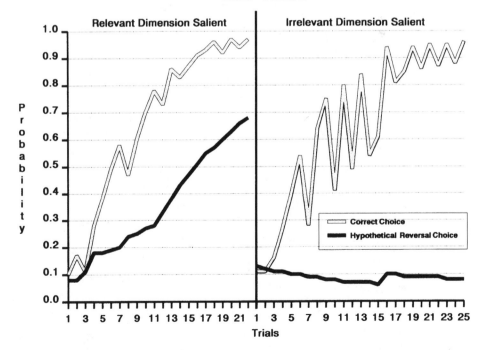

Disparate Intrinsic Salience
Comparing Simulated Performance
Shift Phase

FIG. 8.4b. Comparing the simulated changes in the probability of a correct and a reversal choice during the shift phase under the same two conditions.

Explained Facts

There was no significant difference between the RDS and IDS conditions in the mean trials to criterion on the shift phase of the procedure in the rat experiment where the salience differential was moderate (T. Kendler, 1971). Nor was there any significant difference in learning on the shift phase in the rat experiment where there was a huge salience differential (T. Kendler, Basden, & Bruckner, 1970). Likewise, the children in Smiley's (1972) experiment manifested no significant difference in learning on the shift phase between the RDS and IDS conditions, in spite of the salience differential.

As the model predicts, there was little or no difference in learning attributable to the intrinsic salience differential during the shift phase.

Comparing Simulated Performance (Probe Pair)

The dark gray curve in the same Fig. 8.4a represents the hypothetical probability of a reversal choice on the probe pair in the shift phase, as if this pair had been displayed after each learning trial. Recall that this is a computed measure, referred to as hypothetical because the probe pair was never presented during the shift phase. The critical observation here is the striking difference under the two conditions. The hypothetical $p_{reversal}$ in the RDS condition rose from below .10 at the outset to well above chance by the end of the shift phase and would have continued to rise if overtraining trials has been added. In the IDS condition the hypothetical $p_{reversal}$ also began near .10 at the outset but never climbed any higher throughout the shift phase.

The implication is that, if actual probe trials were presented throughout the shift phase, the $p_{reversal}$ would be different for the two conditions. In the RDS condition this probability should increase gradually as the training trials increase. The extent of this increase should depend jointly on the number of training trials in the shift phase and on the magnitude of the intrinsic salience differential. On the other hand, in the IDS condition the $p_{reversal}$ should, if anything, decrease gradually.

Predicted Facts

These implications were tested in the T. Kendler, Basden, and Bruckner (1970) rat experiment by actually presenting a probe trial after a fixed number of learning trials spaced throughout the shift phase of the procedure. The rats were trained to criterion. Then, to test the effect of overtraining, they were also given 300 overtraining trials after criterion on the shift phase was attained. As predicted, in the RDS condition the mean $p_{reversal}$ increased gradually as training on the shift proceeded until it reached .82 at criterion. During the overtraining the mean $p_{reversal}$ gradually increased to .91.

The mean $p_{reversal}$ for the IDS condition, on the other hand, decreased gradually dropping to .04 at criterion. During overtraining there was a further drop to .03. The substantial difference between the two conditions was attributable the sizable intrinsic salience differential.

Test Phase

The last phase of the optional shift procedure used an opposed-cues test for dimensional dominance which compares the relative weights exerted by the initially relevant and irrelevant visual dimensions on choice behavior. The weight of each dimension is represented in the ICD model by the strength of the associated differential tendency.

Comparing Simulated Weights

Figure 8.5a presents the simulated weight exerted by each dimension during each trial on the test phase. In the RDS condition both the initially relevant and *ir*relevant dimensions exerted some weight but the relevant dimension exerted the most weight throughout the entire phase. In the IDS condition the opposite was true; the *ir*relevant dimension exerted considerable weight throughout the test phase while the relevant dimension exerted practically none. Position contributed to the noise in both conditions in roughly similar degree.

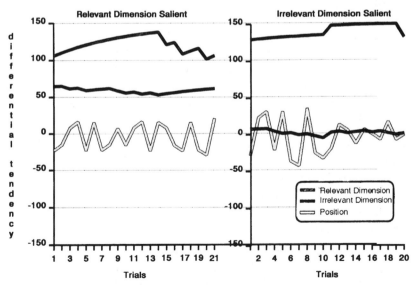

FIG. 8.5a. Comparing the simulated differential tendencies associated with each represented dimension during the test phase under the same two conditions.

Comparing Simulated Performance (Learning Pair)

The next step in the simulation translated the weights into probabilities. The test phase provides for two performance measures, namely the probability of a correct choice on the learning pair ($p_{correct}$) and the probability of a reversal choice ($p_{reversal}$) on the interspersed probe pair.

Consider first the simulated performance on the learning pair, represented in Fig. 8.5b by the diamonds. Introducing the probe trials did not markedly interfere with the very good performance on the learning trials under either condition. The $p_{correct}$ (represented by the diamonds) remained very high throughout the test phase under both conditions, although there was a slight difference in favor of the RDS condition.

Explained Fact

Only Smiley's experiment (1972) with first- and third-grade-children bears on this matter. As predicted, the median number of correct choices on the learning trials in the RDS and IDS conditions were 9.0 and 8.7 respectively. This difference was not statistically reliable.

Comparing Simulated Performance (Probe Pair)

The probability of a reversal choice ($p_{reversal}$) on the probe pair is the critical measure in the optional shift procedure because it provides the means for assessing acquired dimensional dominance. This simulation illustrates that, when intrinsic dimensional salience is disparate, $p_{reversal}$ is markedly dependent on which dimension was relevant in the preshift phase. In the RDS condition the simulated $p_{reversal}$, as depicted by the squares in Fig. 8.5b, was well above chance on every probe trial. In the IDS condition the $p_{reversal}$ hovered near zero on most trials. The model also predicts that the magnitude of the difference in favor of the RDS condition should be a function of the magnitude of the differential salience.

Live experiments have measured performance on the probe trials in two ways. One measure compares the mean proportion of reversal choices made by the group of learners trained under each condition. As this simulation demonstrates, the model predicts the mean $p_{reversal}$ should be greater in the RDS condition than in the IDS condition. The difference between the two conditions should be an increasing function of the salience differential.

Predicted Facts

In both previously cited rat experiments the RDS condition produced significantly more reversal choices than the IDS condition. Moreover, when the salience differential was moderate (T. Kendler, 1971) the mean $p_{reversal}$

Disparate Intrinsic Salience
Simulated Performance
Test Phase

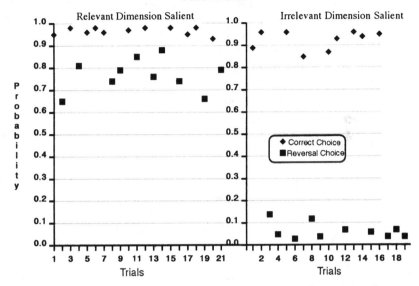

FIG. 8.5b. Comparing the simulated in the probabilities of a correct and a reversal choice during the test phase under the same two conditions.

on the probe trials for the RDS condition and IDS condition were .50 and .23, respectively. When the salience differential was huge (T. Kendler, Basden, & Bruckner, 1970), the mean $p_{reversal}$ on the probe trials for the RDS and IDS condition were .91 and .03, respectively.

As the model predicts, manipulating disparate dimensional salience has little effect on the probability of a correct choice on the learning pair, but the same manipulation has a measurable effect on the probability of a reversal choice on the test pair.

FROM THE PERSPECTIVE OF THE LEVELS THEORY

Consider now the diagnostic measure that classifies the performance of each learner as either an optional reversal or nonreversal shift on the basis of whether or not a significant preponderance of reversal choices (8 or more) were made on the 10 probe trials. This measure has been particularly useful for investigating development differences because it provides a means for diagnosing acquired dominance in the individual by using the number of reversal choices made on the probe trials. An optional reversal shift has been assumed to imply acquired dominance. However, this simulation demonstrates that, when the relevant dimension is relatively salient, a reversal shift could imply either acquired or intrinsic dominance. For example, the simulated outcome in the RDS condition produced 8 reversal choices in the 10 probe trials. Although there was no selective encoding programmed into this simulation, this performance would be classified as an optional reversal shift. If one were not alerted to the effects of intrinsic salience, such a performance would be interpreted as manifesting acquired dominance of the relevant dimension. The simulated outcome in the IDS condition, however, produced only 1 out of 10 reversal choices.

The empirical counterpart of this simulation can be found in the rat experiment cited earlier, where the salience differential was huge. All of the rats in the RDS and none in the IDS condition made optional reversal shifts. Moreover, counterbalancing for the effect of intrinsic salience would not have produced the desired control because it would have led to the erroneous conclusion that half of the rats manifested acquired dominance.

Another case in point comes from yet another experiment by Smiley (1973) that explicitly compared the effect of the RDS and IDS conditions on the developmental trend that relates the probability of an optional reversal shift to age among humans. Individuals drawn from kindergarten, third grade, sixth grade, and college served as learners and the discriminanda differed simultaneously in color and form. Two sets of stimuli were used; in one set the form differences and in the other set the color differences were made much more intrinsically salient. The two sets of discriminanda were used to explore the effect of intrinsic salience on the proportion of learners who made optional reversal shifts at each of the four grade levels. For half the learners at each grade level *form* was the more salient dimension and for the other half *color* was the more salient dimension. Within each dimension-group, half of the learners were trained in the RDS condition and the other half were trained in the IDS condition.

The slope of the developmental trend obtained under the RDS and IDS condition, reproduced in Fig. 8.6, depended markedly on the experimental condition. In the RDS condition there were no significant age differences; the great majority of the learners at every age level made optional reversal-shifts. There was effectively no developmental trend at all. On the other hand, there was a marked, statistically significant, developmental trend in the IDS condition.

Smiley (1973) concluded "These results suggest that the predictions of a developmental . . . theory are applicable only to those conditions for which the nondominant dimension is relevant" (p. 456). Actually the difference between the two conditions would be predicted by the levels theory. Consider first the behavior of the youngest children in the IDS condition, where intrinsic salience and relevance were opposed. In this condition nonreversal

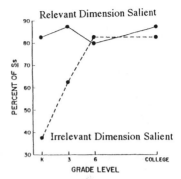

FIG. 8.6. Comparing the empirical percent of human learners at different grade levels who made optional reversal shifts under the RDS and IDS conditions. From Smiley (1973).

shifts should predominate, as they did among the kindergartners. Now consider the behavior of the older humans under the same IDS condition. Intrinsic salience had hardly any effect on their behavior: The great majority of both the sixth graders and the college student made optional reversal shifts. Apparently, among the relatively mature humans the disposition to selectively encode the relevant dimension was strong enough to overcome both the considerable intrinsic salience differential in favor of the irrelevant dimension as well as the reversed reinforcement contingencies.

Looking at the whole developmental trend in the IDS condition we see that the tendency for the acquired dominance of the relevant dimension to override the intrinsic salience differential increased with age. This outcome has two pertinent implications. One implication is that intrinsic and acquired dominance can be opposed, which is consistent with the premise that these two forms of dominance are produced by different processes. The second implication is that the degree to which acquired dominance prevails depends on the developmental status of the learner. This outcome supports the assumption that the higher, selective encoding level, which produces acquired dominance, develops later and more slowly than the lower nonselective level, which produces intrinsic dominance.

Consider now the RDS condition, where salience and relevance are conflated. The youngest children in this condition mostly made reversal shifts. This outcome demonstrates that, if there is an intrinsic salience differential, the RDS condition is likely to underestimate developmental differences. The greater the differential, the less useful this condition is for diagnosing selective encoding. That's the bad news; the good news is that the IDS condition, which opposes intrinsic salience and relevance, provides a rigorous measure of selective encoding. If the learner makes a reversal shift in this condition, then it is quite safe to conclude that relevance is operative. In fact, it is possible to develop a titration measure of the strength of the disposition to encode selectively by manipulating the relative intrinsic salience of the relevant dimension in the IDS condition.

CONCLUSIONS

Dimensional dominance refers to the relative weight exerted on learned behavior by the different dimensions represented in the discriminanda. Two forms of dimensional dominance can be differentiated. Intrinsic dimensional dominance is determined by the intrinsic salience differential. Intrinsic salience is the automatic product of a nonselective, lower level encoding process that determines both the perceived vividness of the difference between the values on a given dimension and the weight this dimension will exert on learned behavior. This lower level encoding process is regulated by a sensory system molded by natural selection to the eco-niche of the species. Stimulus generalization is the mechanism that produces both the relative intrinsic salience and relative weight exerted on learned behavior. Intrinsic dimensional dominance is a relatively stable, automatic reaction to the psychophysical difference between the values on the dimension.

Acquired dimensional dominance is a more flexible reaction determined by relevance. Relevance changes with the nature of the task or the intention of the learner. This kind of dominance is the output of a more complex higher level, selective encoding process, more closely related to conception than perception, that increases the weight of the relevant dimension on behavior. Acquired dominance can be measured by the optional shift procedure which first establishes one dimension as relevant and the other as irrelevant and then puts the two dimensions into opposition in order to test which exerts the greater weight on choice behavior. Accurate measures of acquired dominance, however, require careful control of intrinsic salience lest the two forms of dominance be conflated.

CHAPTER NINE

About Higher
Level Processes

Some psychologists have talked as if all behavior was cognitive: meaning that it involves thought. *Others have talked as if all behavior fitted the* S–R formula: *meaning that thought does not enter into it, that all behavior is fully controlled by the stimulation from the environment. In the light of what has been said about the nervous system, the student will see that both kinds of behavior do occur and that the real question is the directness of the connections between stimulus and response.*
—Hebb (1972, p. 77)

The ICD model explains lower level discrimination learning by postulating that the features in the discriminanda are encoded nonselectively and the correct choice is learned by means of a gradual, associative process. The capacity of this model to explain lower level operations provides a basis for a more clear-cut differentiation between higher and lower level processes. In the best of all possible worlds I would now present a comparably detailed model of the higher level operations. But the higher level remains elusive, touching as it does on deep and baffling epistemic issues. My aim is merely to present some hypotheses about these operations by contrasting them with their lower level counterparts, within the organized perspective provided by the levels theory.

INFORMATION PROCESSING COMPONENT

In discrimination learning the information to be processed refers to the discriminable features—each value on each represented dimension—that distinguish between the compounded discriminanda. While the lower level

141

is assumed to encode these features nonselectively, the higher encoding level is assumed to operate on the output of the lower level in a manner that selectively encodes the relevant aspects of the information. Relevance, a key concept in this theory, has both a general connotation and a specific operational definition. The general connotation refers to the applicability to the matter in hand as jointly determined by past experience, the immediate requirements of the situation, and the present intentions of the individual. Relevance is operationally defined in discrimination learning by the relationship between the discriminanda and the reinforcement contingencies. The relevant features are those that enable the learner to distinguish between a correct and an incorrect choice. The effect of relevance in discrimination learning is measured by setting one dimension relevant and the other dimension irrelevant to the reinforcement contingencies and comparing the relative weight the two dimensions exert on choice behavior. If intrinsic salience is controlled, selective encoding is instantiated when the relevant dimension exerts significantly more weight than the *ir*relevant dimension. Specifically, the disposition to make a reversal shift in the optional shift procedure measures the relative weight exerted by the relevant and irrelevant dimensions, which in turn measures the tendency for the higher encoding level to prevail over the lower encoding level.

How is selective encoding of the relevant features produced? The experimental literature bearing on selective encoding is voluminous and contentious, but most current researchers agree that two information-processing stages can be distinguished: a preattentive stage and focal attentive stage. The preattentive stage is thought to provide a fast, preconscious, effortless, involuntary, inflexible, automatic, parallel response to the impinging stimuli that produces a "spreading activation" in the central nervous system. The preattentive stage, so conceived, shares many of the properties the levels theory assigns to information processing in the nonselective mode.

The more controversial focal attentive stage is assumed to depend on a limited capacity central processor that can operate on only a selected portion of the information. This stage is considered to be slow, voluntary, effortful, and conscious (e.g., Collins & Quillian, 1969; Kahnemann, 1973; Posner & Snyder, 1975). However, beyond invoking intuitive notions about the constraints produced by the limited character of "focal attention," "awareness," or "consciousness," there is unfortunately no consensus after decades of voluminous research about what exactly occurs in this stage (Velmans, 1991).

Some theorists have made a clarifying distinction between two conceptions of selective attention (e.g., Hebb, 1972; Kahnemann & Treisman, 1984). According to one conception, selective attention reduces the complexity of information presented to the senses by attenuating the perceived salience of irrelevant cues. Presumably some mechanism filters out the irrelevant components before awareness occurs (e.g., Broadbent, 1958). The effect of such a mechanism applied to discrimination learning, would be to increase the perceived salience of the relevant cues at the expense of the irrelevant cues. According to the other conception, selection is a matter of choosing the most important of the many responses that could be instigated by the information at the same time (e.g., Posner, 1978; Shallice, 1972). Selective encoding, from this vantage, increases the strength of the tendency for the behavior under the control of the relevant component of the information.

Unfortunately, after decades of intensive research there as yet is no general agreement about whether the selection is produced by affecting perception or by affecting action. Allport (1989) suggests there is no agreement because both views are based on a false premise, namely that consciousness is a singular, limited processing system. Current knowledge about the multiplicity of parallel channels and about quasi-modular cognitive subsystems and their connections in the brain is incompatible with the characterization of one subsystem as uniquely central to consciousness. Moreover, we now also know that sensory input is able to control actions at many different levels. As a consequence, Allport would abandon the notion of consciousness as a limited capacity system but would retain a modified version of the notion of selection for the "potential control of action."

The question is which, if any, of these alternative conceptions applies to the selective encoding manifested in the optional shift procedure? Chapter 3 presents evidence of a developmental trend in selective encoding, as measured by the proportion of optional reversal shifts, under several different experimental conditions. In each case this trend was fitted to a simple log function. The same data, expressed by comparing the fitted developmental functions, are now reconsidered from the experimental perspective in order to provide insights into the nature of the selection process.

Effect of Verbal Labels

One experiment investigated the effect of requiring the learners to use spoken labels (T. Kendler, 1974, 1979b). Specifically, a combined experimental-developmental design compared the shift performance of a relevant label group, an irrelevant label group, and a no-label control group at each of five age levels between 4 and 18 years. The dependent variable was the proportion of reversal shifters in the test phase of the optional shift procedure.

Control Group. Learners in the control group were trained in the standard manner on the three phases of the procedure using the size-form discriminanda illustrated in Fig. 8.1.

Relevant Label Group. Learners in the relevant label group differed from the control group only in that they were instructed at the outset of the preshift phase to say aloud on each trial which value on the relevant dimension they were going to choose. For instance, among those learners for whom *form* was the relevant dimension, each individual learner was instructed to say aloud, before each manual choice, whether he or she would choose the "circle" or the "triangle." A learner who omitted the label on a given trial during the preshift phase was reminded once again to "say aloud. . . ." These reminders were limited to the preshift phase, where the selective encoding would presumably occur. Labeling the relevant cues was expected to potentiate selective encoding at the younger ages. The effect of such potentiation would be to flatten the developmental function.

Results. Although some youngsters substituted more familiar terms such as *round* for circle and *pointy* for triangle, all learners, even the youngest, quickly understood the instructions to label the stimulus features. Moreover, they all proved fully capable of using the spoken labels to correctly signify the stimulus attributes. Even the 4-year-olds matched their manual to their spoken choice on 97% of the trials. For instance, if they said *circle* they practically always chose the circle. Nevertheless, the younger children needed constant reminders during the preshift phase to continue saying the labels aloud, while they needed no reminders at all to make the manual choices. In contrast, all of the adults, not only needed no reminders during the preshift phase, but they spontaneously continued to use the labels throughout the three phases. This spontaneous tendency to continue labeling throughout proved to be a monotonic function of age. Apparently the manual choice for the younger children was fun; using the spoken label was not.

Labeling the relevant features had two measurable effects on choice behavior; both effects interacted significantly with age. Relative to the no-label condition, relevant labeling markedly facilitated learning on the preshift phase at the younger age levels, but the facilitation decreased with age. Relevant labeling also significantly potentiated selective encoding at the younger age levels. But, as expected, this potentiation also decreased gradually over age until at the adult levels there was a slight, statistically nonsignificant, attenuation. In other words, as seen in Fig. 9.1, overt labeling of the relevant features reduced the slope of the developmental function but did not eliminate the developmental trend. Apparently verbal representation can potentiate selective encoding.

Irrelevant Label Group. The *ir*relevant label group differed from the relevant label group in that the learners were instructed to label the cues on the *ir*relevant dimension. Because the discriminanda differed in both *size* and *form*, a learner could choose the correct value on the relevant dimension manually while correctly naming the value on the *ir*relevant dimension. For instance, if *triangle* were correct in the preshift phase one could learn to choose the triangle consistently while saying "big" when the triangle was big and "small" when the triangle was small.

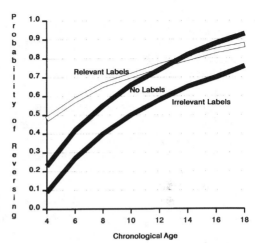

FIG. 9.1. Compares the fitted developmental trends in the proportion of optional reversal shifts under three different training conditions.

Results. To no one's surprise labeling the *ir*relevant features markedly interfered with learning on the preshift phase for the younger children. There was, however, scarcely any effect on the adults, who quickly adapted to labeling the appropriate value on the irrelevant dimension, which changed from trial to trial, while consistently choosing the correct value on the relevant dimension.

On the shift phase of the procedure both dimensions became relevant and redundant. Consequently what had been the *ir*relevant label during the preshift was no longer *ir*relevant to the reversed reinforcement contingencies. For instance, when *big-triangle* became the correct choice, the label "big" was no longer *ir*relevant. If verbal labels were effective determining factors, labeling the *ir*relevant features should *de*crease the disposition to respond selectively to the previously relevant dimension. The decrement should vary *inversely* with age, if only because of the ceiling effect. The result should have been a flattened developmental function.

Figure 9.1 shows that, relative to the control group, there was some decrement in selective encoding at every age level. But instead of varying inversely with age the slope of the fitted development function was hardly changed. Note that .75 of the adults made reversal shifts on the relevant dimension despite the fact that they continued to label the irrelevant features throughout the entire procedure.

Discussion. This experiment was designed to test the effect of linguistic representation on selective encoding. Relevant labels had the expected potentiating effect on selective encoding at the younger age levels and irrelevant labels had an attenuating effect at all age levels. Nevertheless, the data provide no support for the notion that linguistic representation of the relevant features is the basic ingredient of the selective encoding process. Nor do these data support the notion that selective encoding is due to the increased awareness of the relevant features at the expense of the irrelevant ones. Consider the adult performance in the *ir*relevant label condition. In the preshift phase, these adults easily learned to make the correct manual choice on the relevant dimension while they labeled the correct value on the ir- relevant dimension. To perform this feat they had to be well aware of both the relevant and irrelevant features. In the shift phase, when both dimensions became redundant and relevant, all of the adults spontaneously continued to label the *initially ir*relevant dimension. Therefore, they had to continue to be at least as well aware of the values on the *ir*relevant as on the relevant dimension in the shift phase. During the test phase the adults also continued to spontaneously label the *ir*relevant features on all of the test and the learning trials. Nevertheless, the great majority made optional reversal shifts on the relevant dimension, indicating that their manual choice behavior was controlled by the relevant features, while their verbal behavior was controlled by the irrelevant features. These data are incompatible with the notion that selective encoding of the relevant features is based either on a filter that attenuates the awareness of the irrelevant features or a searchlight that po- tentiates the perception of the relevant features. Nor are they consistent with the notion that consciousness is a limited capacity system that could only focus on one dimension at a time, since the adults had so little difficulty in simultaneously using the values on the relevant dimension to control choice behavior and the values on the *ir*relevant dimension to control linguistic behavior. The data are more consistent with the selection-for-action formu- lation in which the features on each dimension can have access to different actions as long as the actions, like walking and talking, are compatible.

Intradimensional Shifts

Another experiment trained learners at the same five age levels on an optional *intra*dimensional shift procedure (H. Kendler, Kendler, & Ward, 1972). The *intra*dimensional shift differs from the reversal-shift procedure only in that the discriminanda in the shift and test phases of the procedure are changed to different values on the same dimensions. This procedure is designed to diagnose whether the learner makes an optional *intra*dimensional shift to the new values on the initially relevant dimension. The original purpose of the experiment was to determine whether the developmental trend obtained with the reversal shift procedure would be replicated under these conditions.

The discriminanda, which differed in *color* and *form*, are illustrated in Fig. 9.2. During the preshift phase the discriminanda in the illustration dif- fered in *color* (green vs. red) and *form* (circle vs. triangle). *Circle* was correct and *triangle* incorrect; hence *form* was relevant and *color* was *ir*relevant in the preshift phase. (Which dimension was relevant and which value was correct was, of course, counterbalanced across learners.)

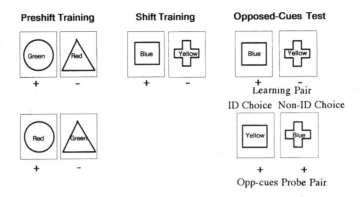

FIG. 9.2. An example of the discriminanda and reinforcement contingencies in the three phases of the optional intradimensional shift procedure.

After attaining criterion on the preshift, the shift phase was introduced. Only one pair of discriminanda was presented but both *colors* and both *forms* were changed. The forms in this example were changed to *square* and *cross*, the colors were changed to *blue* and *yellow*. *Blue square* became the correct choice. When criterion was attained on the shift phase, the test phase introduced a probe pair that opposed the values on the color and form dimensions in order to test for the effect of relevance on choice behavior. In our example form was relevant hence choosing the yellow *square* 8 or more times on the 10 test trials was classified as an *intra*dimensional shift. This kind of shift, like the reversal shift, instantiates selective encoding of the values on the initially relevant dimension (Zeaman & House, 1963, 1974).

Results.   The light gray fitted function in Fig. 9.3 shows that, while only about half of the youngest children made *intra*dimensional shifts, the proportion increased gradually until at the adult level it was over .95. The darker

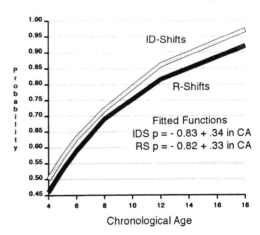

FIG. 9.3. Compares the fitted developmental trends in the proportion of selective encoders as measured in the optional intradimensional and reversal shift procedures.

gray curve in the same figure represents the fitted developmental function applied to the comparable data from an earlier experiment that used the optional reversal shift procedure with the same color and form dimensions (T. Kendler & Kendler, 1970). Comparing the two curves shows a remarkable similarity except for the small but consistent difference in favor of the *intra*dimensional shift at every age level because no reversal of the previously learned response was required. The more interesting outcome is that the developmental functions produced by the reversal and *intra*dimensional shift procedures were so similar.

Discussion. This outcome is also incompatible with the notion that the selective encoding process potentiates the perceived salience of the relevant *features*. In the *intra*dimensional shift procedure, the selection process is grounded in the relevant dimension, rather than in the directly perceptible values on the relevant dimension (Harrow, 1964; Sutherland & Mackintosh, 1971; Zeaman & House, 1963, 1974). These data suggest that, instead of an operation that filters out the perception of the irrelevant features or amplifies the perception of the relevant features, the operation underlying selective encoding sorts the information in a manner appropriate to the required action.

A Sorting Operation

The behavior to be explained is the disposition to make reversal and *intra*dimensional shifts. In the optional reversal shift procedure, the question is why do human adults, who have learned in the preshift that, say, *circle* is correct and *triangle* is incorrect, spontaneously reverse their choices in the shift phase—do the opposite of what they had previously learned to do? In the *intra*dimensional shift procedure, the question is why do human adults spontaneously transfer control of their choice behavior to new values on the relevant dimension? Finally, why does the disposition to behave in this way increase systematically over age?

A plausible answer to these questions would invoke a sorting operation that categorizes the discriminanda as correct or incorrect on the basis of the abstracted features on the relevant dimension. The term *dimension*, as used in psychology, refers to one of a number of measurable properties, such as color, size, or form, that enable one to make useful distinctions between discriminanda. A given value on one of these dimensions, such as a particular color or form, is referred to as a cue or a feature. A feature is directly observable; one sees the color red and the triangular form. A dimension is a highly derived, abstract construct. That the selection process manifested in the optional shift procedure is grounded in the relevant dimension is not consistent with a mechanism that operates by attenuating the vividness or awareness of the particular, directly perceived feature or features. The relevant features may become more noticeable but, if so, this effect is probably a by-product rather than the causal mechanism. Nor does the invocation of a sorting operation deny an important role to language in facilitating the process. But the basic operation appears to be one that categorizes the discriminanda as correct or incorrect on the basis of the abstracted features on the relevant dimension. Such categorization implies the subordination of the abstracted, relevant features into a yet more abstract, superordinate class which, in this case, is the dimension. Superordination by dimension organizes the information by relating the two abstracted features on the relevant dimension to each other as members of the same more inclusive class, without blurring the distinction between them. Viewed in this light, the disposition to make reversal and *intra*dimensional shifts would be a measure of the capacity to sort the information in the discriminanda into subordinate and superordinate categories. And the developmental increase in the proportion of reversal shifts would be explained in terms of an ontogenetic increase in this capacity. The increase in reversal shifts produced by requiring the younger children to label the relevant cues would suggest that linguistic representation increases the probability of activating the sorting operation.

There is converging evidence, based on other experimental procedures, for an ontogenetic increase among humans in the disposition to spontaneously classify information in terms of the values on whatever dimension happens to be relevant to the task in hand. Piaget's class-inclusion problem is one such procedure and Garner's classification task is another.

Piaget's Class-Inclusion Problem

Piaget's procedure begins by acquainting the individual child with a superordinate class of objects, then demonstrating how the superordinate class can be divided into two subordinate classes. After this demonstration the experimenter asks a question that compares the magnitude of the subordinate class with the superordinate class. For instance, in a class-inclusion experiment in our laboratory (Tabor & Kendler, 1981) each child was shown a superordinate class of objects, for example triangles, that were divisible into two subordinate classes, namely four big and two small triangles. Then the child was asked, "Are there more big ones than triangles?" Piaget regarded the correct answer to this question as the *sine qua non* of logical classification. The supposition is that a child who implicitly organizes the information into subordinate and superordinate classes will, of course, answer "More triangles." A child who answers "Big ones" is misled by the perceptible fact that there are more big than small triangles. This response indicates either a relatively weak or no tendency at all to superordinate.

The children in our experiment ranged between 6 and 12 years. Each child was given a series of four class-inclusion problems administered on separate days. We found, among other things that hardly any of the youngest children gave the correct answer but the proportion of correct responses increased monotonically with age. This experiment is only one example. Winer (1980) reviewed an impressive accumulation of evidence showing that: First, the proportion of successes on the class-inclusion task increases monotonically with age and, second, the parameters of these developmental trends depend on task variables, such as the type of objects used, the way the questions are framed, previous training, etc. These class-inclusion experiments present evidence that the spontaneous disposition to sort information into superordinate and subordinate categories increases ontogenetically among humans.

Garner's Classification Procedures

These procedures were first designed by Garner and his collaborators to investigate the difference between the perception of *integral* and *separable* dimensions. Separable dimensions, such as color and form, are easily distinguished. Integral dimensions, such as saturation and brightness, are difficult to distinguish. The data produced by these different kinds of classification procedures provide another body of evidence that converges on the ontogenetic transition from nonselective to selective encoding obtained with the use of discrimination learning procedures.

The stimuli in the Garner classification procedures, as in the discriminative shift procedures, consisted of sets of abstract, visual, bidimensional compounds. But instead of learning to choose between these compounds the subjects were instructed to sort them. The many germane experiments in this genre can be distilled by describing one representative procedure first used with human adults and later with children. Handel and Imai (1972) used sets of three bidimensional compounds (triads) in one of their experiments. Each set was composed of either integral or separable dimensions. The subjects, adult humans in this case, were simply told to sort the stimuli into two classes. As illustrated by the schematic diagram in Fig. 9.4, each triad was formed by combining these features in a manner that provided the classifier with the option of sorting the stimuli by dimension or by overall similarity.

Suppose that dimension 1 is brightness and dimension 2 is size. Let *A* be small-light, *B* be small-dark, and let *C* be only slightly larger and slightly darker than *A*. There are three possible ways these stimuli could be partitioned into two classes:

1. They could be partitioned according to the two values on the size dimension. In that case *A* and *B* (small) would be put in one class and *C* (large) would be put in the other. Such a partition implies selective encoding by dimension.

2. The stimuli could also be partitioned according to overall similarity. In that case *A* and *C*, which share no common value on either dimension

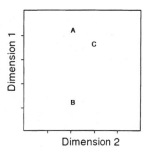

FIG. 9.4. One example of the structure of a stimulus triad that pits overall stimulus similarity against common dimensionality.

but are relatively similar overall, would be put into one class. *B*, which is relatively different, would be put in the other class. Such a partition implies nonselective encoding because it takes into account all of the values on both dimensions.

3. *B* and *C* could be put together for no apparent reason. In practice these two stimuli were hardly ever sorted together by adults and only occasionally by the younger children.

How adults sorted the bidimensional compounds depended on whether the dimensions were integral or separable. Separable compounds were primarily sorted by dimension, indicating that most human adults spontaneously used the abstracted features on one of the dimensions as the basis for their classification. The values on the other dimension became irrelevant to their sorting behavior. This is evidence that adults spontaneously classify easily differentiated features by dimension.

However, when the compounds were composed of integral (difficult to distinguish) dimensions, the adults primarily sorted by overall similarity. Such sorting implies nonselective encoding since both dimensions are taken into account. That adults under certain conditions encode selectively and under other conditions encode nonselectively is consistent with the premise of the levels theory that both levels are operative in human adults. These data would also indicate that, if the two encoding levels lead to opposing actions, which level will prevail depends, among other things, on the separability of the dimensions. As Garner noted (1974):

> We must remember that (adult) subjects can differentiate integral dimensions, since that is how after all, the Munsell color system was developed. . . . Perhaps the best way of considering the difference between integral and separable dimensions is to ask what is the primary process for each, and what is the more derived or cognitive process. For integral dimensions, similarity is the primary process . . . but a dimensional structure can be extracted, certainly by a sophisticated experimenter, and probably by a less sophisticated subject. (p. 120)

According to the levels theory, primary and secondary could refer to which information-processing level controls the action. When the dimensional structure is obvious human adults spontaneously sort by dimensions, indicating that the higher encoding level prevailed. Abstracting the values on integral dimensions is more difficult than on separable dimensions and consequently requires more concerted effort; but obviously it can be done. The implication is that among adults the spontaneous disposition to classify on the basis of an abstracted dimension is influenced by how easily the relevant and irrelevant features are perceptually differentiated and, as Garner suggests, the motivation of the subject.

Smith and Kemler (1977) adapted this sorting procedure for use with children at three age levels between 5 and 11. Their experiments used only separable dimensions because they were investigating developmental change in the spontaneous disposition to sort by dimension. A representative experiment in this line of research also used stimulus triads, structured as illustrated in Fig. 9.4. Instead of being told to sort the stimuli into two classes the children were asked to "put together in one group the two that go together." How the children sorted depended on their age level. The 5-year-olds were disposed to sort the separable compounds by overall similarity; the 10-year-olds were disposed to sort them by dimension and the 7-year-olds were about as likely to do one as the other. A subsequent experiment (Kemler, 1982) found that 4-year-olds, exposed to the same procedure, were least likely to sort by dimension.

The increasing developmental tendency to sort by dimension has since been verified under a range of different conditions. This long-term, gradually increasing, ontogenetic disposition to sort by dimension converges neatly on the ontogenetic trends to make reversal shifts. To account for these and other related results Kemler and Smith concluded that young children "apprehend in an integral manner stimuli that are perceived separably by adults" (p. 295). Kemler (1983) later interpreted these findings as indicating that development proceeds from a relatively undifferentiated state in which information is processed in a global holistic mode to a differentiated state in which information is processed analytically. Whether this interpretation represents a real or merely semantic difference from mine depends on further articulation of both conceptions. Meanwhile, these data provide converging evidence for the existence of two qualitatively different encoding modes. One mode is nonselective and the other is selective and the disposition for the selective mode to prevail to increases ontogenetically in humans. These data are also consistent with the hypothesis that underlying selective encoding is a sorting operation.

Articulating Higher Level Encoding

A mechanism that could conceivably explain both the experimental and developmental data would look to a higher level neural network that matures relatively slowly and provides for the capacity to sort the output from the information encoded by the lower level into categories or classes with respect to some abstracted property or properties selected for the potential control of action.

Thus, while the higher level processes is selective, in that only a part of the perceptible input is utilized, the process is also integrative, in that it combines the information from all of the compounds, present or absent, to arrive at the classification appropriate to the given context. The relationship between selection and context provides the system with the flexibility to classify the same discriminanda in different ways for different purposes, as when the learner classifies the discriminanda on the basis of whichever dimension happens to be relevant. This very flexibility would require many more neural connections than the less flexible processing at the cognitively impenetrable, nonselective encoding level, where the representation is relatively fixed. The requisite increase in neuronal connectivity could ultimately help to explain the observed developmental differences in the probability of selective encoding reported in chapter 3.

EXECUTIVE COMPONENT

While the function of the information-processing component is to encode the information impinging on the sensory system into usable form, the function of the executive component is to use the output of the information processor to produce an appropriate response. In discrimination learning procedures the appropriate response has to be learned. The levels theory assumes that, while the lower level executive mode allows for gradual learning in the associative mode, there is among humans—and possibly other animals—a higher executive level that solves problems in a more intelligent mode. Understanding exactly how this higher mode functions presents science with the most complex problem it has yet faced. There must be some advantage to approaching this complexity, as Mendel approached heredity, by studying its simplest manifestation. Bidimensional discrimination learning is a very simple problem for the intelligent mode. The commensurately simple supposition, is that in this mode the learner applies the win-stay-lose-shift rule to test successive hypotheses about which features predict the reinforcement contingencies.

An hypothesis is defined here as an informed guess about an impending event. Discovering the correct hypothesis produces a quantum leap from a presolution to a solution state. A rule is regarded as a prescribed guide for conduct mediated by a cognitive process partly determined by the agent's intentions. Rules may be formally adopted, as in the rules of a game, or they may come to serve as a guide for practice through experience, as in the acquisition of grammatical rules. Rules are generative; they can generate appropriate responses to novel situations.

Hypothesis-Testing Theory

The notion that hypothesis testing could be investigated with the use of discrimination learning procedures was earlier proposed by Levine to investigate learning sets in monkeys and later applied to adult humans. (See Levine, 1975, for an overview of this research program.) The typical procedure used with adult humans required choosing between pairs of stimuli that differed on four to eight visual dimensions. Only one value on one dimension was correct, the remaining dimensions were irrelevant. During the training phase the learner was told whether each choice was correct or incorrect. The training trials were followed by a set of blank trials, so-called because no further information about correctness was given. The discriminanda on the blank trials were arranged in a manner that enabled the experimenter to use the pattern of choices to discern the learner's guiding hypothesis. With this procedure Levine was able to show that the adults' solutions followed the win-stay-lose-shift rule.

To explain this behavior, Levine proposed that each adult arrives at the solution by sampling *hypotheses* (*H*'s) from some universe of *H*'s. The universe is partitioned into a correct domain, which contains the solution *H*, and a variety of incorrect domains. A subject will be in one of two states; he or she may be sampling from an incorrect domain in which case nothing will be learned about the solution during the training trials. For example, a suspicious subject may assume the experimenter has some hidden purpose and set about testing *H*'s about what that purpose might be. Such a subject may break out of this nonproductive state when none of the *H*'s are confirmed. A subject in the productive state will be sampling *H*'s from the correct domain to form a subset of *H*'s that can vary from one to all of those in the domain. How many *H*'s are sampled can vary with the individual or the type of problem. Because each *H* leads to a different choice response, the subject mostly chooses from this subset a single *H*—referred to as the working hypothesis—to serve as a basis for responding on a given trial. Confirmation causes the correct working *H* to be retained. Disconfirmation causes an incorrect working *H* to be abandoned, and weakens in lesser degree the other disconfirmed *H*'s in the set. Levine (1975, p. 280) was prescient enough to remark that this theory presupposes a problem-solving orientation and is, therefore, probably not the proper conception for rats, monkeys or young children. He went on to suggest that a different model would seem more appropriate for their behavior in comparable situations but considered the form of such a model to be a problem for the future.

As for how the information in the discriminanda is processed by adult humans, Levine proposed a mediating response theory. His premise was that the learner whose *H* is in the correct domain implicitly verbalizes only one or more of the *features* of the chosen stimulus and rehearses them until the feedback appears. After a correct choice is produced, the learner will have memorized a set that contains the correct H. If an incorrect choice is produced all of the memorized H's are disconfirmed and the learner can arrive at a subset containing the correct H by memorizing the complement of the disconfirmed set. As a result of the confirmation and disconfirmation the learner gradually reduces the set until only the correct working H remains.

Although the H's in Levine's theory refer to features rather than dimensions, he also reports that prior to solution the adults in his experiments sampled neither the correct H nor the other H on the same dimension (Levine, Miller, & Steinmeyer, 1967). For instance, if *small* were the correct feature, the subject would try neither *large* nor *small* before attaining solution. In other words, an adult who tests the incorrect value on the relevant dimension, almost invariably tests the correct value on the same dimension next trial.

These data are consistent with the premise that the higher level problem-solving process entails (a) successively categorizing the information in discrimanda in terms of the represented dimensions, and (b) using the win-stay-lose-shift rule to determine which dimension is relevant and which value on the dimension is correct.

Selective Attention Theory

Trabasso and Bower (1968) also used a discrimination learning procedure with human adults. Their purpose was to test a mathematical model of selective attention that was intended originally to apply to learning in infrahuman as well as human learners. This model was introduced in chapter 5 to describe problem solving in the higher mode, as manifested in the optional shift procedure. Now the theory underlying the model and some related experiments are discussed in greater detail. The theory assumed the discriminanda are perceived by the learner as an assemblage of stimulus *dimensions* each of which has two values. Learning entails alternating between a search and test mode. In the search mode the learner decides which dimensions to select from the array and how to classify the values on the selected dimensions. The product is a set of plausible hypotheses regarding the correct rule for the classification of responses. This set of hypotheses is referred to as a focus sample. In the test mode, which operates on the following trial, the subject checks the correctness of the current focus sample. When the response is confirmed the hypotheses in the focus are retained; when in error the hypotheses are rejected and a new focus sample is generated. The alternation between search and test goes on until a solution focus is arrived at that provides for the criterion run of errorless solutions. Dimensional salience enters only in determining the composition of the focus sample during the search operation. According to this theory learning occurs only after an error. Such a formulation could be consistent with levels theory's conception of problem solving in the higher mode, except for a crucial difference. No allowance was made for lower level learning.

Trabasso and Bower also performed a series of experiments to test their theory from which I selected the most pertinent to discuss. All of the selected experiments used a redundant-relevant-cue (RRC) discrimination learning procedure with abstract geometric discriminanda. The basic RRC procedure entailed a learning phase in which the discriminanda were compounded of two relevant and redundant dimensions along with a number of other irrelevant dimensions. The learning phase was followed by a transfer phase designed to determine what was learned about the previously relevant dimensions. Unlike the learners in our experiments, these learners were explicitly told the purpose of the research was to learn how students make classifications. Moreover, they were shown examples of the discriminanda and all the *dimensions were named*. After this they were shown a deck of cards on which the discriminanda were drawn, told the cards could be divided into two classes, and informed that their job was to *learn a rule* that would enable them to presently classify every card correctly. They were also told to begin by guessing, after which they would be informed about the correct answer and allowed a few seconds to study each card before the next card would be shown.

The discriminanda in the first set of experiments differed on five binary geometric dimensions, three of which were always irrelevant. In the training phase two dimensions were relevant and redundant and three were irrelevant. The students were instructed to learn the rule that would classify each card in the deck into either an Alpha or a Beta. They were then trained to a criterion of 32 consecutive correct responses before the test phase was instituted. After the preliminary training the students were shown a new deck of cards, told the deck was similar to the previous deck, and instructed to sort all of the cards in the new deck into Alpha's and Beta's according to the rule they had just learned, but this time they would not be told whether they were right or wrong.

The purpose of the test phase was to determine what had been learned about the two redundant relevant dimensions in the training phase. Half the cards in the new deck tested for learning on the basis of *one* of the relevant dimensions by simply eliminating the other relevant dimension. The learner who responded correctly on these cards could be presumed to have learned to classify on the basis of the remaining relevant dimension. The other half of the deck tested for learning on the basis of the other relevant dimension in the same manner. After the entire test deck was sorted, the adult completed a questionnaire that asked what rule was learned with the first deck and what rule was used to sort the second deck.

There were three experiments in this set. One experiment tested the learners on the two phases of the basic RRC procedure described earlier.

On the test deck most learners (.85) classified on the basis of either one or the other of the two previously relevant dimensions. These learners sorted the cards with the selected dimension almost perfectly correctly and performed close to chance on the rest. A much smaller group (.15) classified nearly perfectly on the basis of both dimensions. The correspondence between how learners sorted the test deck and their verbalized description on the questionnaire was almost perfect. Apparently, most adults tested one dimension at a time and stopped testing when they discovered a rule that worked. Whether the two-dimension solvers tested two dimensions at a time, or went on to test others after finding one that worked, was not revealed.

The second experiment used a procedure that, like the optional shift, consisted of three phases. In the first phase only one dimension was relevant and all of the others were irrelevant. These adults were trained to a criterion of ten successive correct responses before the RRC phase was introduced. Here the initially relevant dimension remained relevant and correct, but one of the previously irrelevant dimensions became relevant and redundant. The RRC phase, which consisted of 32 trials, was followed by the test phase just described. In the test phase *all* of these adults solved the two-relevant-dimensions problem on the basis of the single relevant dimension on which they had been pretrained. Apparently adults are not likely to sort on the basis of a redundant relevant dimension that was previously made irrelevant. Recall that almost all of the adults in the optional shift experiments behaved in the same way although the represented dimension were never named and they were neither instructed to classify the discriminanda nor find the underlying rule.

The third experiment of this set also trained adults on the basic RRC procedure but they were pretrained with one of the two to-be-relevant dimensions absent. Thus, in this condition, the second relevant dimension in the RRC phase was novel. Only a few adults (.08) subsequently sorted on the basis of the novel cue; that small proportion was highly skewed in favor of the more salient novel cue. This result demonstrated again that a confirmed hypothesis continues for a while to control adult's sorting behavior, except possibly if the newly relevant dimension is more intrinsically salient than the older one. Apparently adults are not insensitive to intrinsic salience, which is, however, mostly overridden by relevance.

All of these results are consistent with the assumption that, when are confronted with a problem for which there is no appropriate automatic response available, adult humans are likely to invoke higher level processes. The higher encoding level will then classify the discriminanda by dimension and the higher executive level will use a rule to test hypotheses about which dimension is relevant and which overt response is correct.

The last pertinent experiment concerns the effect of overtraining on the transfer phase of the RRC procedure. The instructions to the learners in this experiment were similar to those described before, but the response differed. Instead of naming the discriminanda Alpha or Omega, the learners pressed a button marked "One" or "Two." Feedback lamps, one above each button, provided the information about the correct response. After pretraining that established one dimension as relevant, half of the students were trained to a criterion of 10 successive correct choices in the RRC training phase, where both dimensions were redundant and relevant. The other half were trained to the same criterion followed by 50 overtraining trials with both dimensions still present. Training under both experimental conditions was followed by 20 test trials in which one dimension was eliminated, interspersed with 20 test trials in which the other dimension was eliminated. No feedback was presented on the test trials.

Overtraining significantly increased the proportion of two-cue learners from .17 to .46. The behavior of the learners in the control condition confirms the previous finding; the number of hypotheses tested usually is restricted to one dimension at a time. If there is not much time or additional training between the attainment of criterion and testing, behavior continues to be controlled by that selected dimension. The difference between the behavior of the learners in the overtrained and control condition indicates, however, that increasing the number of trials after criterion is attained increases the tendency to also respond to the other relevant dimension, which did not initially control choice behavior. This outcome is inconsistent with the attention theory because learning did occur on the correct overtraining trials. The adults in the overtraining condition were increasing the tendency to respond correctly to the unselected dimension, while they continued to respond correctly to the selected dimension.

On the other hand, this outcome is consistent with the assumption of the levels theory that both modes will function in concert as long as they do not lead to incompatible behaviors. During overtraining the disposition to associate the correct choice with the appropriate value on the second relevant dimension was not incompatible with continuing to respond to the first one. At the same time the overtraining provided the opportunity for the relatively slow, gradual, lower level, automatic learning, which applies to all of the perceptible dimensions, to become manifest. The magnitude of this increase should be a joint function of the number of overtraining trials and the degree of intrinsic salience of the represented dimensions.

Trabasso and Bower (1968) finally concluded that to propose a theory supposedly valid for animals and men may be unrealistic "given the apparently vast differences between men and even primates in their categorization capabilities and their competence in transforming information. . . . Possibly more rapid advances will come from the development of learning theories having specific phylogenetic reference" (p. 233).

ARTICULATING THE EXECUTIVE LEVELS

The cumulative data, taken together, suggest the following tentative conception of how the higher level system operates. The higher level information-processing system sorts the output of the lower level into appropriate, hierarchically organized, mutually exclusive categories. In discrimination learning the appropriate superordinate categories are the dimensions represented in the discriminanda. The higher executive level uses the output of the higher level information processor to determine which dimension is relevant and which responses to the values on that dimension are appropriate. The output of the higher executive level is transmitted to the lower executive level, which sets in motion the overt response.

What activates the higher level modes? As Levine (1975) proposed, the activation of the higher level depends on a problem-solving orientation. Such orientation may be regarded as a motivational state aroused by a new problem for which, by definition, the learner has no appropriate automatic response available. The motivational state may also be aroused by instructions, for instance instructions to classify the discriminanda. The lack of an appropriate automatic response may either refer to the absence of any automatic response or to the availability of an inappropriate one. In the latter case, control by the higher mode implies the capacity to inhibit incompatible lower level responses. Given that the activation of the higher mode is based on a motivational state aroused by a *new* problem, the degree of arousal can be expected to diminish with repetition. Thus, while control by the higher level is gradually weakened, the lower level connection between *all* of the relevant cues and the correct response is gradually strengthened. In the cited overlearning experiment the increasing strength of the lower level connection manifests itself in the increase in two-cue learners. The magnitude of two-cue solutions should be an increasing function of the number of overtraining trials and of the intrinsic salience of the represented dimensions.

How does the higher level determine which dimension is relevant and which response is appropriate? Presumably by successive hypothesis testing, a higher level trial-and-error process that successively classifies the compounded stimuli in terms of the available *mutually exclusive* features until the correct features are encountered. I suspect that, as Johnson-Laird (1993) proposed, this process is tacit rather than explicit. The reinforcement contingencies, instead of automatically strengthening or weakening response tendencies, sooner or later disclose which dimension is relevant and which feature is correct. As noted by Trabasso and Bower (1968), and supported by our own data, intrinsic salience enters into the order in which the dimensions are tested for relevance. We found that, if the relevant dimension is salient, the solution among adults occurs sooner. Another variable that would affect higher level problem solving would be the number of irrelevant dimensions simply because there are more potentially tenable hypotheses to test. Nevertheless, while learning to make the correct choice in the lower level mode is gradual, solutions in the higher level mode are all-or-none. In principle, the higher level can not only solve simple problems more efficiently than the lower level but can also solve difficult problems beyond the scope of the lower level.

Family Resemblance and Classical Categories

The evidence for differentiating between higher and lower level operations comes from well-controlled, simple, laboratory experiments. Outlining how the levels notion could clarify the difference between family resemblance and classical categorization illustrates how these ideas can extend to a wider arena.

Family Resemblance Categories

Single sets of entities with many highly correlated features, where no one feature or set of features serves to sharply differentiate members from non-members, are referred to as family resemblance categories. Most natural categories—such as birds or fruits, and common artifacts—such as furniture or clothing—take the family resemblance form (Rosch, 1973; Wittgenstein; 1953). Membership in such categories is based on the overall similarity of the member to a prototype (Mervis & Rosch, 1981). The similarity is variable; some members are very close to the prototype and some are so different as to questionable. Consequently the borders of family resemblance categories are said to be fuzzy (Massaro, 1987) or unbounded (Harnad, 1987). Human adults generally agree about how typical or representative of the category a given entity is (Malt & Smith, 1984). *Apple* is, for instance, rated as somewhat more typical of the *fruit* category than *raisin* and much more typical than *pumpkin*. Typicality predicts how quickly a member of such a category can be named. *Apples*, for instance, would be named quicker than *pumpkins*. Typicality is a function of the number and salience of the properties an instance shares with the exemplar. (Smith, 1989). For instance *robin* would be closer to the exemplar of the *bird* category than *ostrich*. Especially pertinent is the fact that children learn to name the typical instances of a category before atypical instances (Rosch, 1978).

The levels theory could be extended to account for the formation of family resemblance categories, and for the related evidence, by showing that nonselective encoding and associative learning are both operative. The information in this kind of category is encoded nonselectively—as opposed to selectively—in that all of the perceptible features enter into the determination of membership. Others have made a similar observation expressed in different terms. Kemler (1983) refers to the instances in family resemblance categories as being perceived holistically as opposed to analytically. Harnad (1987) refers to them as analog, as opposed to categorical, representations of the sensory input. Markman (1989) suggests they are based on nonanalytic strategies.

Associative learning is operative in learning to identify—make a common response—to the different instances in the category. In humans the common response to different instances is likely to be a verbal label, as when a toddler learns to apply the word *fruit* to apples, peaches, and pears. Each rewarded coupling of the label to an instance of the category would increase the strength of the association between the label and all of the impinging features of each instance regardless of how typical the instance is or how characteristic the features are. However, according to continuity theory, how quickly and how strongly the association is formed is learned should depend on how many times the label is associated with a given instance, the ratio of relevant to irrelevant features, and the relative salience of the relevant dimension. Hence the typical instance is named more rapidly by adults and learned more easily by children because it is relatively common or it has more relevant or more salient features. This strength would also be reflected in the typicality measure.

Furthermore, if only nonselective encoding and associative learning need be invoked, infrahuman animals should be capable of acquiring family resemblance categories. Operant learning experiments (e.g., Cerella, 1979; D'Amato & Van Sant, 1988; Herrnstein, 1979; Schrier & Brady, 1987) demonstrated that animals—mostly pigeons but in some cases monkeys—can learn to respond differentially to members and nonmembers of natural categories such as bodies of water, trees, fish, oak leaves, and people. The typical procedure in these experiments was to use many different photographs of natural settings as discriminanda. Half of the photographs contained different members of a given natural category (positive instances) and half did not (negative instances). The animals were rewarded for responding in the presence of the positive instances but received no reward for responding in the presence of negative instances. As a result, they presently learned to respond more frequently to the positive than to the negative instances. Training was followed by transfer tests that compared the response to new positive and negative instances. In most cases the animals responded somewhat more frequently to the new positive instances than to the new negative instances.

This learning required a great many trials and the transfer to new instances, although usually statistically reliable, was also usually weak for two reasons. The naturalistic photographs contained a great many irrelevant features and the salience of the relevant features in the selected photographs was often low. Nevertheless, as Herrnstein (1990) concluded, there is evidence that infrahuman animals can form something akin to family resemblance categories. At the same time he was careful to distinguish "open-ended categorization," which is based on past experience, from "categorization based on abstract relations." He also noted that "we see the largest gaps in comparative performance at the level of abstract relations" (p. 163).

Classical Categories

Although family resemblance categories have fuzzy borders and no one set of features sharply differentiates members from nonmembers, classical categories can be defined by a set of necessary and sufficient properties and membership is sharply defined. For instance, an *even number* is a number that can be divided by two without leaving any remainder. This property is sufficient to define any even number. An uncle is the brother of a parent is another example. Classical categories are often invented for some axiomatic field, like mathematics, or for some technical purpose, such as codifying family relations (Smith, 1989).

There are other important differences between family and classical categories. A family category, such as trees, refers to a single set of entities. Classical categories differentiate between two or more sets of entities. If there were no even numbers there would be no point in a category of odd numbers. If there were no other categories in a family, an uncle would have no meaning. While membership in a fuzzy category is based on the overall resemblance of an instance to a prototype, membership in a classical category depends on an abstracted set of properties. This set of properties is selected on the basis of a rational superordinate structure that serves to reliably sort the individual instances into distinctive sets. For instance, an even number can be sharply differentiated from an odd number on the basis of its divisibility. Divisibility is a rational superordinate structure of the number system.

Also, family resemblance categories are insensitive to context—a rose is a rose is a rose—while the selected features subserving classical categories are highly context sensitive. As defined by Harnad (1987), to be context sensitive means that the categories are formed by selectively encoding the features sufficient to sort the negative and positive instances appropriately in terms of some rational superstructure. The rational superstructure can be different in different contexts and hence the same entities can be formed into different categories. Numbers, for instance, can be classified in terms of many different rational superstructures.

The implication of this analysis is that the acquisition of family resemblance categories, particularly among infrahuman animals and young children depends only on the capacity to invoke *lower level* nonselective encoding and associative learning processes. But the formation of classical categories requires the capacity to invoke the *higher level* processes that sort the information into categories on the basis of selected properties and use hypothesis testing to determine which of the selected properties are relevant to the task in hand. Assuming the higher level capacities develop later than the lower ones, both phylogenetically and ontogenetically, helps to explain why adult humans are more capable than any other animals in the formation and use of classical categories and why, among humans, this same capacity can take many years to attain its ultimate level.

The implication for further research is that simple discrimination learning procedures, like the optional shift, can provide a controlled way to investigate the nature and development of the complex capacities that underlie classical categorization. Understanding this development is especially worthwhile because, while family resemblance categorization may be more common, classical categorization plays a more important role in human intellectual enterprises, including science, mathematics, and logic.

CONCLUSIONS

Higher level selective encoding, as manifested in discrimination learning, could be characterized in terms of three alternative kinds of operations performed on the feature output of the lower encoding level. One kind of operation directs attention to the relevant features by increasing their perceived salience. A second operation attaches verbal labels to the relevant features, which serve to mediate choice behavior. The third operation implicitly sorts the discriminanda as correct or incorrect on the basis of the abstracted features of the relevant dimension. The evidence presented here favors a sorting operation, which leaves the perception of the features unaltered, but can be elicited or directed by verbal labels.

The saltatory learning, which characterizes discrimination learning in the higher level executive mode, determines which dimension is relevant by using a win-stay-lose-shift rule to test successive hypotheses about which features predict the reinforcement contingencies until the correct hypothesis is discovered. This mode is presumably activated by a motivational state that can be aroused by the presentation of a new problem, for which no appropriate response is automatically available. The difference between higher and lower level functioning elucidates the difference between family resemblance and classical categorization.

CHAPTER TEN

An Overview

Any large computation should be split up and implemented as a collection of small sub-parts that are as nearly independent of one another as the overall task allows. If a process is not designed in this way, a small change in one place will have consequences in many other places. This means that the process as a whole becomes extremely difficult to debug or improve, whether by a designer or in the course of natural evolution, because a small change to improve one part has to be accompanied by many simultaneous compensating changes elsewhere.

—Marr (1976, p. 485)

All the data reviewed in the previous chapters can be explained by the few premises that together form the levels theory. The premises are broadly stated in the expectation that subsequent investigation will amplify, specify, and modify them as the data demands. Because cognitive and cortical development must in some way be related, the theory is modeled, in the substantive sense, after the central nervous system. Granted, as potential steps to an inclusive neuroscience theory, these ideas require further articulation. Nevertheless, in research of this kind it is well to maintain the perspective of a long-term strategy that seeks ultimately to relate behavioral phenomena to their biological substrates.

Strictly speaking the theory is about the structure, function, operation, and development of the system that governs discrimination learning. The structural aspect identifies the components of the system and describes their interrelations. The functional aspect describes the purpose served by each component part. The operational aspect specifies how the components fulfill their functions. The developmental aspect describes the progressive and cumulative changes within the system during the course of human ontogeny and phylogeny. Although the theory is anchored in observable behaviors, it also includes indirectly defined theoretical constructs. The constructs conform to what is known about the neurological infrastructures in the anticipation that psychological and neurological theorizing about cognitive development will gradually coalesce.

The basic premise of is that, like the central nervous system, the psychological system governing behavior is differentiated into separable but interacting subsystems. The primary differentiation is into an afferent, information-processing system and an efferent, executive system. The overall function of the information-processing system is to encode the impinging sensory input into usable form. The overall function of the executive system is to produce the appropriate action, based on the input from the information-processing system.

Another general premise is that each of these two systems has become differentiated into overlaid structural levels, with the higher levels developing later than the lower levels. Each successive level increases the capacity of the system to function in a more flexible and voluntary mode. The term *levels* has three different but interrelated meanings in this theory, where it refers to way-stations in the central nervous system, to stages in the evolution of the human nervous system, and to aspects of human ontogenetic development.

In modern biology, development can refer to ontogenetic changes within the individual or to phylogenetic changes in the historical evolution of the species. Some linkage is assumed to exist between the two forms of development but precisely how the ontogeny and phylogeny of different systems are related has been controversial since Darwin's theory of evolution was first proposed. The linkage assumed by the levels theory is that, when more than one level is present in a species, the previously evolved level develops earlier in the individual than the more recently evolved higher level. This assumption extends a generalization about prenatal development, formulated by von Baer in 1828, to postnatal development. According to Baer's law, the more general structures common to all members of a superordinate class of animals develop earlier in the individual than the more special structures that distinguish the various, more recently evolved, subordinate classes (Balinsky, 1970).

As noted by S. J. Gould (1977), ". . . von Baer's theory of increasing differentiation calls only upon a conservative principle of heredity to preserve stubbornly the early stages of ontogeny in all members of a group, while evolution proceeds by altering later stages" (p. 3). For example, the paleocortex, a structure common to all vertebrates, develops earlier than the neocortex, which distinguishes mammals from the rest of the vertebrates. Likewise, there are structures within the cortex, such as the prefrontal lobe and secondary association areas, that distinguish primates, especially humans, from the other mammals. Using neuronal myelination and arborization as measures, there is evidence that these earlier emerging structures mature earlier in the human individual. The levels theory proposed here makes the common assumption that, in the central nervous system, the more recently developed structures are overlaid on the earlier ones and function to successively increase the capacity of the organism to adapt to change. These general premises, applied to discrimination learning, serve to differentiate two functional levels within the information processing and executive components.

In the information-processing component there is a lower nonselective, feature detection level and a higher selective, classification level. The function of the lower level is to detect all of the perceptible features in the discriminanda. The features that are detected, and their perceived salience, are determined by their physical properties, in concert with the biological sensory system of the learner. The function of the higher level is to abstract only the relevant information for further processing. The higher level operates on the input from the lower level by sorting the information on the basis of the features on the relevant dimension. Which dimension is relevant can vary with the demands of the task and the intentions of the learner. The distinction between lower and higher level information processing is consistent with the general agreement among neuroscientists that sensory information is processed at successive, hierarchically organized levels in the central nervous system.

Likewise, two executive levels can be differentiated. The function of the lower level is to produce stable, automatic, learned behavior, which it accomplishes by means of an incremental, associative process. The associative process provides a gradual, automatic increase in the relative tendency of the correct value on the relevant dimension to evoke the appropriate response. Although associative learning is usually regarded as slow, stupid, and tedious it has the advantage of producing stable behavioral change. Moreover, associative learning can be rapid and efficient if the ratio of relevant to *ir*relevant dimensions is substantial, or if the intrinsic salience differential markedly favors the relevant dimension, or both. For these reasons associative learning can be expected to work well among species whose sensory capacities are well adapted to a reasonably stable eco-niche where, by virtue of natural selection, the important things would be composed of either many relevant or highly salient dimensions.

But the inverse is also true; automatic, associative learning can be very slow and inefficient if the *ir*relevant dimensions either greatly outnumber the relevant dimensions or are much more intrinsically salient, or both. Species like humans, who create their own environments, are likely to encounter problems in which relevant dimensions are neither intrinsically salient nor numerous. Consequently, circumstances can arise that require adjustments to situations in which associative learning is not at all efficient. As a result another, less automatic, more intelligent mode of learning presently evolved. When applied to discrimination learning, this mode entails testing successive hypotheses about how the discriminanda should be classified in order to solve the problem. The outcome is faster and more efficient problem solution. However, the more facile, rational, higher level solution has one disadvantage. Unlike a well-learned association, the intelligent solution is not necessarily recalled when the same problem arises again at some later time.

An optimal system would allow for two learning modes. One mode provides for rational but easily forgotten solutions to new problems and the other mode provides for automatic but well-retained responses to recurring problems. Both modes are available to humans. The lower level executive component operates in the associative mode to produce adaptive, gradual, and sustained behavioral change. The higher level executive component operates in a rational mode to provide relatively rapid, intelligent, but not well remembered, solutions to problems.

Each successive, superimposed level extends the repertoire of the organism without depriving the lower level of its function. The two encoding levels work together in that the lower nonselective provides the information on which the higher level operates. The two executive levels also work together in an integrated fashion. Higher level problem solving is invoked when a situation arises for which there is no satisfactory, automatic, lower level response. During higher level problem solving, lower level learning remains operative. With repetition of the correct response, control by the higher level gradually decreases and control by the lower level gradually increases. Thus, the two levels work together in harmony unless they lead to incompatible behaviors. In that case, which level will prevail depends jointly on the developmental status of the system as well as on the previous experience and current motivation of the individual.

The final set of premises concerns development within the system. The higher and lower encoding and executive levels are assumed to be mediated by different structures in the central nervous system. The lower level structures develop earlier and faster than the higher level structures both ontogenetically and phylogenetically. Among humans the higher levels continue to mature until young adulthood. The disposition for behavior to be controlled by the higher levels is a function of the system's developmental status. Of course, providing a role for maturation by no means precludes either the proximal effect of environment on behavior or the distal effect of experience on subsequent cognitive development. Rather, a levels theory can produce a vehicle for differentiating between the variables that influence immediate performance and those that determine ultimate development. Such a differentiation could have considerable practical value.

Although these assumptions are plausible in the light of the data, there is a potential criticism that should be addressed before closing. Because almost all of the evidence cited in support of the various premises was drawn from discrimination learning methodology, it could appear that the theory concerns discrimination learning and not cognitive development. Actually this theory is about the system that governs discrimination learning and about how this system develops. Discrimination learning allows for comparisons between infrahuman and humans at different age levels under well-controlled conditions. Just as Mendel used peas and Morgan used fruit flies to investigate the system that produces the transmission of hereditary characteristics, one can use discrimination learning to investigate the system that produces simple problem solving.

Moreover, a number of cognitive psychologists, using a variety of different data bases, have also distinguished between two qualitatively different forms of information processing that bear on the differences between selective and nonselective encoding. To name a few, Broadbent (1977) proposed a model in which information processing occurs in levels specifically traced back to Hughlings Jackson. Shiffrin and Schneider (1977) differentiated between automatic and controlled processes. Posner (1984) distinguished "automatic, unattended" from "active" processing of information. Pylyshyn (1980) argued for a fundamental distinction between noncognitive and cognitive processing, Fodor (1983, 1985) carried this argument further by proposing a "principled distinction" between perception and cognition. Schachter (1987) distinguished between implicit and explicit memory. Although these various distinctions were not necessarily related to developmental change, they easily could be.

There are also a number of neuroscientists who posited distinctions that bear on the dual executive modes proposed in the levels theory. To mention a few: Warrington and Weiskrantz (1982) distinguished between horizontal and vertical association. Mishkin and Petri (1984) distinguished between habit and memory. Squire (1987) distinguished between procedural (knowing how) and declarative (knowing what) memory. Goldman-Rakic (1990) distinguished between working and reference memory. According to Petri and Mishkin (1994), the upshot of much neuropsychological research is that there is more than one system in the brain for learning and retention: one system is consistent with the behaviorist and the other with the cognitivist approaches.

The various cited formulations come to the issue from different theoretical vantages and cover a wide range of behavioral and neurological evidence, yet all conclude there are two different modes of information processing or two different modes of executive control, not unlike those proposed by the levels theory. However, these theories and their evidential bases are so divergent they have not coalesced into a widely accepted, common formulation. Relating them to each other in a clear and cogent manner, and hence to the distinctions made in this levels theory, is not yet feasible, except for one thing. In each case, the two modes can be described in terms of levels in which one level functions in a more flexible, voluntary, and efficient manner than the other. The point is that other behavioral and neurological evidence points to qualitatively different modes of information processing and executive control. Only one small step is needed to cast these modes into a developmental format.

The conclusion all this leads up to is that the proposed levels theory provides a plausible account of some critical aspects of cognitive development and may eventually provide a few stepping stones toward understanding the underlying structure, function, and development in the brain.

References

Altman, J. (1978). Three levels of mentation and the hierarchic organization of the human brain. In G. A. Miller & A. E. Lenneberg (Eds.), *Psychology and biology of language and thought* (pp. 87–105). New York: Academic Press.

Allport, A. (1989). Visual attention. In M. I. Posner (Ed.), *Foundations of cognitive science* (pp. 632–682). Cambridge, MA: MIT Press.

Anderson, J. R. (1982). Acquisition of cognitive skill. *Psychological Review, 89,* 369–406.

Balinsky, B. I. (1970). *An introduction to embryology.* Philadelphia: Saunders.

Basden, B. H., & Kendler, T. S. (1976). Dominance as a function of cue similarity: A test of the intrinsic cue dominance model. *Learning and Motivation, 7,* 132–140.

Bessemer, D. W. (1967). *Retention of object discriminations by learning set experienced monkeys* (Doctoral dissertation, University of Wisconsin). Ann Arbor, MI: University Microfilms No. 67-16, 893.

Bessemer, D. W., & Stollnitz, F. (1971). Retention of discriminations and an analysis of learning set. In A. M. Schrier & F. Stollnitz (Eds.), *Behavior of nonhuman primates* (Vol. 4). New York: Academic Press.

Block, K. K., Erickson, J. R., & McHoes, L. N. (1973). Quantitative models for children's concept learning from a developmental perspective. *Developmental Psychology, 8,* 187–201.

Bourne, L. E., & Restle, F. (1959). Mathematical theory of concept identification. *Psychological Review, 66,* 278–296.

Bower, G. H., & Trabasso, T. (1964). Concept identification. In R. C. Atkinson (Ed.), *Studies in mathematical psychology* (pp. 32–94). Stanford, CA: Stanford University Press.

Broadbent, D. E. (1958). *Perception and communication.* Elmsford, NY: Pergamon Press.

Broadbent, D. E. (1977). Level, hierarchies, and the locus of control. *Quarterly Journal of Experimental Psychology, 29,* 181–201.

Brookshire, K. H., Warren, J. M., & Ball, G. G. (1961). Reversal and transfer learning following overtraining in rat and chicken. *Journal of Comparative and Physiological Psychology, 54,* 98–102.

Bush, R. R., & Mosteller, F. A. (1951) A mathematical model for simple learning. *Psychological Review, 58,* 313–321.

170

Buss, A. H. (1953). Rigidity as a function of reversal and nonreversal shifts in the learning of successive discriminations. *Journal of Experimental Psychology, 45*, 75–81.

Buss, A. H. (1956). Reversal and nonreversal shifts in concept formation with partial reinforcement eliminated. *Journal of Experimental Psychology, 52*, 162–166.

Capaldi, E. J., & Stevenson, H. W. (1957). Response reversal following different amounts of learning. *Journal of Comparative and Physiological Psychology, 50*, 195–198.

Cerella, J. (1979). Visual classes and categories in the pigeon. *Journal of Experimental Psychology: Human Perception and Performance, 5*, 68–77.

Changeux, J. (1985). *Neuronal man: The biology of mind.* New York: Pantheon.

Collins, A. M., & Quillian, M. R. (1969). Retrieval time from semantic memory. *Journal of Verbal Learning and Verbal Behavior, 8*, 240–247.

Coutant, L. W., & Warren, J. M. (1966). Reversal and nonreversal shifts by cats and rhesus monkeys. *Journal of Comparative and Physiological Psychology, 61*, 484–487.

D'Amato, M. R., & Fazzaro, J. (1966). Attention and cue-producing behavior in the monkey. *Journal of Experimental Analysis of Behavior, 9*, 460–478.

D'Amato, M. R., & Jagoda, M. R. (1962). Overlearning and position reversal. *Journal of Experimental Psychology, 64*, 117–122.

D'Amato, M. R., & Van Sant, P. (1988). The person concept in monkeys (*Cebus apella*). *Journal of Experimental Psychology: Animal Behavior Processes, 14*, 43–55.

Dawkins, R. (1986). *The blind watchmaker.* New York: Norton.

Deese, J., & Hulse, S. H. (1967). *The psychology of learning* (3rd ed.). New York: McGraw-Hill.

Eimas, P. D. (1969a). Attentional processes in optional shift behavior. *Journal of Comparative and Physiological Psychology, 69*, 166–169.

Eimas, P. D. (1969b). A developmental study of hypothesis behavior and focusing. *Journal of Experimental Child Psychology, 8*, 160–172.

Eimas, P., Siqueland, E. R., Juszyk, P., & Vigorito, J. (1971). Speech perception in infants. *Science, 171*, 303–306.

Eninger, M. U. (1952). Habit summation in a selective learning problem. *Journal of Comparative and Physiological Psychology, 46*, 604–608.

Flechsig, P. (1901). Developmental (myelogenetic) localization of the cerebral cortex in the human subject. *Lancet*, 1027.

Fodor, J. A. (1983). *The modularity of mind.* Cambridge, MA: MIT Press.

Fodor, J. A. (1985). Multiple book-review of "The Modularity of Mind." *Behavioral and Brain Sciences, 8*, 1–42.

Garner, W. R. (1974). *The processing of information and structure.* Hillsdale, NJ: Lawrence Erlbaum Associates.

Gholson, B., Levine, M., & Phillips, S. (1972). Hypotheses, strategies and stereotypes in discrimination learning. *Journal of Experimental Child Psychology, 13*, 423–446.

Goldman-Rakic, P. S. (1990). Cortical localization of working memory. In J. L. McGaugh, N. M. Weinberger, & G. Lynch (Eds.), *Brain organization and memory: Cells, systems, and circuits.* New York: Oxford University Press.

Gormezano, I., & Grant, D. A. (1964). Progressive ambiguity in the attainment of concepts on the Wisconsin Card Sorting Test. *Journal of Experimental Psychology, 64*, 621–627.

Gottlieb, G. (1983). The psychobiological approach to developmental issues. In P. H. Mussen (Ed.), *Handbook of child psychology* (pp. 1–19). New York: Wiley.

Gottlieb, G. (1984). Evolutionary trends and evolutionary origins. Relevance to theory in comparative psychology. *Psychological Review, 91*, 448–456.

Gough, P. B. (1962). Some tests of the Hullian analysis of reasoning in the rat. Doctoral dissertation. *The study of mediation in animals.* University of Minnesota, 1961, Minneapolis, MN.

Gould, S. J. (1977). *Ontogeny and phylogeny.* Cambridge, MA: Harvard University Press.

Guttman, N., & Kalish, H. J. (1956). Discriminability and stimulus generalization. *Journal of Experimental Psychology, 51,* 79–88.

Handel, S., & Imai, S. (1972). The free classification of analyzable and unanalyzable stimuli. *Perception & Psychophysics, 12,* 108–116.

Hara, K., & Warren, J. M. (1961). Stimulus additivity and dominance in discrimination performance in cats. *Journal of Comparative and Physiological Psychology, 54,* 86–90.

Harlow, H. F. (1949). The formation of learning sets. *Psychological Review, 56,* 51–65.

Harlow, H. F. (1950). Analysis of discrimination-learning by monkeys. *Journal of Experimental Psychology, 40,* 36–39.

Harlow, H. F., Harlow, M. K., Rueping, R. R., & Mason, W. A. (1960). Performance of infant rhesus monkeys on discrimination learning, delayed, response, and discrimination learning set. *Journal of Comparative and Physiological Psychology, 53,* 113–121.

Harlow, H. F., & Hicks, L. H. (1957). Discrimination-learning theory: Uniprocess versus duoprocess. *Psychological Review, 64,* 104–109.

Harnad, S. (1987). Category induction and representation. In S. Harnad (Ed.), *Categorical perception: The groundwork of cognition.* New York: Cambridge University Press.

Harrow, M. (1964). Stimulus aspects responsible for the rapid acquisition of reversal shifts in concept formation. *Journal of Experimental Psychology, 67,* 330–334.

Harrow, M., & Friedman, G. B. (1958). Comparing reversal and nonreversal shifts in concept formation with partial reinforcement controlled. *Journal of Experimental Psychology, 55,* 592–598.

Hebb, D. O. (1972). *Textbook of psychology: 3rd Edition.* Philadelphia: Saunders.

Herrman, T., Bahr, E., Bremner, B., & Ellen, P. (1982). Problem solving in the rat: Stay vs. shift solutions on the three-table task. *Animal Learning and Behavior, 10,* 39–45.

Herrnstein, R. J. (1979). Acquisition, generalization, and discrimination reversal of a natural concept. *Journal of Experimental Psychology: Animal Behavior Processes, 5,* 116–129.

Herrnstein, R. J. (1990). Levels of stimulus control: A functional approach. *Cognition, 37,* 133–166.

Hull, C. L. (1930). Knowledge and purpose as habit mechanisms. *Psychological Review, 37,* 511–525.

Hull, C. L. (1943). *Principles of behavior.* New York: Appleton-Century.

Hull, C. L. (1952). *A behavior system.* New Haven, CT: Yale University Press.

Huxley, J. S. (1957). The three types of evolutionary progress. *Nature, 180,* 454–455.

Ingalls, R. P., & Dickerson, D. J. (1969). Development of hypothesis behavior in human concept identification. *Developmental Psychology, 1,* 707–716.

Jackson, J. H. (Ed.). (1932). *Selected writings of John Hughlings Jackson.* London: Hodder & Stoughton.

James, W. (1892). *Psychology (Briefer course).* Republished 1948; Cleveland, OH: World.

Johnson-Laird, P. N. (1993). *Human and machine thinking.* Hillsdale, NJ: Lawrence Erlbaum Associates.

Kahneman, D. (1973). *Attention and effort.* Englewood Cliffs, NJ: Prentice-Hall.

Kahneman, D., & Treisman, A. (1984). Changing views of attention and automaticity. In R. Parasuraman & D. R. Davies (Eds.), *Varieties of attention* (pp. 29–61). New York: Academic Press.

Kelleher, R. T. (1956). Discrimination learning as a function of reversal and nonreversal shifts. *Journal of Experimental Psychology, 51,* 379–384.

Kemler, D. G. (1982). Classification in young and retarded children: The primacy of overall relations. *Child Development, 53,* 768–799.

Kemler, D. G. (1983). Holistic and analytic modes in perceptual and cognitive development. In T. J. Tighe & B. E. Shepp (Eds.), *Perception, cognition and development: An interactional analysis* (pp. 77–102). Hillsdale, NJ: Lawrence Erlbaum Associates.

Kendler, H. H., & D'Amato, M. F. (1955). A comparison of reversal shifts and nonreversal shifts in human concept formation behavior. *Journal of Experimental Psychology, 49*, 165–174.

Kendler, H. H., Hirschberg, M. A., & Wolford, G. (1971). Spence's prediction about reversal shift behavior. *Psychological Review, 78*, 354.

Kendler, H. H., & Kendler, T. S. (1961). Effect of verbalization on reversal shifts in children. *Science, 134*, 1619–1620.

Kendler, H. H., & Kendler, T. S. (1962). Vertical and horizontal processes in problem solving. *Psychological Review, 69*, 1–16.

Kendler, H. H., Kendler, T. S., & Ward, J. W. (1972). An ontogenetic analysis of optional and intradimensional shifts. *Journal of Experimental Psychology, 95*, 102–109.

Kendler, T. S. (1964). Verbalization and optional reversal shifts among kindergarten children. *Journal of Verbal Learning and Verbal Behavior, 3*, 428–436.

Kendler, T. S. (1971). Continuity theory and cue dominance. In H. H. Kendler & J. T. Spence (Eds.), *Essays in neobehaviorism: A memorial volume to Kenneth W. Spence* (pp. 237–264). New York: Appleton.

Kendler, T. S. (1974). The effect of training and stimulus variables on the reversal-shift ontogeny. *Journal of Experimental Child Psychology, 17*, 87–106.

Kendler, T. S. (1979a). The development of discrimination learning: A level of functioning explanation. In H. W. Reese & L. P. Lipsitt (Eds.), *Advances in child development and behavior* (Vol. 13, pp. 83–117). New York: Academic Press.

Kendler, T. S. (1979b). Cross-sectional research, longitudinal theory, and a discriminative transfer ontogeny. *Human Development, 22*, 235–254.

Kendler, T. S. (1983). Labeling, overtraining, and levels of function. In T. J. Tighe & B. R. Shepp (Eds.), *Perception, cognition and development: Interactional analyses*. Hillsdale, NJ: Lawrence Erlbaum Associates.

Kendler, T. S., Basden, B. H., & Bruckner, J. B. (1970). Dimensional dominance and continuity theory. *Journal of Experimental Psychology, 83*, 309–318.

Kendler, T. S., & Hynds, L. T. (1974) A reply to Brier and Jacob's criticism of the optional-shift methodology. *Child Development, 45*, 208–211.

Kendler, T. S., & Kendler, H. H. (1959). Reversal and nonreversal shifts in kindergarten children. *Journal of Experimental Psychology, 58*, 56–60.

Kendler, T. S., & Kendler, H. H. (1962). Inferential behavior in children as a function of age and subgoal constancy. *Journal of Experimental Psychology, 4*, 460–466.

Kendler, T. S., & Kendler, H. H. (1967). Experimental analysis of inferential behavior in children. In L. P. Lipsitt & C. C. Spiker (Eds.), *Advances in child development and behavior* (Vol. 3, pp. 157–189). New York: Academic Press.

Kendler, T. S., & Kendler, H. H. (1970). An ontogeny of optional shift behavior. *Child Development, 41*, 1–27.

Kendler, T. S., Kendler, H. H., & Carrick, M. A. (1966). Verbal labels and inferential problem solution of children. *Child Development, 37*, 749–763.

Kendler, T. S., Kendler, H. H., & Learnard, B. (1962). Mediated responses to size and brightness as a function of age. *American Journal of Psychology, 75*, 571–586.

Kendler, T. S., Kendler, H. H., & Silfen, C. K. (1964). Optional shift behavior of albino rats. *Psychonomic Science, 1*, 5–6.

Kendler, T. S., Kendler, H. H., & Wells, D. (1960). Reversal and nonreversal shifts in nursery school children. *Journal of Comparative and Physiological Psychology, 53*, 83–88.

Kendler, T. S., & Ward, J. W. (1972). Optional reversal probability is a linear function of the log of age. *Developmental Psychology, 7*, 337–348.

Koranakos, C. (1959). Inferential learning in rats: The problem-solving assembly of behavior segments. *Journal of Comparative and Physiological Psychology, 52*, 231–235.

Krechevsky, I. (1932a). "Hypotheses" versus "chance" in the presolutions period in sensory discrimination learning. *University of California Publications in Psychology, 6*, 27–44.

Krechevsky, I. (1932b). "Hypotheses" in rats. *Psychological Review, 39,* 516–532.

Krechevsky, I. (1938). A study of the continuity of the problem-solving process. *Psychological Review, 45,* 107–133.

Kuenne, M. R. (1946). Experimental investigation of the relationship of language to the transposition behavior of young children. *Journal of Experimental Psychology, 35,* 471–490.

Kuhn, T. S. (1970). *The structure of scientific revolutions (2nd ed.).* Chicago: University of Chicago Press.

Lashley, K. S. (1929). *Brain mechanisms and intelligence.* Chicago: University of Chicago Press.

Lashley, K. S. (1938). The mechanism of vision: XV. Preliminary studies of the rat's capacity for detailed vision. *Journal of General Psychology, 18,* 123–193.

Lassek, A. M. (1970). *The unique legacy of Doctor Hughlings Jackson.* Springfield, IL: Thomas.

Lawrence, D. H. (1950). Acquired distinctiveness of cues. II. Selective association in a constant stimulus situation. *Journal of Experimental Psychology, 40,* 175–188.

Levine, M. (1959). A model of hypothesis behavior in discrimination learning set. *Psychological Review, 66,* 353–366.

Levine, M. (1963). Mediating responses in humans at the outset of discrimination-learning. *Psychological Review, 70,* 254–276.

Levine, M. (1966). Hypothesis behavior in humans during discrimination learning. *Journal of Experimental Psychology, 71,* 331–338.

Levine, M. (1975). *A cognitive theory of learning: Research on hypothesis-testing.* Hillsdale, NJ: Lawrence Erlbaum Associates.

Levine, M., Miller, P., & Steinmeyer, C. H. (1967). The none-to-all theorem of human discrimination learning. *Journal of Experimental Psychology, 73,* 568–573.

Levinson, B., & Reese, H. W. (1967). Patterns of discrimination learning set in preschool children, fifth graders, college freshmen, and the aged. *Monographs of the Society for Research in Child Development, 32,* (7, Whole No. 115).

Luria, A. R. (1973). *The working brain: An introduction to neuropsychology.* New York: Basic Books.

Luria, A. R., & Yudovich, F. Ia. (1959). *Speech and the development of mental processes in the child.* London: Staples Press.

Mackintosh, N. J. (1964). Overtraining and transfer within and between dimensions in the rat. *Quarterly Journal of Experimental Psychology, 16,* 250–256.

Mackintosh, N. J. (1975). A theory of attention: Variations in the associability of stimuli with reinforcement. *Psychological Review, 82,* 276–298.

MacLean, P. D. (1968). *A triune concept of the brain and behavior.* Toronto, Canada: University of Toronto Press.

Maier, N. R. F. (1929). Reasoning in white rats. *Comparative Psychology Monographs. No. 29.*

Malt, B. C., & Smith, E. E. (1984). Correlated properties in natural categories. *Journal of Verbal Learning and Verbal Behavior, 23,* 250–269.

Markman, E. M. (1989). *Categorization and naming in children: Problems of induction.* Cambridge, MA: MIT Press.

Marr, D. (1976). Early processing of visual information. *Philosophical Transactions of the Royal Society of London. B. Biological Sciences, 275,* 483–524.

Massaro, D. W. (1987). *Speech perception by ear and eye: A paradigm for psychological inquiry.* Hillsdale, NJ: Lawrence Erlbaum Associates.

Maxwell, A. E. (1961). *Analysing qualitative data.* London: Methuen.

Mcguigan, F. J., Culver, V. I., Kendler, T. S. (1971). Covert behavior as a direct electromyographic measure of mediating responses. *Conditional Reflex, 6,* 145–152.

Mervis C. B., & Rosch, E. (1981). The categorization of natural objects. *Annual Review of Psychology, 32,* 89–115.

Miles, C. G., & Jenkins, H. M. (1973). Overshadowing in operant conditioning as a function of discriminability. *Learning and Motivation, 4,* 11–27.

Miles, R. C. (1965). Discrimination-learning sets. In H. F. Schrier, H. Harlow, & F. Stollnitz (Eds.), *Behavior of nonhuman primates, Vol. 1.* New York: Academic Press.

Miller, N. E. (1951). Learnable drives and rewards. In S. S. Stevens (Ed.), *Handbook of experimental psychology.* New York: Wiley.

Miller, N. E. (1959). Liberalization of basic S-R concepts: Extensions to conflict behavior, motivation and social learning. In S. Koch (Ed.), *Psychology: A study of a science* (Vol. 2, pp. 196–293). New York: Wiley.

Mishkin, M., Malamut, B., & Bachevalier, J. (1984). Memories and habits: Two neural systems. In G. Lynch, J. L. McGaugh, & N. M. Weinberger (Eds.), *Neurobiology of learning and memory* (pp. 65–77). New York: Guilford Press.

Mishkin, M., & Petri, H. L. (1984). Memories and habits: Some implications for the analysis of learning and retention. In L. R. Squire & N. Butters (Eds.), *Neuropsychology of memory* (pp. 287–296). New York: Guilford Press.

Nagel, E. (1961). *The structure of science.* New York: Harcourt Brace & World.

Norman, D. A., & Shallice, T. (1980). *Attention to action: Willed and automatic control of behavior* (Tech. Rep. 8006). La Jolla, CA: University of California, San Diego, Center for Human Information Processing.

Pavlov, I. (1927). *Conditioned reflexes* (G. V. Anrep, Trans.). London: Oxford.

Petri, H. L., & Mishkin, M. (1994). Behaviorism, cognitivism and the neuropsychology of memory. *American Scientist, 82,* 30–37.

Piaget, J. (1970). Piaget's theory. In P. H. Mussen (Ed.), *Carmichael's manual of child psychology* (pp. 703–732). New York: Wiley.

Posner, M. I. (1978). *Chronometric explorations of mind.* Hillsdale, NJ: Lawrence Erlbaum Associates.

Posner, M. I., & Snyder, C. R. (1975). Attention and cognitive control. In R. L. Solso (Ed.), *Information processing and cognition: The Loyola Symposium* (pp. 55–85). Hillsdale, NJ: Lawrence Erlbaum Associates.

Pylyshyn, Z. W. (1980). Computation and cognition: Issues in the foundation of cognitive science. *The Behavioral and Brain Sciences, 3,* 111–169.

Reid, L. S. (1953). The development of noncontinuity behavior through continuity learning. *Journal of Experimental Psychology, 46,* 107–112.

Rensch, B. (1959). *Evolution above the species level.* New York: Columbia University Press.

Rescorla, R. A., & Wagner, A. R. (1972). A theory of Pavlovian conditioning: Variations in the effectiveness of reinforcement and nonreinforcement. In A. Black & W. F. Prokasy (Eds.), *Classical conditioning II.* New York: Appleton-Century-Crofts.

Reynolds, G. S. (1961). Attention in the pigeon. *Journal of the Experimental Analysis of Behavior, 4,* 203–208.

Riley, D. A. (1968). *Discrimination learning.* Boston: Allyn & Bacon.

Riopelle, A. J., & Chinn, R. McC. (1961). Transfer suppression and learning sets. *Journal of Comparative and Physiological Psychology, 54,* 178–180.

Rosch, E. (1973). On the internal structure of perceptual and semantic categories. In T. E. Moore (Ed.), *Cognitive development and the acquisition of language* (pp. 111–144). New York: Academic Press.

Rosch, E. (1978). Principles of categorization. In E. Rosch & B. B. Lloyd (Eds.), *Cognition and categorization.* Hillsdale, NJ: Lawrence Erlbaum Associates.

Rust, K. J., & Kendler, T. S. (1987). Lower level encoding: Holistic or nonselective? *Developmental Review, 7,* 326–362.

Schacter, D. J. (1990). Perceptual representation systems and implicit memory: Toward a resolution of the multiple memory systems debate. *Annals of the New York Academy of Sciences, 608,* 543–571.

Schade, A. F., & Bitterman, M. E. (1966). Improvement in habit reversal as related to dimensional set. *Journal of Comparative and Physiological Psychology, 62,* 43–48.

Schaie, K. W. (1970). A reinterpretation of age-related changes in cognitive structure and functioning. In P. B. Goulet and L. R. Baltes (Eds.), *Life-span developmental psychology.* New York: Academic Press.

Schrier, A. M., & Brady, P. M. (1987). Categorization of natural stimuli by monkeys (*Macaca mulatta*): Effects of stimulus set size and modification of exemplars. *Journal of Experimental Psychology: Animal and Behavioral Processes, 13,* 136–143.

Schulte, F. J. (1969). Structure-function relationships on the spinal cord. In R. J. Robinson (Ed.), *Brain and early behavior.* New York: Academic Press.

Schusterman, R. J. (1961). The use of strategies in the decision behavior of children and chimpanzees. *American Psychologist, 16* (Abstract).

Seward, J. P. (1949). An experimental analysis of latent learning. *Journal of Experimental Psychology, 10,* 177–186.

Shallice, T. (1972). Dual functions of consciousness. *Psychological Review, 79,* 383–393.

Shepp, B. E., & Adams, M. J. (1973). Effects of amount of training on type of solution and breadth of learning in optional shifts. *Journal of Experimental Psychology, 101,* 63–69.

Shepp, B. E., & Turissi, F. D. (1966). Learning and transfer of mediating responses in discrimination learning. In N. R. Ellis (Ed.), *International review of research in mental retardation, 2,* 85–121.

Shepp, B., & Zeaman, D. (1966). Discrimination learning of size and brightness by retardates. *Journal of Comparative and Physiological Psychology, 62,* 55–59.

Shiffrin, R. M., & Schneider, W. (1977). Controlled and automatic human information processing. II. Perceptual learning. *Psychological Review, 84,* 419–512.

Silverman, I. W. (1966). Effect of verbalization on reversal shifts in children. *Journal of Experimental Child Psychology, 4,* 1–8.

Smiley, S. S. (1972). Optional shift behavior as a function of dimensional preference and relative cue similarity. *Journal of Experimental Child Psychology, 14,* 313–322.

Smiley, S. S. (1973). Optional shift behavior as a function of age and dimensional dominance. *Journal of Experimental Child Psychology, 16,* 451–458.

Smiley, S. S., & Weir, M. W. (1966). Role of dimensional dominance in reversal and nonreversal shift behavior. *Journal of Experimental Child Psychology, 4,* 296–307.

Smith, E. E. (1989). Concepts and induction. In M. I. Posner (Ed.), *Foundations of cognitive science* (pp. 501–526). Cambridge, MA: MIT Press.

Smith, L. B., & Kemler, D. G. (1977). Developmental trends in free classification: Evidence for a new conceptualization of perceptual development. *Journal of Experimental Child Psychology, 24,* 279–298.

Spence, K. W. (1936). The nature of discrimination learning in animals. *Psychological Review, 43,* 427–449.

Spence, K. W. (1937). The differential response in animals to stimuli varying within a single dimension. *Psychological Review, 44,* 430–444.

Spence, K. W. (1960). *Behavior theory and learning.* Englewood Cliffs, NJ: Prentice-Hall.

Spiker, C. C. (1970). An extension of Hull–Spence discrimination learning theory. *Psychological Review, 77,* 496–515.

Squire, L. R. (1987). *Memory and brain.* New York: Oxford University Press.

Strong, P. N. (1959). Memory for object discrimination in the rhesus monkey. *Journal of Comparative and Physiological Psychology, 52,* 333–335.

Suchman, R. G., & Trabasso, T. (1966). Stimulus preference and cue function in young children's concept attainment. *Journal of Experimental Child Psychology, 3,* 188–198.

Suppes, P., & Ginsberg, R. (1963). A fundamental property of all-or-none models, binomial distribution of responses prior to conditioning, with application to concept formation in children. *Psychological Review, 70,* 139–161.

Sutherland, N. S., & Mackintosh, N. J. (1966). The learning of an optional extradimensional reversal shift problem by rats. *Psychonomic Science, 5,* 343–344.

Sutherland, N. S., & Mackintosh, N.J. (1971). *Mechanisms of animal discrimination learning.* New York: Academic Press.

Tabor, L. E., & Kendler, T. S. (1981). Testing for developmental continuity or discontinuity: Class inclusion and reversal shifts. *Developmental Review, 1,* 330–343.

Thompson, R. F. (1965). The neural basis of stimulus generalization. In D. J. Mostofsky (Ed.), *Stimulus generalization.* California: Stanford University Press.

Tighe, T. J. (1964). Reversal and nonreversal shifts in monkeys. *Journal of Comparative and Physiological Psychology, 58,* 324–326.

Tighe, T. J. (1965). Effect of overtraining on reversal and extradimensional shifts. *Journal of Experimental Psychology, 70,* 13–17.

Tighe, T. J., Brown, P. I., & Youngs, E. A. (1965). The effect of overtraining on the shift behavior of albino rats. *Psychonomic Science, 2,* 141–142.

Tighe, T. J., & Tighe, L. S. (1966). Overtraining and optional shift behavior in rats and children. *Journal of Comparative and Physiological Psychology, 62,* 49–54.

Tolman, E. C., & Honzik, C. H. (1930). "Insight" in rats. *University of California Publications in Psychology, 4,* 215–232.

Trabasso, T., & Bower, G. H. (1968). *Attention in learning theory and research.* New York: Wiley.

Velmans, M. (1991). Is human information processing conscious? *Behavioral and Brain Sciences, 14,* 651–726.

Vygotsky, L. S. (1962). *Thought and language.* Cambridge, MA: M.I.T. Press.

Warren, J. M. (1965). Primate learning in comparative perspective. In A. M. Schrier, H. F. Harlow, & F. Stollnitz (Eds.), *Behavior of nonhuman primates* (Vol. 1, pp. 249–281). New York: Academic Press.

Warrington, E. K., & Weiskrantz, L. (1982). Amnesia: A disconnection syndrome? *Neuropsychologia, 20,* 233–248.

White, S. H. (1965). Evidence for a hierarchical arrangement of learning processes. In L. P. Lipsitt & C. C. Spiker (Eds.), *Advances in child development and behavior* (Vol. 2). New York: Academic Press.

Winer, G. A. (1980). Class-inclusion reasoning in children: A review of the empirical literature. *Child Development, 51,* 309–328.

Wittgenstein, I. (1953). *Philosophical investigations.* New York: Macmillan.

Wolff, J. L. (1967). Concept-shift and discrimination learning in humans. *Psychological Bulletin, 68,* 369–408.

Yakovlev, P. I., & Lecours, A. R. (1967). The myologenetic cycles of regional maturation of the brain. In A. M. Minkowski (Ed.), *Region-development of the brain in early life.* Oxford, England: Blackwell Scientific Publications.

Zeaman, D., & Hanley, P. (1983). Stimulus preferences as structural features. In T. J. Tighe & B. E. Shepp (Eds.), *Perception, cognition and development: An interactional analysis* (pp. 103–128). Hillsdale, NJ: Lawrence Erlbaum Associates.

Zeaman, D., & House, B. J. (1963). The role of attention in retardate discrimination learning. In N. R. Ellis (Ed.), *Handbook of mental deficiency.* New York: McGraw-Hill.

Zeaman, D., & House, B. J. (1974). Interpretation of developmental trends in discriminative transfer effects. In A. Pick (Ed.), *Minnesota symposia on child psychology Vol. 8.* Minneapolis: University of Minnesota Press.

Author Index

Subject Index